STRUCTURE AND FUNCTION
IN CRIMINAL LAW

Structure and Function in Criminal Law

PAUL H. ROBINSON

CLARENDON PRESS · OXFORD
1997

Oxford University Press, Great Clarendon Street, Oxford OX2 6DP
Oxford New York
Athens Auckland Bangkok Bogota Bombay
Buenos Aires Calcutta Cape Town Dar es Salaam
Delhi Florence Hong Kong Istanbul Karachi
Kuala Lumpur Madras Madrid Melbourne
Mexico City Nairobi Paris Singapore
Taipei Tokyo Toronto Warsaw
and associated companies in
Berlin Ibadan

Oxford is a trade mark of Oxford University Press

Published in the United States by
Oxford University Press Inc., New York

British Library Cataloguing in Publication Data
Data available

Library of Congress Cataloging in Publication Data
Robinson, Paul H., 1948–
Structure and function in criminal law / Paul H. Robinson.
p.   cm. — (Oxford monographs on criminal law and criminal
justice)
Includes bibliographical references.
1. Criminal law—Methodology.   I. Title.   II. Series.
K5025.R63   1997
345'.001—dc21   97–8004
ISBN 0–19–825886–0

1 3 5 7 9 10 8 6 4 2

Typeset by Graphicraft Typesetters Ltd., Hong Kong
Printed in Great Britain by
Bookcraft Ltd., Midsomer Norton, Somerset

Dedicated To
Sarah McAlpine Robinson

In Memoriam
Glanville Williams
1911–1997

General Editor's Introduction

In this original and distinctive book, Paul Robinson presents an integrated statement of the results of several years of criminal law theorising and of practical experience of working with and drafting criminal codes. It begins with an analysis of the existing structure of systems of criminal law in the Anglo-American tradition. This is followed by an exploration of the structure of criminal law in terms of its functions, identifying and elaborating the separate functions of articulating rules, establishing grounds of liability, and grading offences. The final part of the book develops some principles for drafting criminal codes using the insights gained, and two appendices contain actual drafts prepared on this basis. Anyone who has reflected on the organisation of the criminal law will find this a rewarding book which challenges assumptions and points new ways. For those charged with reform and/or codification of the criminal law, it sets out standards and distinctions which will command attention for many years to come. I am delighted that Paul Robinson has been able to write such a powerful book for the series.

Andrew Ashworth

Preface

During the past fifteen years I have struggled with the question of how best to organize criminal law: what is the interrelation among the rules and doctrines of criminal law? How can those interrelations best be described in a comprehensive conceptual framework? Inevitably, the inquiry came to face the question of what 'best' means in this context: what should be the guiding principle in conceptualizing criminal law? To track as closely as possible the distinctions shown to be most significant by moral philosophy? To replicate how common people intuitively decide issues of criminal liability and punishment? To provide the organizational system that most effectively performs the functions we want a criminal code to perform? To increase the rationality of the conceptualization that history has given us, recognizing how difficult it is in the real world to change something so fundamental as how lawyers and judges have come to conceptualize criminal law? Some combination of these goals?

This book claims to answer the first question: what is the interrelation among the rules and doctrines of criminal law? It offers several alternative answers to the second question: how can those interrelations best be described in a comprehensive conceptual framework? The need for alternative answers is created by the complexity of the third question: what should be the guiding principles in conceptualizing criminal law? People will not agree upon the answer to that question. Thus, to speak to a full range of people and goals alternative conceptualizations are needed.

The book's contribution is less in its new ideas and more in its pulling together into a coherent whole my fifteen years of thought on the subject. First was an attempt to organize the area of criminal law defences, in 'Criminal Law Defenses: A Systematic Analysis' (1982), which was later elaborated in *Criminal Law Defenses* (2 volumes, 1984). Then came a similar organizing expedition for offence definitions, in 'Element Analysis in Defining Criminal Liability: The Model Penal Code and Beyond' (1983), with Jane Grall. The final piece of the trilogy came in 'Imputed Criminal Liability' (1983), which argued for recognition of a class of doctrines that operate in the reverse of general defences and ought to be given equal prominence. Just as general defences exempt an actor from liability despite the satisfaction of offence elements, so these doctrines impose liability despite the absence of an offence element. In this present work, I claim that, taken together, these three efforts offer a comprehensive framework for criminal law. A few other articles incorporated here provide refinements on important issues, most notably 'Competing Theories of Justification: Deeds v. Reasons' (1996).

This thread of work is the subject of Part II of this volume. As the Introduction explains, the broad approach is to improve upon, but generally to give deference to, the current structure and conceptualizations implicit in current law.

Part III gives no such deference. It pulls together conceptualization work written on a blank slate. First, 'Rules of Conduct and Principles of Adjudication' (1990) suggested that criminal law, and criminal codes in particular, serve several functions and that current conceptualizations are the poorer for ignoring those different functions. It offers a vision of how current doctrines could be reorganized better to serve each function. In part, its claim is that different doctrines serve different functions and that doctrines of similar function should be formulated analogously and should as a group be segregated from groups of doctrines serving other functions. The theory of that piece is worked out in full doctrinal detail in 'A Functional Analysis of Criminal Law' (1994). And that theoretical detail is translated in turn into criminal code drafting rules in 'Making Criminal Codes Functional: A Code of Conduct and a Code of Adjudication' (1996), with Peter D. Greene and Natasha R. Goldstein. That project, with the help of a large group of students, ultimately generated a sample draft criminal code to illustrate the drafting principles. Again, other pieces incorporated here took up special problems in this thread, most notably 'Should the Criminal Law Abandon the Actus Reus–Mens Rea Distinction?' (1993).

I think the whole offered in this volume provides insights that the collected pieces do not. I know that the process of producing the whole required me to refine some earlier claims and to rethink others.

Part of my hope here is to make a case for the importance of such conceptualization work generally. Sorting out the similarities and differences between specific doctrines often leads to reformulation of one or both. By defining the interrelation among doctrines, a conceptual framework suggests specific reforms, an effect well documented here.

But conceptual framework building also has a more subtle, and perhaps more important long-term effect of improving the quality and even the possibility of debate. Debate of criminal law issues without some degree of an articulated framework too often ends in an argument in which both sides misunderstand the significance of the other's arguments, and even the other's questions. Real debate can start only when a shared conceptual structure frames the issues in a way that all understand.

Further, public debate among scholars over criminal law's proper conceptual framework would lay bare the most fundamental points of disagreement and thereby set a valuable scholarly agenda. A developed consensus from such public debate eventually would affect the way students are taught and the way code drafters and judges think about criminal law, and therefore the way criminal law rules are formulated and applied. Conceptualization is both the starting point for debate and the vehicle for refinement and reform.

PAUL H. ROBINSON

Acknowledgements

My thanks go to Andrew Ashworth, for being a patient and insightful editor, to Ethan Skerry, Scott England, and Mary Tait, for their research and editing assistance, and to Mike Przyuski for secretarial assistance. As usual, my greatest debt is to my family.

PAUL H. ROBINSON

Contents

Table of Authors

Table of Cases

Table of Statutes

Model Penal Code

Arizona

Revised Statutes Annotated

Alaska

Statutes

Table of Statutes

FLORIDA

Table of Statutes

New Hampshire

Revised Statutes Annotated

New Jersey

Statutes Annotated

New York

Penal Law

North Carolina

General Statute

North Dakota

Century Code

OHIO

Revised Code Annotated

OREGON

Revised Statutes

PENNSYLVANIA

Consolidated Statutes Annotated

PUERTO RICO

Laws Annotated

RHODE ISLAND

General Laws

Proposed Criminal Code

Table of Statutes

South Carolina

Code

Tennessee

Code Annotated

Texas

Penal Code Annotated

Utah

Code Annotated

Washington

Revised Code Annotated

West Virginia

Code

WISCONSIN

Statutes Annotated

WYOMING

Statutes

UNITED STATES FEDERAL

United States Code

Other

Part I
Introduction

1

Structure and Function in Criminal Law

This book has two themes. First, it argues that how we conceptualize the criminal law is not just a matter of theoretical interest but has important real-world practical effects. Legislators, policy makers, and people concerned about crime, not just criminal law scholars, ought to be concerned about the way in which we distinguish criminal law doctrines and define their interrelation.

A second theme is to demonstrate that there are any number of ways in which one could structure criminal law. This book focuses on two possibilities. Using as a starting point the outline that current law appears to follow, Part II of the book examines the operation of current law to develop a complete conceptual framework. The exercise is partially descriptive and partially apologetic. It constructs a conceptual framework from the actual distinctions that current law uses, at least up to the point where the current distinctions are fuzzy, irrational, or internally inconsistent. Where a weakness in current law is apparent, it makes necessary adjustments, while trying to stay within the spirit of current law's general approach. That is, it makes as good (in the sense of rational and logical) a presentation of current law's current conceptualization as is possible.

The book uses current American criminal law as its work base. Because of common roots—and because roots often determine conceptualization—English criminal law has a generally similar structure, although there are important differences in detail. Other legal systems use more obviously different conceptual structures. The German conceptualization, for example, which has been influential worldwide, is different from the American structure in many fundamental and important ways.[1] One could perform a similar reconstruction/refinement exercise for any legal system's criminal law, and each exercise would generate a different result. There are many conceptualization approaches that are better than others, Part II argues, but the advantages of each must be weighed against the practicality of making

---

[1] See e.g. Wolfgang Naucke, 'An Insider's Perspective on the Significance of the German Criminal Theory's General System for Analyzing Criminal Acts' [1979] *Brigham Young ULR* 1.

such a change, and the dislocation that would result, given that legal system's history and tradition.

Part III takes on the same inquiry free of these practical constraints, and the resulting proposed structure is, on paper, far superior. But while Part II may actually provide a useful guide to today's criminal code drafters, Part III is not likely to be seriously considered as a useful guide, at least not in my lifetime. It seeks to demonstrate that much of the current conceptualization, even in the rationalized form laid out in Part II, is built on questionable organizational devices like the mens rea–actus reus distinction or the more modern culpability–objective elements distinction. Frequently these distinctions result more from the vagaries of history than from thoughtful and rational planning. While the rationalized structure developed in Part II has the considerable virtue of being generally familiar to current judges, lawyers, and law teachers, a better structure, Part III argues, relies upon a different set of basic organizing distinctions and principles. Part III looks at the functions that criminal law performs and uses these to create a conceptual structure designed to maximize effective performance of those functions, what it calls a 'functional structure' of criminal law.

Part IV shows how the principles of Part III can be used to draft a working criminal code, an example of which is given in the appendices.

A. The Formal Structure of Current Criminal Law

The distinctions between offences and defences and between actus reus and mens rea are criminal law's basic organizing distinctions for most lawyers, judges, and code drafters. The offence–defence distinction is reflected in the structure of modern codes. The American Model Penal Code, for example, groups offences in Part II of the Code, leaving defences for Part I. The Code recognizes three kinds of defences. Those relating to an actor's irresponsibility, such as mental illness and infancy, are contained in Article 4 of Part I, entitled 'Responsibility'. Those relating to the justification of an actor's conduct, such as self-defence and law enforcement authority, are grouped in Article 3 of Part I, 'General Principles of Justification'. Other miscellaneous defences, such as duress, statute of limitations, consent, and the *de minimis* defence, are included in Article 2 of Part I entitled 'General Principles of Liability'.

The mens rea–actus reus distinction is another basic organizing distinction of current law. The mens rea of an offence typically consists of the culpable state of mind or culpable negligence required for liability. The actus reus of an offence consists of the other offence requirements, including the objective elements, any causation requirements, the voluntary act requirement,[2] or, in the absence of an act, any special requirements for omission liability.[3]

To summarize, the current conceptual structure of American criminal law looks something like this:

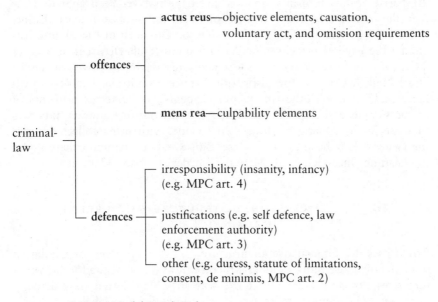

MPC = Model Penal Code

English criminal law reflects a similar structure. This is apparent in the proposed Criminal Code for England and Wales, which is essentially a codification of existing law, at least in terms of its basic structure and principles.[4] The Draft Code was published by the Law Commission in 1989, based on an earlier draft prepared by a team of three law professors that was then re-worked in light of comments received from practitioners and other law teachers. It is now recognized that the Draft Code will not be enacted as a whole, and so the Law Commission has been attempting in the 1990s to persuade governments to set aside legislative time for a series of smaller bills dealing with offences against the person, etc. in the hope that they could ultimately link the bills together to constitute a code. However, this approach has not yet met with any success, and the codification process appears to be stalled.

---

[2] See e.g. Model Penal Code, § 2.01.

[3] See e.g. Model Penal Code, § 2.03. The term 'actus reus' sometimes is used to refer only to the voluntary act or omission requirement, sometimes to the conduct, circumstance, and result elements of an offence, and sometimes to both. See Ch. 3, sect. A.

[4] The proposed Criminal Code for England and Wales will hereinafter be referred to as the 'Draft English Code.'

It is convenient in this work to refer to the Draft English Code as representing current English criminal law, in order to be able to address structural issues without becoming embroiled in the details of statutes and case law. It is recognized, however, that some parts of the Draft English Code are based on law reform proposals that have not yet been approved.

In the structure of the Draft English Code, the offence–defence distinction can be seen as the Code defines 'Specific Offences' in Part II, and lists among the general principles of Part I a number of 'Defences' in clauses 41 to 46.[5] A form of the mens rea–actus rea distinction lives on in the Draft English Code as the distinction between 'fault elements' of an offence and 'elements other than fault elements'[6] or 'external elements of offences'.[7] General defences are distinguished from one another, much as they are in the American Model Penal Code, with some collected under the General Part heading 'Defences' (clauses 41 to 46) and others under the heading 'Incapacity and Mental Disorder' (clauses 33 to 40).

B. The Operational Structure of Current Criminal Law

Part II uses this familiar overall structure as a starting point for building a more detailed and more rational structure. It argues that the formal structure does not accurately reflect the way in which current law actually operates. For example, most American criminal codes label as a 'justification' defence both an objective justification and a mistaken (subjective) justification, yet the same codes do in fact treat these two kinds of defences quite differently. Use of force under the former may not lawfully be resisted; force under the latter may.[8] Thus, to describe a conceptualization that captures how the law actually works, one must distinguish these two kinds of justifications even though the formal structure reflected on the face of the code does not.

To give another example, many doctrines impute to an actor a required offence element that is not satisfied; that is, the actor is treated as if he or she satisfies the required element even if he or she does not, as long as the actor satisfies the requirements of the doctrine that impute the missing element. The doctrine of complicity, for example, imputes another's conduct to the actor and thereby allows the actor to be convicted of an offence whose definition requires proof of an act that the actor did not

---

[5] The Draft English Code's general part includes a number of other general defences in other cll. For example, cl. 33 defines a defence of automatism and physical incapacity; cl. 35 defines a defence of mental disorder.

[6] See e.g. cl. 20(1) of the Draft English Code: 'Every offence requires a fault element of recklessness with respect to each of its elements other than fault elements, unless otherwise provided'.

[7] See heading for cll. 15–17 of the Draft English Code.   [8] See Ch. 5, sect. C.

in fact perform. The formal doctrine does not recognize the similarity in the operation of the many such doctrines of imputation, but a conceptualization of criminal law that attempts accurately to describe the law's operation sets these doctrines of imputation apart as an operational group, a group as basic and distinct as defences.[9]

After a brief introduction, each of the three chapters of Part II takes up one of the three basic ways in which a criminal law doctrine operates: defining an offence definition, imputing an offence element and thereby imposing liability despite the absence of a required element, or providing a general defence and thereby avoiding liability although the actor satisfies all required offence elements. Taken together, these three operational groups include most criminal law doctrines, and in that sense they represent a comprehensive conceptual scheme. The resulting conceptual structure will seem familiar to lawyers, for it only attempts to refine and rationalize the formal structure.

Does it matter whether the law's formal conceptualization accurately represents the way in which the law actually operates? The formal conceptualization typically serves as the basis for organizing a criminal code, and provides the structure for teaching criminal law. Where the formal framework does not mirror the actual operational structure, errors and confusion are inevitable. For example, how does one refer to objective justifications, which cannot lawfully be resisted, without including mistaken (subjective) justifications, which can lawfully be resisted, if the formal structure uses the same term, 'justification', to refer to both? For another example, should voluntary intoxication rules, which impute recklessness, be criticized because they treat an actor as having a culpable state of mind that he or she does not in fact have? Or is such imputation simply analogous in operation to the imputation that occurs when the complicity doctrine is used to convict an actor of an offence although he does not satisfy the conduct element of the offence definition? (Chapter 5 argues that the proper grounds for criticizing doctrines of imputation lie in an assessment of whether the special conditions that are required justify the imputation, not in a criticism of the process of imputation itself.)

Beyond the potential for confusion and misunderstanding arising from a formal structure that does not match actual operation, Part II shows that a conceptualization of existing law that matches its operation gives insights into the better formulation of many doctrines. As one attempts to construct an accurate conceptual framework, one sees ambiguities and inconsistencies among the doctrinal formulations that were not previously apparent. Once one sees the similarities among and common function of excuse defences, for example, one may notice that some such defences have special provisions governing an actor's culpability in causing the excusing

---

[9] See Ch. 4.

conditions, such as voluntary intoxication, but others do not. If there is a practical possibility that an actor might cause the conditions of his or her excuse in other ways (for example, failing to take a prescribed anti-psychotic medication), ought not other excuse defences address the possibility?

C. A FUNCTIONAL STRUCTURE OF CRIMINAL LAW

The 'operational structure' set out in Part II concerns itself with accurately capturing the operation of current law in a framework that helps us better understand the law's operation. It only suggests changes to the formal structure that are called for by its own internal inconsistencies and ambiguities; it does not alter the basic assumptions or organizing principles of current law. Part III builds a different conceptual framework, one that starts with a different base assumption of what a criminal law and a criminal code should look like. It argues that criminal law must perform a number of different and sometimes conflicting functions, and that current doctrine's failure to appreciate these distinct functions has made current doctrine less able to perform them.

Specifically, a criminal code must announce to the general public, *ex ante*, the rules of conduct that are to be enforced with criminal penalties. At the same time, a criminal code must adjudicate, *ex post*, any violation of those rules. In performing the latter function, the law's primary audience is not the general public but the trained or specially instructed participants of the criminal justice system, primarily lawyers, judges, and jurors. The substance and the form of these two kinds of rules—rules of conduct and principles of adjudication—are very different. The differences suggest that what are needed are two different and distinct kinds of codes: a code of conduct written in a way the general public can understand and apply, and a code of adjudication for the adjudicators, lawyers, judges, and juries that is more complex and subjective.

Chapter 6 describes how most current criminal law doctrines contain aspects that perform different functions. The three remaining chapters of Part III illustrate the kinds of errors and confusions in formulating and interpreting doctrine that arise from a failure to appreciate the different functions of criminal law. A conceptual framework that reflects the different functions of different doctrinal requirements would differ greatly from the current formal structure described above or even from the more refined and rationalized conceptual framework developed in Part II. It will seem foreign to criminal lawyers, judges, and law teachers. But, if a conceptual framework has significant practical effects, as Part II argues, a framework that reflects the different functions of criminal law is a framework that can bring a higher level of clarity, understanding, and effectiveness in serving those functions.

Part II

The Current Operational Structure

2

The Basic Organizing Distinctions of Current Law

Using as a starting point the general outline of current law diagrammed in Chapter 1, this Part examines the operation of current law to develop a complete and internally consistent conceptual structure. As noted, the exercise is partially descriptive and partially apologetic. It constructs a conceptual framework from the actual distinctions that current law uses, at least up to the point where the current distinctions are fuzzy, irrational, or internally inconsistent. Where a weakness in current law is apparent, it makes necessary adjustments, while trying to keep current law's general thrust. That is, it presents current law's conceptualization in the best light possible.

A. THE OFFENCE–DEFENCE DISTINCTION

The most basic organizing distinction in current law is between offences and defences, but that distinction is problematic when one examines how current law actually operates. In casual language, anything that prevents conviction of a defendant is called a 'defence', but this term includes doctrines that are very different from one another. An 'alibi defence', for example, simply refers to the presentation of facts that suggest the defendant was somewhere else when the offence was committed, and therefore cannot be the perpetrator. It is not a legal doctrine but a form of factual counterclaim. A defence of diplomatic immunity, on the other hand, may admit commission of the offence (although it need not), yet suggest that the defendant nonetheless cannot be prosecuted for the offence. The legal doctrines that we refer to as defences typically are one of five sorts.[1]

Like the alibi defence, many defences simply prevent proof of the requirements of an offence. Mistake or mental illness negating a culpability ('fault') element are of this sort. Where they do not provide complete exculpation but only a reduction in liability, they sometimes are referred

---

[1] See also Paul H. Robinson, 'Criminal Law Defenses: A Systematic Analysis' (1982) 82 *Columbia LR* 199 at 204–43.

to as 'mitigations'. In truth, such mitigations are simply instances where a factor—such as mistake or mental illness—negates a culpable state of mind for one offence but not for a lesser included offence. It is true that the effect of these doctrines is to prevent or reduce liability, but such is not the result of a doctrine of 'defence' or 'mitigation'. It is, rather, the result of applying the normal rules for proof of offence elements. These 'defences' may be called *absent element defences*.[2]

Other defences and mitigations may be defined separately from an offence definition. They do more than simply describe the negation of an offence element. Many apply only to a particular offence or group of offences, such as renunciation as a defence to inchoate liability and 'inevitably incident' conduct as a defence to complicity liability. While they are independent in form, the nature of these defences suggests that, in essence, they are part of the criminalization decision underlying the offence. In other words, what we mean by complicity does not include conduct that is inevitably incident to the offence. These defences might be called *offence modification defences*.

Other defences, in contrast, have general application to all offences. Such *general defences* represent general principles that are not dependent upon a particular offence or group of offences. They exist to bar liability for a reason unrelated to the criminalization decisions embodied in the offence definition. General defences are of three sorts: justifications, excuses, and nonexculpatory defences. The nature of these defences is the subject of Chapter 5. The potential for ambiguity in the term 'defences' suggests that the offence–defence distinction is best defined as the distinction between offence definitions (as modified by offence modification 'defences') and *general* defences.

An even more important qualification of the offence–defence distinction is that it is not the most fundamental distinction upon which the doctrine is built. It includes only two of the three most basic organizing groups of criminal law doctrines. The doctrines of imputation represent a third fundamental conceptual group. Let me sketch this basic tripartite structure, a structure around which Part II of this book is organized.

B. The Current Operational Structure: Offence Definitions, Doctrines of Imputation, and General Defences

Most criminal law doctrines operate in one of three ways. First, a doctrine may define what constitutes an *offence*. Secondly, a doctrine may define

---

[2] In earlier writings, I have recommended that these defences be called 'failure of proof defences', but experience with students suggests that that label easily misleads readers into thinking that these defences concern special evidentiary rules.

the conditions under which an actor will be acquitted even though he satisfies the elements of an offence. As noted, such a doctrine typically is called a *defence*, and perhaps more accurately is called a *general defence*. Thirdly, a doctrine may define the conditions under which an actor will be held liable even though he does not satisfy the elements of an offence— the reverse of a defence. Such a doctrine may be called a doctrine of *imputation*. Within each of these three groups of doctrines, the law relies upon a variety of other organizing distinctions.

As noted in Chapter 1, the definition of an offence typically is comprised of two kinds of elements: objective elements—e.g. conduct, its attendant circumstances, or its results—and culpability ('fault') elements— e.g. purpose, knowledge, recklessness, or negligence—as to each objective element. Thus, the objective elements of murder require that an actor engage in *conduct* that causes the *death* of *another human being*. The culpability elements require that the actor *know* the nature of his conduct, that it will cause a death, and that the death caused is that of a human being (e.g. not that of an inviable foetus). The culpability requirements may be different for different elements of the same offence. A jurisdiction might, for example, require that an actor *know* the nature of his conduct and that it will cause a death, but only require that the actor be reckless as to whether the death is that of a human being. Current law's organization of the definition of offences is the subject of Chapter 3.

An actor may be held liable for an offence, even if he does not satisfy the elements of the offence definition, if he satisfies the requirements of a doctrine of imputation that impute to him the missing element. For example, an actor may participate in a bank robbery in which it is planned that another accomplice will kill the bank guard if the guard resists. Although the accomplice does the killing, the robber may be liable for the murder. This is true even if the definition of murder requires that the actor engage in the conduct that causes the death. While the robber did not engage in the conduct that caused the death, the accomplice's conduct will be imputed to him under the doctrine of complicity. That is, the doctrine of complicity allows the actor to be treated as if he had engaged in the conduct constituting the offence.

Just as the complicity doctrine can impute an objective element to the defendant, such as another's conduct, the doctrine of voluntary intoxication can impute a culpability element. An actor who voluntarily intoxicates herself, and in that drunken state strikes and kills a pedestrian with her car, in fact may lack the culpability as to causing death required for the offence of manslaughter—e.g. an awareness of a substantial risk that her conduct will cause the death of another human being. Yet, such awareness of a risk of causing a death (i.e. recklessness as to causing death) may be imputed to the actor under the doctrine of voluntary intoxication. That is, because of her voluntary intoxication, she may be treated as if she satisfies the required element of recklessness as to causing death, and therefore may be convicted of manslaughter. Chapter 4 examines current law's doctrines of imputation.

Where an actor satisfies all of the elements of an offence, actually or through imputation, he nonetheless may be acquitted of the offence if he satisfies the conditions of a general defence. As discussed at the beginning of this Chapter, defences typically are of one of five sorts—absent element defences, offence modification defences, justifications, excuses, or non-exculpatory defences—but only the last three of these operate as general defences, independent of the offence definition.

Because both absent element and offence modification defences serve to refine the offence definition, they tend to apply to a single offence or group of offences. The general defences—justifications, excuses, and non-exculpatory defences—in contrast, are unrelated to a particular offence; they theoretically apply to all offences. The recognition of each general defence rests upon reasons extraneous to the criminalization goals and policies of the offence. A general defence is provided, not because there is no criminal wrong, but rather despite the criminal wrong. The community may be displeased with the occurrence of the offence, yet the special conditions establishing the defence support a decision not to punish the violator. Justifications, excuses, and non-exculpatory defences each represent a different kind of special condition.

An actor may satisfy all of the elements of an offence and his conduct may clearly be a legally recognized harm or evil of the sort that generally is prohibited, yet the circumstances of the offence may suggest that, because of the justifying circumstances, this particular offence conduct ought to be tolerated or even encouraged. An unconsented-to striking of another constitutes assault and generally is prohibited, yet it ought not to result in liability if done in self-defence against an aggressor to protect one's life. Burning another's farm constitutes arson, yet it ought to be tolerated and even encouraged if it creates a firebreak that saves a town from a raging forest fire. Providing a justification defence in such cases is not meant to lessen the general prohibition against assault and arson but only to recognize that the harm or evil of even such serious offences as these may be outweighed by a greater good that flows from the commission of such an offence under the special justifying circumstances.

Even if an actor's conduct is both harmful or evil in itself and is not justified by special circumstances, an acquittal nonetheless may be appropriate. An actor who is acting involuntarily, who is insane, involuntarily intoxicated, or immature, or who is acting under duress or under a reasonable mistake of law or mistake as to a justification may be blameless for his or her admittedly wrongful conduct. That is, we may feel that such an actor in such a situation could not reasonably have been expected to remain law-abiding. The excuse defences are designed to exculpate such blameless offenders.

Even blameworthy actors may be acquitted if they satisfy the requirements of a non-exculpatory defence. Such defences are disfavoured, yet recognized, because each is said to further an important societal interest, judged by the law-maker as more important than punishing the offender at hand. Diplomatic immunity, for example, shields criminal offenders because by recognizing such a defence we make the defence available to our diplomats abroad, and this in turn allows the establishment of diplomatic relationships between nations. That a societal benefit is derived from the defence may seem to make non-exculpatory defences similar to justifications, but note that the benefit in non-exculpatory offences flows not from the actor's offence conduct, as is the case with justifications, but rather from foregoing his or her conviction despite the undesirability of the conduct and despite the actor's blameworthiness. Chapter 5 examines each of these three kinds of general defences.

3

Offence Requirements

The most basic organizing distinction of offence requirements in current law has been the actus reus–mens rea distinction. The Chapter begins with an exploration of the weaknesses of and the potential for confusion in the use of that distinction. It advocates that use of the distinction be abandoned. The Chapter then offers as a replacement an alternative three-part conceptualization of offence requirements, distinguishing what it calls objective, culpability, and act–omission requirements. Each of these three groups of doctrines is then examined. The current conceptualization of each is summarized and refinements of it suggested.

A. The Conceptual Difficulties of the Actus Reus–Mens Rea Distinction

Many criminal lawyers, judges, and law teachers see the distinction between actus reus and mens rea as one of the most basic of criminal law.[1] Along with the offence–defence distinction, it helps us organize the way we conceptualize and analyse liability. It is said to be 'the corner-stone of discussion on the nature of criminal liability'.[2] And, the concepts of actus reus and mens rea have 'justified themselves by their usefulness'.[3] This section argues that this most basic organizing distinction is not coherent. Rather than being useful to criminal law theory, it is harmful because it creates ambiguity in discourse and hides important doctrinal differences of which criminal law should take account.

No doubt the actus reus–mens rea distinction is a logical and natural extension of the obvious empirical difference between an actor's conduct, which we can directly observe, and the actor's intention, which we cannot. In the simple case, the actor shoots another person, with the intention of injuring him. Both the actor's conduct and intention are prerequisites to liability. The concepts of actus reus and mens rea adequately capture these

---

[1] See generally Paul H. Robinson, 'Should the Criminal Law Abandon the Actus Reus–Mens Rea Distinction?' in S. Shute, J. Gardner, and J. Horder (eds.), *Action and Value in Criminal Law* (Oxford, 1993).

[2] A. C. E. Lynch, 'The Mental Element in the Actus Reus' (1982) 98 LQR 109 at 111.

[3] *Lynch* v. *DPP for Northern Ireland* [1975] AC 653 at 690.

two facts and reflect the empirical difference. Having created such a distinction in the paradigm case, it is natural to extend the mens rea required for liability beyond an intention to injure, to include knowledge, recklessness, or negligence as to injuring another (as when a person target-shoots in the woods without paying adequate attention to the possibility of campers in the overshot zone). It also is natural to extend the actus reus required for liability beyond an affirmative act of shooting another, to include cases of injuring another by failing to perform a legal duty (as in failing to feed one's child) and to include possession of contraband.

While such an evolution is understandable, even logical, it does not follow that the resulting distinction is one around which current doctrine should be conceptualized. We may be able to explain how we came to rely upon the distinction, but that in itself may not be adequate reason to keep it. If we are to rely upon it, we should be able to identify something that the doctrine gains by conceiving of the actus reus doctrines as representing a single concept and by conceiving of the mens rea doctrines as a single concept. We should be able to articulate a common denominator among each group that makes it more convenient or more enlightening to speak of them as a group. What is the unifying characteristic of actus reus doctrines and of mens rea doctrines?

1. Conceptual Diversity Within Actus Reus and Within Mens Rea

While there are sometimes different uses of the phrase, 'actus reus' commonly is used to include four kinds of requirements. First, the 'actus reus' of an offence includes the conduct required to constitute the offence, as well as any circumstances or results that are required to make the conduct criminal. Secondly, where a result is one of these offence elements, proof of the actus reus requires proof that the actor's conduct and the result stand in a certain relation, as defined by the doctrine of causation. A third part of the actus reus is the requirement that liability be based on conduct that includes a voluntary act. Finally, in the absence of an act, the actus reus of an offence may be found in the omission to perform a legal duty of which the actor is physically capable, or in an actor's knowing possession of contraband for a period of time sufficient to terminate the possession. To summarize, actus reus is said to include the conduct, circumstance, and result elements of an offence, as well as the supporting doctrines of causation, voluntary act, and omission and possession liability.

The 'mens rea' of an offence typically is said to be the actor's required mental state at the time of the conduct constituting the offence. Under the American Model Penal Code, for example, this generally requires proof that the actor was intentional (purposeful), knowing, reckless, or negligent as to each conduct, circumstance, and result element, as the offence definition may require.[4] The required mens rea also may include proof of additional culpable mental states beyond that required for each objective element. The offence may require, for example, that the actor have a purpose to do something more than the conduct required for the offence or that the actor engaged in the offence conduct for a particular reason.[5]

What is the unifying characteristic of the actus reus requirements? Are they all 'objective' in nature? A circumstance element of an offence may be entirely abstract, such as 'being married' in bigamy or 'without licence' in trespass. Indeed, an 'objective' element may include a purely subjective state of mind, such as the requirement of causing 'fear' in robbery or the requirement in rape that the victim does not 'consent'.[6] The 'subjective' nature of mens rea requirements and their common character as 'mental states' is similarly chequered. Negligence is neither subjective nor a state of mind, of course, but rather a failure to meet an objective standard of attentiveness.

Perhaps the common denominator among actus reus requirements and among mens rea requirements is not found in the descriptive characteristics of the requirements (e.g. 'objective' or 'subjective'), but rather is found in their common function. It is common to conceive of the actus reus–mens rea distinction in a general way as the distinction between the functions of defining the prohibited conduct and defining the conditions under which the actor is to be held blameworthy and therefore liable for engaging in such prohibited conduct. This is the approach taken by the Model Penal Code drafters. The requirements of intention (purpose), knowledge, recklessness, and negligence have different characteristics from one another—subjective, objective, state of mind, legal abstraction, etc.—but they serve a single function in the drafters' view: to assess whether the actor is sufficiently culpable for his prohibited conduct to be held criminally liable for it.[7] Indeed, the Code refers to these requirements—intentionally (purposely), knowing, recklessly, and negligently—as 'culpability' levels, emphasizing this common function. The Draft English Code similarly defines terms of 'fault' in clause 18.

The objective elements of conduct, circumstance, and result, in contrast, describe the prohibited (or required) conduct, the definition of which

---

[4] Model Penal Code, § 2.02(1).

[5] See e.g. *ibid.*, §§ 221.1(1) (defining burglary as entering a building with 'purpose to commit a crime therein'), 213.5 (defining indecent exposure as exposing genitals with 'purpose of arousing or gratifying [his] sexual desire').

[6] See e.g. Texas Penal Code, § 29.02(a)(2) (Vernon 1974) (defining robbery as placing another in 'fear' of bodily injury or death during the course of a theft); Del. Code Ann., tit. 11, §§ 767, 770(1), 771(1) & (3), 773(1), 774(1) & (2) (all defining sex offences to include absence of 'consent' as an element); 18 Pa. Cons. Stat. Ann., § 3922(a)(1) (Purdon 1983) (defining theft by deception to require creation or reinforcement of a 'false impression').

[7] Model Penal Code, § 2.02 explanatory note and comment 1 (Official Draft and Revised Comments 1985).

may be modified or refined by the supporting actus reus doctrines. But this apparent functional similarity among 'actus reus' requirements and among 'mens rea' requirements also is an illusion. As Part III of this book demonstrates in some detail, 'actus reus' requirements serve several different functions, as do 'mens rea' requirements.[8]

What we refer to as 'actus reus' requirements in fact are a collection of entirely distinct doctrines with important conceptual differences: the act requirement, the rules governing omission liability, the voluntariness requirement, and the objective elements of offence definitions. The Chapter documents this point and argues that these distinct doctrines ought not be grouped together as 'actus reus' requirements, because such a grouping suggests a conceptual similarity between them that does not exist.

'Mens rea' requirements also include diverse doctrines, although the reconceptualizations needed to distinguish them are sufficiently far from our current conceptualizations that they are appropriately a subject of Part III; that is, the reconceptualization required could not be claimed to be simply a refinement of current conceptualization. Current law seems obliged to retain the concept of 'mens rea', unless it undertakes a conceptual overhaul like that proposed in Part III.

2. Terminological Confusion Among the Doctrines of 'Actus Reus'

Perhaps because of the conceptual confusion inherent in the grouping of doctrines as part of the offence actus reus, the phrase 'actus reus' suffers considerable terminological confusion. The confusion arises from two sources: first, the label 'actus reus' is used to refer to one of the four doctrines typically included within the concept without identifying which of the four is the intended reference; secondly, there are some who disagree with the majority view of what is included within that label.

To illustrate the first, consider the entries from several good scholars in a debate on 'The Actus Reus Requirement'. One writer, defending 'the traditional conception of the actus reus requirement',[9] takes the issue to be whether *the act requirement* is defensible: 'what objections are there to the contention that criminal liability is never imposed in the absence of such an act?'[10] It turns out that the writer means the term to refer to both the act requirement and the voluntariness requirement, for he defines an 'act' as 'a bodily movement [caused] by the actor's will'.[11] Later in the

---

[8] See Ch. 6, sect. A.

[9] Michael Gorr, 'The Actus Reus Requirement: A Qualified Defense', (Winter–Spring 1991) 10 *Criminal Justice Ethics* 11 (hereinafter 'Actus Reus Requirement').

[10] *Ibid.*   [11] *Ibid.*

same discussion, however, the phrase 'actus reus' is used to mean *the specific conduct prohibited by each specific offence*: 'there exists, for the vast majority of crimes, a clear and separate actus reus requirement'.[12]

Another writer in the same debate similarly takes 'the actus reus principle' to mean the act requirement. He notes agreement 'for abandoning the actus reus principle . . . because there are many cases—status crimes, possessory offences, omissions—in which liability is sometimes imposed despite the absence of an act'.[13] But later in the same discussion, this writer too uses the phrase 'actus reus' to mean the specific prohibited conduct of a specific offence: 'Actus reus refers to the outer, physical, behavioral, objective ingredient of crime; mens rea refers to the inner, mental, subjective ingredient of crime'.[14]

The potential problems from such loose language are substantial. For example, part of the debate among these scholars concerns whether the 'actus reus requirement' is a universal principle.[15] The answer depends, of course, on what one means by 'the actus reus requirement'. The act requirement is not a universal requirement; the use of omission liability is generally accepted. The offence conduct requirements are not universal (the specific conduct required for each offence is different). But the voluntariness requirement is universal.

Another part of the debate concerns whether a 'control principle' is preferable to the 'actus reus requirement'. A control principle is a proper substitute for the actus reus requirement, one argues, because the control principle performs most of the functions usually assigned to 'actus reus'.[16] But whether this is true or not again depends on what one is referring to by the phrase 'actus reus'. Certainly a 'control principle' is an appropriate substitute for the voluntariness requirement. Some would say that the voluntariness requirement, along with the general excuses is a 'control principle'. A 'control principle' would not do well, of course, as a substitute for the act requirement or the special rules governing liability for an omission and for possession, or for the objective requirements of offence definitions.

My point here is not to criticize the substantive points of the debaters: I agree with many of the points. I am concerned, rather, that use of the phrase 'actus reus' makes it more difficult to engage in useful debate about the doctrines referred to by that label. In reading the debate, one wonders how many of the disagreements would melt away if the participants agreed upon a single terminology.

---

[12] *Ibid.* 13 (emphasis in original).

[13] Douglas N. Husak, 'The Orthodox Model of the Criminal Offense', (Winter–Spring 1991) 10 *Criminal Justice Ethics* 20 (hereinafter 'Orthodox Model').   [14] *Ibid.*

[15] Douglas N. Husak, *Philosophy of Criminal Law* (Totowa, NJ, 1987), 78 (hereinafter *Philosophy of Criminal Law*); Gorr, 'Actus Reus Requirement', n. 9 above, at n. 3; Jeffrie G. Murphy, 'Gorr on Actus Reus', (Winter–Spring 1991) 10 *Criminal Justice Ethics* 18 at 19; Husak, 'Orthodox Model', n. 13 above, at 22.   [16] *Ibid.* 21.

The potential for confusion is exacerbated by disagreement among writers as to which issues are included under the label. All agree that the act requirement is included.[17] The voluntariness requirement is included by most.[18] While this requirement may seem to be frequently omitted, it often is subsumed in the act requirement, as noted above, by defining an 'act' as a 'willed bodily movement'. (The Model Penal Code defines an act as 'a bodily movement, whether voluntary or involuntary', then explicitly adds a separate voluntariness requirement when it requires a '*voluntary* act'.)

Most writers also use 'actus reus' to refer to the objective elements of an offence definition, but in this usage too there is disagreement as to exactly which elements are included. Some writers mean to refer to the conduct element, the behaviour required for the offence, and perhaps its attendant circumstances, but not its results.[19] Others mean to include the results of the conduct as well, in other words, to include all of the objective elements of the offence definition: '(a) A willed movement (or omission). (b) Certain surrounding circumstances (including past facts). (c) Certain consequences'.[20] Finally, some writers go further to include the collateral doctrines sometimes required to establish liability for an offence. '[L]iability may rest on (and the actus reus may accordingly consist of) an *omission*, a *status*, or a *possession*'.[21]

With this much disagreement as to what is included within the concept, it should be no surprise to find ambiguity, confusion, and disagreement in discussing 'actus reus'. As noted above, the actus reus requirement, in the narrow act-requirement sense, is not a universal requirement. Omission liability is the obvious exception. In its act-or-omission sense, the actus

[17] The actus reus principle means that no crime can be committed simply by one's thoughts or mental states: Husak, 'Orthodox Model', n. 13 above; see Gorr, 'Actus Reus Requirement', n. 9 above, at 12; Glanville Williams, *Criminal Law: The General Part* (2nd edn., London, 1961), §§ 1–3 (hereinafter General Part).

[18] The actus reus principle is invoked to disallow liability for involuntary conduct: Husak, 'Orthodox Model', n. 13 above; see also Gorr, 'Actus Reus Requirement' n. 9 above, at 12; Joshua Dressler, *Understanding Criminal Law* (New York, 1987), 63 (hereinafter Understanding Criminal Law); Williams, *General Part*, n. 17 above, at § 8.

[19] Husak seems to suggest that some writers take this view but does not cite them.

'[D]eath is not part of the actus reus. The actus reus of homicide *causes* death, so that death is a consequence of the proscribed act rather than a component of it. According to this view, an element of liability is part of neither the actus reus nor the mens rea. It may seem odd to suppose that one can commit the actus reus of homicide before anyone has died, but this first view entails this oddity': Husak, *Philosophy of Criminal Law*, n. 15 above, at 124–5 (emphasis added).

[20] Williams, *General Part*, n. 17 above, at § 11. See also J. C. Smith and Brian Hogan, *Criminal Law* (8th edn., London, 1996), 33; Gorr, 'Actus Reus Requirement', n. 9 above, at 13; Dressler, *Understanding Criminal Law*, n. 18 above, at 63. Dressler also includes causation in actus reus: *ibid*. 63, n. 2.

[21] Meir Dan-Cohen, 'Actus Reus' in Sanford Kadish (ed.), *Encyclopedia of Crime and Justice* (London, 1983), 15 (hereinafter 'Actus Reus'). See also Dressler, *Understanding Criminal Law*, n. 18 above, at 63, n. 3.

reus requirement is universal. In its objective–offence–elements sense it is universal in application but every application, every offence, is different.

In its narrow act-requirement or even its voluntary-act-requirement forms, the actus reus is a minor part of the requirements of liability. It is the unusual case in which it raises issues that are in dispute. In its broader forms—'the actus reus designates all the elements of the criminal offense except the mens rea'[22]—it raises a disputed issue in many, if not most, cases.

The concept of 'mens rea' is somewhat less problematic than the concept of 'actus reus' in some respects, but more problematic in others. There is no significant disagreement about the reference of the phrase 'mens rea'. It may be a misleading phrase when used to include reference to negligence, but the modern phrases of 'culpability' or 'fault' requirements seem to avoid the problem. The difficulties with the concept of 'mens rea' arise instead from the fact that it groups together doctrines with important differences in their requirements and rationales. As noted above, this discussion generally is put off until Part III.[23]

3. Conclusion and Proposal: Objective, Culpability, and Act-Omission Requirements

It seems we have not made much progress since Jerome Hall's 1960 lament for the confusion inherent in the use of the term 'actus reus'.[24] The potential for clarity and understanding for lawyers, judges, and theorists alike would improve if the phrase 'actus reus' were never used again. The actus reus–mens rea distinction reflects no discernible underlying concept; neither 'actus reus' requirements nor 'mens rea' requirements share a common characteristic or function.

This conclusion does not raise doubts about the value of the requirements themselves that make up the 'actus reus' and 'mens rea' of offences. Is the act requirement useful? Yes, although its contribution is very modest. Is the voluntariness requirement useful? Yes, although, as the next section explains, it is better seen as part of the system of excuses rather than as having some special relationship to the elements of the offence definition. Is it useful to have the objective and culpability elements of offence definitions, the causation requirement, and the omission and possession liability rules? Yes, of course, for these requirements are all important for criminal law to perform its basic functions.

Is the actus reus–mens rea distinction useful? No. That is, by grouping doctrines under these headings we gain no special insights into a characteristic or function that doctrines in each group share. Indeed, the groupings

---

[22] Dan-Cohen, 'Actus Reus', n. 21 above, at 15. [23] See Ch. 6, sect. A.2.

[24] See Jerome Hall, *General Principles of Criminal Law* (2nd edn., Indianapolis, Indiana, 1960), 222.

tend to hide important differences between doctrines. The groupings also create terminological ambiguity—especially among 'actus reus' doctrines—that can impede careful analysis of the doctrines.

A suggested substitute is this three-part scheme:

1. *Objective Requirements.* The objective requirements of conduct, circumstance, and result elements in offence definitions share a conceptual similarity in their nature and roles. The special requirement of a causal connection between the conduct and result elements of an offence also could be usefully included as closely related to these objective requirements; it defines the required relation between two of the requirements.

2. *Culpability Requirements.* What we call 'culpability', or 'fault' requirements are conceptually diverse in many important ways. Chapter 6 in Part III discusses this in some detail. But, as that discussion will show, it is difficult to reconceptualize these requirements without a dramatic change in the current conceptualization. Such a dramatic reconceptualization is within the challenge of Part III of this book, but not within the 'refinement' of current conceptualization that Part II attempts.

3. *Act-Omission Requirements.* The act requirement's primary role, it is argued below, is to trigger the special requirements for omission liability, and should be treated as part of the special requirements for omission. The special rules governing possession liability can be viewed as a specialized case of omission liability. The voluntariness requirement, for reasons discussed later in this Chapter, is best conceptualized as part of the system of excuse defences, as an involuntariness defence, rather than the voluntariness requirement being treated as a part of all offence definitions.

Using this organizational scheme, each of the three groups of doctrines is examined in some detail below. Current law conceptualization is summarized and further refinements suggested.

B. Objective Elements of Offence Definitions

The typical objective elements scheme of modern codes can be summarized as follows. Offence definitions include three kinds of objective elements: (i) conduct, (ii) attendant circumstances of the conduct, and (iii) a result caused by the conduct.[25] Most offence definitions also include one or more circumstance elements. These frequently define the precise nature of the prohibited conduct—e.g. having intercourse with a person *under 16 years old*—or the precise nature of a prohibited result—e.g. causing the death of *another human being*. A minority of offences contain a result element. Homicide offences, personal injury offences, and property destruction offences typically require a resulting physical harm. Such offences as

---

[25] Model Penal Code, § 1.13(9) (defining 'elements of an offense').

endangerment, indecent exposure, and falsification typically require the actor to cause a *risk* of a physical or intangible harm, such as danger, alarm, or a false impression.[26]

When an offence definition includes a result element, as homicide requires a death, implicit in that result element is a causation requirement. That is, it must be shown that the actor's offence conduct caused the prohibited result. This required relation between the actor's conduct and the result derives from our notions of causal accountability. A result ought to affect an actor's liability only if it is a result for which the actor is causally accountable. Specifically, the law appears arbitrary and unfair if it increases an actor's liability because of a result for which the actor is not causally accountable. The rules of the causation doctrine are the means by which the law attempts to define the conditions under which such causal accountability exists.

Current doctrine typically contains two independent requirements to establish a causal connection between an actor's conduct and a result. First, the conduct must be a 'but for' cause of the result. That is, in the language of Model Penal Code section 2.03(1)(a), the conduct must be 'an antecedent but for which the result in question would not have occurred'. This is sometimes called the 'factual cause' requirement. Conduct is a factual ('but for') cause of a result if the result would not have occurred but for the conduct. In other words, the conduct was necessary for the result to occur. The factual cause inquiry is essentially a scientific one and a hypothetical one. It asks what the world would have been like had the actor not performed his conduct. Specifically, would the result still have occurred (when it did)? If the answer is no, then the actor's conduct was necessary for, was a 'but for' cause of, the result.[27] (The Draft English Code takes a different approach, requiring only that the act 'makes a more than negligible contribution to its occurrence'.[28])

The second requirement, 'legal' or 'proximate' cause, assures that the strength and nature of the causal connection between the conduct and the result is sufficient. This requires a finding under the Model Penal Code that the harm 'is not too remote or accidental in its occurrence to have a [just] bearing on the actor's liability or on the gravity of his offence'.[29] This language is sometimes supplemented with an additional requirement that the harm is 'not too . . . dependent on another's volitional act'.[30] The Draft English Code focuses instead upon the foreseeability of the result. An actor's conduct is not the cause of a result 'which he did not foresee,

---

[26] Model Penal Code, §§ 211.2, 213.5, 241.3(1)(b).

[27] The *necessary*-cause test is not the only possible formulation of the factual cause requirement. A sufficient-cause test similarly presents a scientific and hypothetical inquiry: would the actor's conduct have been sufficient by itself to cause the result?

[28] Draft English Code, ¶ 17(a).   [29] Model Penal Code, § 2.03(2)(b) and (3)(b).

[30] e.g. NJ Stat. Ann., § 2C:2-3.

and which could not in the circumstances reasonably have been foreseen' from such conduct.[31]

In contrast to the scientific inquiry of the factual cause requirement, the proximate (legal) cause requirement presents essentially a normative inquiry. Whether a result is 'too remote or accidental in its occurrence' or 'too dependent on another's volitional act' obviously calls for an exercise of intuitive judgment. The inquiry cannot be resolved by examining the facts more closely or having scientific experts analyse the situation. Ultimately, the decision maker must determine how much remoteness is 'too remote' or how much dependence on another's volitional act is 'too dependent' for the result to have a just bearing on the actor's liability. The foreseeability of the result, given the actor's conduct, is one factor that appears to be highly influential in jury determinations of proximate cause.

1. WEAKNESSES IN THE OBJECTIVE ELEMENT CATEGORIZATION SCHEME OF CONDUCT, CIRCUMSTANCE, AND RESULT ELEMENTS

The modern code categorization scheme of conduct, circumstance, and result elements is a significant and useful innovation in the conceptualization of criminal law, but some of the potential benefits of the scheme are lost by the failure of most modern codes to define the categories. When does an element constitute a conduct element, as opposed to a circumstance element or a result element? In the illustrations above, for example, one might argue that 'under 16 years old' is not a circumstance element but rather is part of the conduct element, 'having intercourse with a person under 16 years old'. Similarly, 'another human being' might be interpreted to be part of the result element of 'causing the death of another human being', rather than as an independent circumstance element. Without definitions of the categories that distinguish them, these differences in interpretation cannot authoritatively be resolved.

Adding to the confusion, offence definitions commonly use terms that combine what might be different categories of elements. Verbs like 'kills', 'obstructs', 'destroys', 'falsifies', 'mutilates', and 'desecrates' combine conduct and results. Each would have its meaning unchanged if it were written as 'engages in conduct by which he causes [death, obstruction, etc.]'. Verbs like 'compels' and 'removes' combine conduct with its attendant circumstances. To 'compel' or 'remove' a victim is implicitly to do so 'without his or her consent'.[32]

---

[31] Draft English Code, ¶ 17(2).

[32] For further discussion of these kinds of difficulties in defining elements, see Paul H. Robinson, *Criminal Law Defenses* (St Paul, Minn., 1984), i, § 61(b) (hereinafter *Criminal Law Defenses*); Paul H. Robinson and Jane A. Grall, 'Element Analysis in Defining Liability: The Model Penal Code and Beyond' (1983) 35 *Stanford LR* 681 at 705–19 (hereinafter 'Element Analysis').

The inability authoritatively to distinguish conduct, circumstance, and result elements is of practical significance because the application of several general provisions of a code depends upon the category of an element. Model Penal Code section 2.02(2), for example, defines the culpability terms differently for each kind of objective element. The definitions are asymmetrical. Thus, 'purposely' as to a *result* or *conduct* requires that the result or conduct be the actor's 'conscious object'. Being 'practically certain' of the result or 'aware' that his conduct is of that nature is an instance of the lesser culpability of 'knowingly' as to a result or conduct, which is inadequate to satisfy a requirement of 'purposely'. 'Purposely' as to a *circumstance*, in contrast, requires only that the actor be 'aware' of the circumstance—the same requirement as is required for the lesser culpability of 'knowingly' as to a circumstance.[33] The Draft English Code similarly defines fault requirements differently with reference to circumstance and result elements.[34]

The need to distinguish objective elements is similarly illustrated by the special requirements of causation (as in Model Penal Code section 2.03 and Draft English Code clause 17) that must be shown to be satisfied if an element is a result element, but not when it is a conduct or circumstance element. Thus, if 'obstructs' is interpreted as a pure conduct element, for example, the state need only prove the conduct. It need not prove the traditional requirements of causation, including, for example, proof that the obstruction would not have occurred but for the actor's conduct. If 'obstructs' is viewed as embodying both a conduct element and a result element, then the state would have to satisfy the 'but for' test as well as the other causation requirements.[35]

Here are proposals for definitions of objective element classification that are consistent with the spirit and intention of the modern code scheme. 'Conduct' elements should be defined narrowly to refer to the actual physical acts of the actor. All characteristics of the conduct should be defined as separate 'circumstance' elements. All consequences caused by the conduct should be defined as separate 'result' elements. 'Result' elements should be identified as circumstances changed by the conduct of the actor. As with conduct, the characteristics of a result should be treated as separate 'circumstance' elements.

Thus, an offence of 'obstructing a public highway' essentially requires proof that the actor 'engaged in conduct by which he caused the obstruction of

---

[33] That an actor 'hopes' or desires that a circumstance exists—the analogous requirement to a result or conduct being on actor's 'conscious object'—is adequate to satisfy 'purposely' as to a circumstance but is not required.

[34] See Draft English Code, ¶ 18. For example, it defines 'knowingly' with regard to a circumstance but not with regard to a result.

[35] This includes, for example, the requirement that the result is 'not too remote or accidental in its occurrence to have a [just] bearing on the actor's liability or on the gravity of his offense'.

a public highway'. 'Obstruction' is a result element; the state has to prove that the actor's conduct caused the obstruction, the change in circumstance. That it was a 'public highway' was not changed by the actor but rather is a characteristic of the result of the conduct—what it was that was obstructed—and therefore is treated as a circumstance element. The 'conduct' element here, as in many offences, requires simply some act by the actor. No particular act is required, other than one that causes the required result (obstruction) with the required characteristic (of a public highway). Under this definitional scheme, the conduct element commonly has little or no significance beyond satisfying the act requirement.[36] Section D.4, at the end of this Chapter, discusses these proposals further, to the extent that they influence the application of culpability requirements.

2. Confusion in the Modern Code Conceptualization of Causation Requirements

The natural complexities of causation issues often are exacerbated by the typical American code provisions, which are unnecessarily complex and misleading. Many are modelled after the Model Penal Code causation provision, Model Penal Code section 2.03, which is quoted in the note below.[37] (Most of these problems are avoided in the Draft English Code provision in clause 17.)

First, the Model Penal Code provision uses a triple negative, the need for which is not clear. The required culpability element 'is *not* established if the actual result is not [that which was intended or risked] *unless*'. The first clause—'is not established if'—suggests that the subsection is defining a defence. But the 'unless' clause reveals an opposite intention: while an

---

[36] For a more detailed description of this proposal and the reasons for it, see Robinson, *Criminal Law Defenses*, i, n. 32 above, at § 61(c); Robinson and Grall, 'Element Analysis', n. 32 above, at 719–25. For a discussion of the act requirement, see sect. B.2. of this Ch.

[37] Model Penal Code § 2.03(1) & (2) reads as follows:

'(1) Conduct is the cause of a result when:

    (a) it is an antecedent but for which the result in question would not have occurred; and

    (b) the relationship between the conduct and result satisfies any additional causal requirements imposed by the Code or by the law defining the offense.

(2) When purposely or knowingly causing a particular result is an element of an offense, the element is not established if the actual result is not within the purpose or the contemplation of the actor unless:

    (a) the actual result differs from that designed or contemplated, as the case may be, only in the respect that a different person or different property is injured or affected or that the injury or harm designed or contemplated would have been more serious or more extensive than that caused; or

    (b) the actual result involves the same kind of injury or harm as that designed or contemplated and is not too remote or accidental in its occurrence to have a [just] bearing on the actor's liability or on the gravity of his offense.'

actor might normally get a defence through the absence of the required culpability, this section is designed to take away that defence under the conditions specified in the 'unless' clause in subsections (a) and (b). In other words, subsections 2.03(2) and (3) are doctrines of imputation, not defence.

Subsection (a) concerns cases of divergence between the result intended or risked and the result caused. Such a provision appropriately is a doctrine of imputation. While an actor may not have intended to harm the actual victim or may not have intended the actual harm, it nonetheless is appropriate to treat him as if he had so intended, if he intended the same harm to a different target, or intended a greater harm than that actually caused. Subsection (a) can be faulted only because it does not state the authority for such imputation in the positive form that the legality principle prefers. It would be better phrased: the required culpability is established if the actor intended a greater harm or intended the same harm to a different person.

Subsection (b), concerning cases of remoteness, is more troubling. The introductory language of section 2.03(2) and (3) is improper for these provisions. That a result is 'too remote or accidental' is a defence; it is not a ground for imputation as the introductory language suggests. More important, the limiting language at the beginning of subsection (b)—limiting the remoteness defence to instances where 'the actual result involves the same kind of injury or harm [as that intended or risked]'—is inappropriate. The defence for a result that is 'too remote or accidental' ought to be available in all cases, not just those of the same kind of injury or harm.

Recall the classic case of remoteness: an actor shoots at the victim and misses; the victim then flees and several minutes later is struck and killed by a falling piano. He would not have died when he did but for the actor's shot, but most would agree that the connection between the actor's conduct and the death is too remote to hold the actor accountable. Now assume that the falling piano causes a less serious injury than that intended by the actor's original shot. If the falling piano only maims rather than kills the fleeing victim, the defendant still ought not to be causally accountable for the maiming, any more than he ought to be accountable for causing the death if the victim is killed. Preferable is language requiring that in every instance an actor's conduct must be not only a 'but for' cause but that it also be 'not too remote or accidental'.[38]

For the same reasons, it also is doubtful that the remoteness defence should be limited by the subsection (2) and (3) introductory language restricting the defence to cases where 'the actual result is not within the [purpose or contemplation of the actor]/[risk of which the actor knew or

---

[38] Proposed Rhode Island Criminal Code, § 11A–2–2(2).

should have known]'.[39] Even if the actual result is the result intended, it should be a defence that the result is too remote or accidental.[40]

The causation provision drafters formulated their provision the way they did because of a misunderstanding of how the Code's culpability system works. Let me explain. The Code's peculiar causation provision makes perfect sense if one assumes that the culpability required with respect to a result element is not simply culpability as to the result itself, as defined in the offence definition, but also includes a requirement that the actor be culpable as to the *way in which the result came about*, even though this is not an objective element of the offence. Thus, the causation drafters apparently believed that the Code required for murder proof that the actor wanted to cause the death of another *and wanted to cause it in the way in which it actually came about*. Thus, in *State* v. *Lassiter*, for example, where a prostitute jumped to her death to avoid further beating by her pimp,[41] the drafters imply that proof of murder by the pimp requires proof that he intended to cause the woman's death *by having her jump out the window*; liability for murder could not be sustained, they apparently thought, upon proof that he intended to cause her death by beating her. Thus, they drafted section 2.03(2)(b) to impute to him what they thought was the needed culpability—the intention to cause her death by jumping out of the window—based upon his having another equally blameworthy culpability—the intention to cause her death by beating.

But the causation drafters were trying to solve a problem that exists only in their minds. Nothing in the Code's provisions would suggest that the culpability required as to a result, such as death of another human being, is any more than culpability as to the specific result described in the offence definition. If the offence required more—for example, if the offence specifically punished causing death by poison or death by explosive, as some offences do (or death by causing someone to jump out a window)—then the defendant would have to have not only culpability as to causing the death but also culpability as to causing death *by poison* or causing the death *by explosive* or causing the death *by having another jump out a window*. Absent a more demanding objective requirement such as one of these, there is nothing in the Code to suggest that culpability as to a result requires anything more than culpability as to the result specified in the offence definition, i.e. death of another human being.

The drafters' confusion may stem from the distinction between culpability in the general sense of blameworthiness and culpability in the special sense of offence culpability requirements such as those defined in Model Penal Code section 2.02. As the Code was being drafted scholars

---

[39] Model Penal Code, § 2.03(2) & (3).

[40] Thus, even if the actor sought to kill the victim by dropping a piano on him, we are likely to judge the death too remote and accidental if the fleeing victim is killed by the accidental fall of a piano.　　　　　[41] (1984) 197 NJ Super. 2, 484 A (2d) 13.

came to the significant insight that proximate cause matters were essentially an issue of general blameworthiness.[42] Proximate cause is not subject to determination by applying an apparently empirical assessment of how 'direct' or 'immediate' the cause is to the result, as the common law would suggest.[43] Rather, it calls for a general normative assessment by the decision-maker. As the Model Penal Code usefully expresses it, the result must not be 'too remote or accidental in its occurrence to have a [just] bearing on the actor's liability or on the gravity of his offence'.

But, because proximate cause and remoteness concern blameworthiness (culpability in the general sense) it does not follow that they concern offence culpability elements (culpability in the special sense). The Code distinguishes general blameworthiness issues from offence culpability in other contexts (e.g. excuse defences are independent doctrines of exculpation; they do not negate offence culpability requirements). There is no reason to think that general blameworthiness in the proximate cause context must be treated as an issue of offence culpability elements. Indeed, because the Code elsewhere defines culpability requirements *in relation to an offence's objective elements*,[44] it is unworkable to assume in the causation provision that a culpability element requires something more than proof of culpability *as to the corresponding objective element*.

A causation provision would be better drafted not only to reflect the insight of the Model Penal Code but also to treat proximate cause not as an issue of culpability as to a result but rather as a required relation between conduct and a result. A better formulation follows:

Section 11A–2–2. Causal Relationship Between Conduct and Result.[45]
Conduct is the cause of a result if:
(1) the conduct is an antecedent but for which the result in question would not have occurred; and
(2) the result is not too remote or too accidental in its manner of occurrence or too dependent upon another's volitional act to have a just bearing on the actor's liability or on the gravity of his offence; and
(3) the relationship between the conduct and result satisfies any additional causal requirements imposed by the Code or by the law defining the offence.
(4) *Simultaneous Causes.* Where the conduct of two or more actors each simultaneously contributes to the result and each alone would have been sufficient

---

[42] See H. L. A. Hart and A. M. Honoré, *Causation in the Law* (1st edn., Oxford, 1959), 353–61, (2nd edn., London, 1985), 394–403.

[43] In *The Queen* v. *Pocock*, for example, all of the persons in the nearby village had the legal duty to repair, or have repaired, the potholes in the road so as to ensure safe travel. When a traveller died from an accident caused by the disrepair of the road, the court concluded that the villagers were not criminally accountable for the death. While the omission of each of them may have been a 'but for' cause, the court concluded that the omission was not 'immediately connected with the death', that is, the death was not the 'direct consequence' of their omission. See (1851) 17 QB 34 at 38–9, 117 ER 1194 at 1196.

[44] See Model Penal Code, § 2.02(2).

[45] Proposed Rhode Island Criminal Code, § 11A–2–2.

to cause the result, the requirement of Subsection (1) of this section shall be held to be satisfied.[46]

C. The Act–Omission Requirements and the Involuntariness Defence

Consider next the voluntary act requirement. I argue here that current conceptualization is flawed in two respects. First, close examination suggests that the act requirement does little or nothing to serve the purposes traditionally attributed to it. Instead, the most important role of the statutory act requirement is to trigger the special requirements for omission liability. It ought to be seen as simply an aspect of the omission rules, their trigger. Secondly, the traditional characterization of the voluntariness requirement as an aspect of the act requirement, which is seen as a part of each offence definition, overlooks the conceptual identity of the voluntariness requirement with the excuse defences. I argue below that it is distinct and conceptually different from the act requirement and all offence definition requirements, and that involuntariness should be treated as an excuse defence rather than voluntariness as an offence requirement.

1. The Role of the Statutory Act Requirement

One cannot be held liable for thoughts alone, it is said. Properly construed, the maxim is accurate but may invite too broad an interpretation. Otherwise lawful conduct can be made criminal by an actor's accompanying state of mind. In that sense, one can be punished because of one's thoughts. Lighting one's pipe is not itself an offence but becomes attempted arson if it is a step in a plan to ignite a neighbour's haystack. Giving a young girl a ride is not an offence but becomes attempted sexual assault if it is done with the intention of then sexually assaulting her. Just thinking about committing an offence—arson or sexual assault—is not an offence. But once the actor externalizes his thoughts by performing an act toward

---

[46] A revised divergence provision might look like this:

'*Section 11A–2–4. Divergence Between Consequence Intended or Risked and Actual Consequence*

When the culpability as to a particular consequence is required by an offense definition and the actual consequence is not designed, contemplated, or risked by the actor, as the case may be, the required culpability as to the consequence is nonetheless established if the actual consequence differs from the consequence intended, contemplated, or risked, as the case may be, only in the respect that:

(1) a different person or different property is injured or affected, or

(2) the consequence intended, contemplated, or risked was more serious or more extensive an injury or harm than the actual consequence.

(3) "Consequence", as used in this section, means the result element of the offense definition and the attendant circumstance elements that characterize that result.'

Proposed Rhode Island Criminal Code, § 11A–2–4.

the offence, he may be subject to liability. The act requirement is the criminal law's mechanism for requiring such externalization. Model Penal Code section 2.01(1), for example, provides that, 'A person is not guilty of an offense unless his liability is based on conduct which includes a voluntary act'. This continues the common law rule.[47]

A requirement of externalization is said to be useful for several reasons. By requiring an act, the law excludes from liability those persons who only fantasize about committing an offence and those persons who may indeed form an intention to commit an offence but whose intention is not sufficiently firm to mature into action. One may argue that such people are dangerous, at least more dangerous than persons without such fantasies or intentions, and perhaps the criminal law should take jurisdiction.[48] Many people may fantasise or form irresolute intentions yet never act, and use of criminal sanctions in these cases is inefficient. More important, so long as the criminal law continues to claim a moral foundation, liability is inappropriate in such cases because fantasising and irresolute intentions generally are not viewed as adequate to deserve condemnation and punishment.[49] Condemnation sufficient for criminal conviction typically follows only after an intention matures into action.

Beyond its value in barring punishment for unexternalized thoughts, the act requirement provides some minimal objective confirmation that an actor's intention does exist. Upon observing an action consistent with the intention, we feel more sure of the actor's intention and her willingness to act upon it. But the act requirement by itself performs this role poorly. Admittedly, some conduct may unambiguously manifest a mind bent on crime. There is little ambiguity in the act of strangling another by the neck. But it also is the case that conduct, especially that short of a substantive offence, frequently does little by itself to indicate a culpable state of mind. The farmer lighting his pipe near his neighbour's haystack may have no intention of committing arson.

The act requirement also has been used to establish a time and place of occurrence of an offence. While one's intention may range over a long period of time and many places, the conduct constituting the offence can be identified with a particular time and place. This assists enforcement of the concurrence requirement—i.e. that the required mens rea exist at the time of the conduct constituting the offence. An identifiable time and place also facilitate the application of various procedural rules, such as those governing jurisdiction, venue, and periods of time of limitation. Again,

---

[47] Compare Model Penal Code, § 2.01(1) with 4 William Blackstone, *Commentaries*, *5.

[48] Barbara Wootton, 'Diminished Responsibility: A Layman's View' (1960) 76 LQR 224 at 233.

[49] Among other things, there is some question whether one has sufficient control over one's thoughts to be held responsible for having them. One generally does have control of one's conduct, however, absent dysfunction, that would justify an excuse.

however, the act requirement cannot be relied upon for too much. Frequently, an offence contains many acts and some offences punish so-called 'continuing acts' (such as concealment, criminal agreement, possession, or obstruction). The greater the number of acts or the longer 'a continuing act', the messier the application of the procedural rules.[50] The reason for the procedural rules sometimes may be undercut, as where jurisdiction and venue are appropriate everywhere and where the statute of limitation never begins to run.

Some states, such as California, also have tried to use the act requirement to resolve the thorny issue of liability and punishment for multiple related offences. The California Penal Code purports to allow punishment for only one offence arising from a single act.[51] But the California courts have rejected strict application of this provision where one act causes two results, such as two deaths, or constitutes two violations of the same offence provision, such as two instances of attempted murder.[52] The courts continue to defer to the provision in cases where one act violates different provisions, such as arson and attempted murder,[53] but even this narrow application is problematic. Where an actor sets a house on fire with two people in it, intending to burn the house and the people, why should the state have to elect to punish for arson or for attempted murder? Why is not punishment for both appropriate? To exclude punishment for both is to trivialize the offence not punished. One also may question the logic of allowing multiple liability for the two instances of attempted murder arising from a single act yet denying liability for arson and attempted murder from the same act. Under what theory must the state choose between different kinds of harms from a single act but need not choose between distinct but related harms from a single act? One can conclude from the California experience that the act requirement is of little value in solving the difficult problem of multiple offences. At best, it serves as a starting point for a more complex analysis.[54]

As a practical matter, the most significant purpose of the act requirement is its exclusion from liability of fantasisation and irresolute intentions. But look more carefully at how effectively the act requirement serves this

---

[50] Special rules frequently are constructed to deal with this weakness of the act requirement. In the context of conspiracy, for example, see Model Penal Code, § 5.03(7).

[51] Cal. Penal Code, § 654 provides:

> 'An act or omission which is made punishable in different ways by different provisions of this code may be punishable under either of such provisions, but in no case can it be punished under more than one.'

[52] See e.g. *Neal* v. *State* (1960) 9 Cal. Rptr. 607, 357 P (2d) 839 (defendant convicted on two counts of attempted murder and one count of arson; because arson and attempted murder resulted from one act, defendant's conviction for arson was dismissed, but not two convictions for attempted murder). [53] *Ibid.*

[54] For a discussion of more useful provisions determining when liability is appropriate for multiple offences, see Model Penal Code, §§ 1.07(1) & (4), 5.05(3).

purpose. The act requirement is satisfied by the performance of nearly any act; the act need not be the conduct element of a completed offence. The farmer who lights his pipe by the haystack and the child molester who gives a girl a ride, each have performed an act. Nothing in the statutory requirement requires that the act be the act immediately preceding or contemporaneous with the harm or evil of the offence. The Model Penal Code provision, for example, requires only that the actor's liability be 'based on conduct which *includes* a voluntary act.'[55] The student who thinks about killing his criminal law professor may not actually try to kill her, yet he no doubt has performed acts while having that desire to kill. The thought may have come to him while eating breakfast, a voluntary act.

One would think that we ought to exclude such a collateral act as a basis for liability because it fails to show an *externalization of his intention* to commit the offence. Yet nothing in the Model Penal Code provision seems to limit the act requirement in this way. Perhaps this is so because it is unclear how one might define such a limitation. Would one require an act in furtherance of the actor's intention to commit an offence? Assume the student gets out of bed with the intention of killing his criminal law professor. In fact, the conduct is in furtherance of the intention and, indeed, necessary for commission of the offence. Should it then be adequate for liability? This example illustrates that the problem, an important one in criminal law, has already been tackled by the inchoate offences. How little of what sort of conduct is sufficient for liability if accompanied by an intention to commit an offence? In other words, the act requirement is not necessary to define the minimum conduct required for criminal liability because the inchoate offences—attempt, conspiracy, solicitation, and possession—already do this.

Does the act requirement extend the existing limitations of the inchoate offences? In fact, each of the inchoate offences satisfies the act requirement on its face. For example, Model Penal Code section 5.01(1) requires 'a substantial step' toward commission of the offence. As thin a conduct requirement as that is, it nonetheless insures that every attempt case satisfies the act requirement. Similarly, the offence of conspiracy, defined in section 5.03(1) of the Model Penal Code, contains an act requirement by requiring that the actor 'agree' with another person that one of them will commit an offence. Speaking, as in 'I agree', or even nodding, satisfies the act requirement. Thus, if an actor satisfies the requirements of an inchoate offence, the actor also necessarily satisfies the requirements of the act requirement.

One may ask, then, whether the statutory act requirement has any practical significance. Perhaps the act requirement would be important if the legislature created an offence independent of the inchoate offences that

---

[55] Model Penal Code, § 2.01(1).

contained no conduct element. Of course, if the offence were one of omission, then the special requirements of omission liability would apply.[56] But, what if a legislature gone wild sought to criminalize thinking or a status of some kind? The act requirement might seem to help. But it would take little for the legislature to add a conduct element of some kind to the offence definition. Instead of an offence of imagining the death of the king, the offence could be defined to punish communicating to another that one imagined the death of the king, a fact that would necessarily exist in every instance where we could know that such an offence had occurred. Instead of an offence of Being a Democrat, the offence could be defined to punish Joining the Democratic Party, which presumably would require an act of some sort. These offences might run afoul of other legal or constitutional provisions,[57] but they do satisfy the statutory act requirement. The requirement protects us, then, only from very stupid legislatures (such as those too stupid to simply repeal the requirement).

The inescapable conclusion seems to be that the statutory act requirement has no independent significance other than to trigger the special requirements of omission liability. It is perhaps no surprise that the Draft English Criminal Code contains no such provision.[58] It may continue to exist as an independent provision in modern American codes primarily as a vehicle for the voluntariness requirement, but, as discussed below, that usage is unwise for other reasons. It is suggested, then, that the statutory act requirement ought to be reconceptualized from its current position as an independent requirement to be seen instead as an aspect of the doctrine of omission liability.

2. THE VOLUNTARINESS REQUIREMENT AS AN EXCUSE

The voluntary act requirement, frequently treated as a single aspect of the 'actus reus' requirement, contains two related but distinct doctrines: the act requirement and a voluntariness requirement. Several writers ensure that the two are treated as one by defining an 'act' as a 'willed movement'.[59]

---

[56] The two most important special requirements of omission liability are requirements of the capacity to perform the omitted conduct and the legal duty to perform the omitted conduct. See generally Paul H. Robinson, *Criminal Law* (Boston, 1997), § 3.4 (hereinafter *Criminal Law*).

[57] If there is an act requirement that has some content to it, it is found in constitutional law doctrine, not in the criminal code. In *Scales* v. *United States*, for example, the Court barred the government from criminalizing pure membership in the Communist Party. It did, however, allow liability for 'active' members of the Party: (1961) 367 US 203 at 222. In *Robinson* v. *California*, the Court similarly invalidated a state statute that made it an offence to 'be addicted to the use of narcotics': (1962) 370 US 660 at 667. Yet, these cases limit governmental criminalization authority in a very modest way. It would not be unconstitutional to criminalize *joining* the Communist Party or *taking* drugs.

[58] See generally Draft English Code commentary, vol. 2, ¶¶ 7.6–7.13.

[59] See e.g. Williams, *The General Part*, n. 17 above, at § 8; Oliver W. Holmes, *The Common Law* (Boston, 1881), 54.

Modern codes typically keep the two separate; they define an 'act' to be 'a bodily movement whether voluntary or involuntary'.[60]

The voluntariness requirement with regard to acts upon which liability is based has a counterpart for omission liability (and possession liability). That is, liability must be based upon either a voluntary act or a voluntary omission to perform a legal duty (or voluntary possession of contraband). To be voluntary, an *act* must be 'a product of the effort or determination of the actor'.[61] An actor who injures another through convulsion or reflex muscle action, for example, is excused. Involuntary acts commonly include, for example, 'a reflex or convulsion; a bodily movement during unconsciousness or sleep; conduct during hypnosis or resulting from hypnotic suggestion'.[62] To be voluntary, an *omission to perform a duty* must be an omission 'to perform an act of which [the actor] is physically capable'.[63] To assure that *possession of contraband* is voluntary, modern codes typically require that the actor know he has control 'for a sufficient period to have been able to terminate his possession'.[64] When speaking of the act requirement or omission to perform a duty, one typically refers to a voluntary act or a voluntary omission even if it is not expressly noted. If one rereads the previous discussion of the act requirement, for example, one could substitute the phrase 'voluntary act' each time the term 'act' is used, and the meaning of the passage would likely be just as the reader interpreted it.

This natural connection between the voluntariness requirement and the act requirement helps explain why the voluntariness requirement traditionally is treated conceptually as a part of it, as an aspect of the actus reus. But it is, in truth, an independent doctrine with different requirements and rationales. It applies to the act requirement in the same way that it applies to all conduct requirements, such as the conduct elements of offence definitions. Rather than protecting fantasising and irresolute intentions from liability, or providing an anchor for application of procedural rules, or limiting governmental criminalization authority, or triggering the special requirements of omission liability, as the act requirement claims to do, the voluntariness requirement is designed to protect from liability actors who admittedly have brought about a prohibited harm or evil but who cannot properly be held blameworthy for the violation because they are unable to control their conduct. The assault that results from convulsion, hypnotic suggestion, or somnambulism is harmful and remains prohibited in the future but the actor at hand is not punished for it because he is not morally responsible for the conduct.

The distinction between the act requirement and the voluntariness requirement also appears in United States Supreme Court cases. In *Robinson*

---

[60] See Model Penal Code, § 1.13(2).   [61] Model Penal Code, §§ 1.13(3), 2.01(2)(d).
[62] Model Penal Code, § 2.01(2)(a)–(c).   [63] Model Penal Code, § 2.01(1).
[64] See Model Penal Code, § 2.01(4).

v. *California*, the Supreme Court found a violation of the Fourteenth Amendment's 'cruel and unusual punishment' prohibition in a state's making it a crime for a person to 'be addicted to the use of narcotics'.[65] A mere status or condition may not be punished, the Court concludes. Some commentators took this to mean that the constitution required that criminal liability be based upon a voluntary act. Conviction of the addict in *Robinson* could not be permitted, they argued, because the addict could not control his status as an addict. But in *Powell* v. *Texas*[66] the justices' opinions distinguish the act requirement from the voluntariness requirement. Four of the justices in the majority in *Powell* expressly reject the abovementioned reading of *Robinson*; they see no constitutional requirement of a voluntary act:[67] '[t]he entire thrust of *Robinson's* interpretation of the Cruel and Unusual Punishment Clause is that criminal penalties may be inflicted only if the accused has committed some act, had engaged in some behavior, which society has an interest in preventing'.[68] But the four dissenters in *Powell* would have constitutionalized the voluntariness requirement, and the remaining member, Justice White, indicates some agreement with this position.[69] Nothing further has come of constitutionalizing the voluntariness requirement. That the act requirement has clear constitutional status and the voluntariness requirement does not is simply another example of the distinct and independent nature of the two requirements.[70]

Rather than being similar to the other doctrines of actus reus, the voluntariness requirement is analogous to, indeed is part of, the criminal law's system of excuses. Both the voluntariness requirement and the excuse defences, such as insanity, involuntary intoxication, and duress, hold an actor blameless despite criminal conduct when that conduct is judged too much the product of forces other than the actor's exercise of will. These exculpatory doctrines work upon a continuum of volition, with the voluntariness requirement exculpating the most extreme cases. There is considerable overlap, however, between the range of cases dealt with under the

---

[65] (1962) 370 US 660. It is not the extent of punishment that offends the constitution, but rather its use. 'Even one day in prison would be a cruel and unusual punishment for the "crime" of having a common cold': *ibid.* 667.

[66] (1968) 392 US 514.   [67] *Ibid.* 532.   [68] *Ibid.* 533.   [69] *Ibid.* 548.

[70] The Supreme Court's reluctance to extend constitutionalization to the voluntariness requirement may have come from an appreciation for the doctrine's conceptual identity with the excuse defences, discussed in the text, immediately following. The Court might well have seen that, no matter the wisdom of having such a requirement, to constitutionalize it logically would have drawn the Court into constitutionalizing, or trying to distinguish, the host of other criminal law doctrines that are based upon some degree of impairment of volition. This includes not only the general disability excuses, such as insanity, duress, involuntary intoxication, but also doctrines of mitigation, such as provocation and extreme emotional disturbance. Criminal law theory has struggled with and changed the accepted wisdom on these and other issues central to criminal responsibility many times during the past century. The Court might have thought it unwise to impede this continuing development by constitutionalizing and thereby solidifying matters that ought to remain fluid until we are more certain of their proper formulation.

involuntariness defence and the range of cases dealt with under the excuse defences. The fact is, many excuse defences reflect overwhelming compulsions, while many cases classed as involuntary acts reflect only a mild form of coercion.[71]

While it may have been different in an earlier era, a defence under the voluntariness requirement currently does not require absolute involuntariness. Reflex action and convulsion are certainly instances of involuntary conduct but other less absolute dysfunctions also are recognized. There is in reality a continuum of control dysfunction even within the range of cases treated as involuntary acts. In *Regina* v. *Charlson*,[72] for example, the defendant hit his son over the head with a mallet and threw him out of a window, for no apparent reason. His actions subsequently were attributed to the effect of a brain tumour. While these acts may seem more willed and directed than a convulsion, their physiological explanation persuasively argues that the actor is not accountable for them. Further along the involuntariness continuum is conduct during sleep. In *King* v. *Cogdon*,[73] for example, the defendant stabbed her daughter to death while dreaming that the Korean War was going on in her house and one of the soldiers was attacking her daughter. The psychiatric testimony suggested that her attack manifested a subconscious hostility toward her daughter. Such actions may well be the product of an actor's effort or determination in a narrow sense. But one's subconscious desires and motivations generally are not recognized as an adequate basis for condemnation by criminal sanction. We do not generally treat people as if they can control their subconscious. Still further along the continuum is conduct under hypnosis. While Model Penal Code section 2.01(2)(c) conclusively presumes 'conduct during hypnosis or resulting from hypnotic suggestion' to be involuntary, the weight of modern evidence suggests that the effect of hypnosis on most people is not nearly so dramatic and that its effect is only to create a discernible but not compelling compulsion.[74]

The point here is simply that the voluntariness requirement concerns issues and serves purposes analogous to those of the general excuses and distinct from those of the act requirement. The proper conceptualization of the voluntariness requirement as a general excuse of involuntariness is discussed further in Part III (Chapter 8, section B), which gives examples of the kinds of practical difficulties its misconceptualization can cause.

---

[71] See generally Robinson, *Criminal Law*, n. 56 above, at § 9.2.

[72] [1955] 1 WLR 317, 39 Cr. App. R 37 (jury found defendant was acting as an automaton without any knowledge of or control over his actions).

[73] This unreported case, heard in the Supreme Court of Victoria in 1950, is reported in Norval Morris, 'Somnambulistic Homicide: Ghosts, Spiders, and North Koreans' (1951) 5 *Res Judicata* 29 (defendant acquitted because the act of killing itself was not, in law, her act at all).

[74] For a more detailed discussion, see Robinson, *Criminal Law*, n. 56 above, at § 9.2.

D. Culpability Elements of Offence Definitions

The first section of this Chapter described the objective element 'building blocks' of offence definitions: conduct, circumstance, and result elements. Modern American codes typically follow Model Penal Code section 2.02(1) in providing that 'a person is not guilty of an offence unless he acted purposely, knowingly, recklessly, or negligently, as the law may require, with respect to each material element of the offence'. The Draft English Code similarly provides in clause 20(1) that, 'Every offence requires a fault element of recklessness with respect to each of its elements other than fault elements, unless otherwise provided'. The provisions reflect the criminal law's commitment to requiring not only a breach of society's objective rules of conduct but also an actor's culpability as to the conditions that make the conduct a breach.

As this section explains, the development of modern culpability requirements has brought order and rationality to an area of law that had previously been adrift in confusion. The 'element analysis' innovation was one of the greatest contributions of the Model Penal Code. The use of a limited number of defined culpability terms, as in Model Penal Code section 2.02(2) and Draft English Code clause 18, also brings order and clarity. Both of these advances are briefly described below.

But any such grand reconceptualization creates its own complications. Practical experience with application of the Model Penal Code has revealed a variety of problems with its provisions. While the Draft English Code avoids many of these problems, experience suggests that it will encounter its own unique set. Any culpability scheme sophisticated enough to address that complex area will inevitably produce unforeseen complications. The Model Penal Code scheme is used here to illustrate how even the best planned scheme has its problems. The final conclusion is not, however, that such reforms are doomed to failure. On the contrary; the scope and nature of the problems are sufficiently minor that they only illustrate what great advances have been made. We now have the luxury of arguing about the details, a monumental improvement over being adrift in a sea of culpability confusion.

1. The Evolution to Element Analysis

The law did not always require culpability of an actor. Early Germanic tribes, it is suggested, imposed liability upon the causing of an injury, without regard to culpability.[75] But this was a period before tort law and criminal law divided. As the functional difference between tort and crime appeared —that is, as the distinction of imposing punishment became independent

---

[75] For a history of the development of culpability requirements, see Paul H. Robinson, 'A Brief History of Distinctions in Criminal Culpability' (1980) 31 *Hastings LJ* 816.

of the function of compensating victims—the requirement of culpability took on increasing importance for criminal law.[76]

Changing notions of mens rea are illustrated by the different opinions in *Regina* v. *Prince*.[77] The defendant had taken an under-age girl 'out of the possession' of her father, reasonably believing she was over the age of consent. That the defendant's conduct was generally immoral was sufficient for Bramwell J to find that the defendant had the mens rea necessary for the crime.[78] Brett J on the other hand, would require that Prince at least have intended to do something (anything) that was criminal, not just immoral.[79] A somewhat more demanding requirement is expressed in *Regina* v. *Faulkner*.[80] In the process of stealing rum from the hold of a ship, Faulkner accidentally set the ship afire, destroying it. Fitzgerald and Palles JJ conclude that the mens rea requirement means that Faulkner at least must have intended to do something criminal that reasonably might have been expected to have led to the actual harm caused and charged.[81] Thus, Faulkner ought not be liable for the offence of burning a ship when he intended only to steal rum and could not reasonably have foreseen the ship's destruction.

This last shift in the notion of mens rea meant not only a dramatic increase in the demand of the requirement but also meant a significant qualitative change. No longer did there exist a single mens rea requirement for all offences—the intention to do something immoral or, later, something criminal. Now each offence had a different mens rea requirement. An actor had to intend to do something that reasonably might be expected to lead to the harm of the particular offence. As some have expressed it, there was no longer a *mens rea* for criminal liability but rather *mentes reae*.[82]

The Model Penal Code carried this refinement another step. As section 2.02(1) quoted above makes clear, the Code requires culpability 'with respect to each material element of the offence'.[83] Even the notion of *mentes reae* conceives of each offence as having a single culpability requirement. Indeed, doctrine of that day grouped offences according to the type of culpability that the offence required: general intent offences, specific intent offences, and offences of strict liability.[84] In what may be described

---

[76] For centuries, admittedly, tort law remained tied to notions of fault, generally negligence, but the nature of the fault required for tort recovery was never set at the level that would justify condemnation of the actor, as was and is generally required at criminal law. Nor, admittedly, has criminal law completely forsaken the imposition of liability in the absence of subjective awareness of wrongdoing. Criminal liability sometimes is still permitted for 'gross negligence' or a 'gross deviation' from the standard of care of a reasonable person. See e.g. Model Penal Code, § 2.02(2)(d).

[77] (1875) 13 Cox CC 138.   [78] *Ibid.* 141–2.   [79] *Ibid.* 146.
[80] (1877) 13 Cox CC 550.   [81] *Ibid.* 557, 561.
[82] Francis Bowes Sayre, 'The Present Significance of Mens Rea in the Criminal Law' (1934) *Harvard Legal Essays* 399 at 404.
[83] Model Penal Code, § 2.02(1).
[84] For an attempt to define and illustrate these distinctions, see *Linehan* v. *State* (1983) 442 So. (2d) 244.

as a shift from *offence analysis* to *element analysis*,[85] the Model Penal Code introduced the requirement of culpability as to each element of an offence. The Code also permits the level of culpability to be different for different elements of the same offence. This element analysis approach provides, for the first time, a fully comprehensive statement of the culpability required.

Early conceptions of mens rea were not simply undemanding; they were hopelessly vague. They failed to tell courts enough about the required culpability for an offence to enable courts to resolve the cases that commonly arose. The vague conceptualizations left it for courts to 'fill in' the culpability requirements that the statutes did not provide.[86] Element analysis permits legislatures to reclaim from the courts the authority to define the conditions of criminal liability.[87] It allows them to give a comprehensive definition of an offence, a definition that makes clear to a reader every objective and culpability element that is required.

The shift to element analysis did not so much represent an attempt to change offence requirements as an attempt accurately and fully to define those requirements. That is, common law lawyers and judges were wrong to think that their offence-analysis view of offence culpability requirements was adequate to describe the culpability that the common law required. Their misconception stemmed in part from their conceptualization of an independent 'law of mistake', which they saw as supplementing the culpability requirements of an offence definition. Under this view, an actor might satisfy the requirements of theft but might have a defence if the law of mistake allowed a defence in the actor's particular situation. The Model Penal Code drafters, in contrast, recognized that a mistake defence and a culpability requirement generally are one and the same, simply two ways of describing the same thing. The Code states that mistake provides a defence if it negates an offence culpability requirement.[88] The Draft English Code has a similar provision.[89]

---

[85] See generally Robinson and Grall, 'Element Analysis', n. 32 above.

[86] This occurs most commonly in determining whether an actor's mistake should provide a defence. See Robinson, *Criminal Law*, n. 56 above, at § 4.4.

[87] Despite these recent dramatic developments, most American courts have failed to take note of the modern criminal code shift to element analysis. Dulled by generations of offence analysis, courts ignore general code provisions that, together with offence definitions, define every objective and culpability element required for liability. They continue to define unstated culpability requirements according to their own view of the public policy interests. The result is that in nearly every criminal case in the United States the statement of the law defining the offence charged suffers a significant risk of inaccuracy.

While it does not explain or excuse the slow judicial re-education, the Model Penal Code's implementation of element analysis is admittedly haphazard and, in many respects, seriously flawed. See sects. D.3. and D.4. of this Ch. So too are the criminal codes of most states, modelled as they are after the Code. Yet the virtues of element analysis make it worth salvaging. The feasibility of such a task is confirmed by the proposals made here. See sect. D.4. of this Ch.

[88] See Model Penal Code, § 2.04(1).   [89] See Draft English Code, ¶ 21.

2. THE CULPABILITY DISTINCTIONS .

Aside from their insight into the relation between mistake defences and culpability requirements, the Code drafters' greatest contribution in this area is their use of a limited number of culpability terms. In place of a plethora of common law terms—wantonly, heedlessly, maliciously, etc.[90] —the Code defines four levels of culpability: purpose, knowledge, reck-lessness, and negligence.[91] (The Draft English Code does not formally re-cognize or define the lowest level, negligence.) Ideally, all offences are defined by designating one of these levels of culpability as to each object-ive element. If the objective elements of an offence require that an actor take property of another, the culpability elements might require, for ex-ample, that the actor know that he is taking property and that he be at least reckless as to it being someone else's property.[92] Each of the four culpability levels of the Model Penal Code is specifically defined. The Draft English Code definitions are similar in concept but different in many important respects.[93]

To use an actor's culpability as to causing a result as an example, a person acts 'purposely' with respect to a result, under the Code, if his conscious object is to cause such a result. A person acts 'knowingly' with respect to a result if it is not his conscious object yet he is practically cer-tain his conduct will cause that result. The anti-war activist who sets a bomb to destroy the draft board offices may be practically certain the bomb will kill the night watchman but may wish that the watchman would go

---

[90] The current federal criminal law, which has never undergone the modernization via the Model Penal Code that a majority of state codes have, uses 78 different culpability terms. 'Present federal criminal law is composed of a bewildering array of terms used to describe the mental element of an offence': S Rep. No 605, 95th Cong, 1st Sess, pt 1, at 55.

[91] Some jurisdictions have adopted the Model Penal Code scheme, which uses the four defined culpability terms described above, but have altered the definition of some offences to use terms other than the defined terms. New Jersey, for example, adopted a code based upon the Model Penal Code but continued for some time to use terms such as 'carelessly', 'heedlessly', 'wanton', 'willful', 'intent', and 'criminal negligence', without definition: NJ Stat. Ann., § 2C:11–5 (amended 1981). This error has been corrected recently. The New Jersey death-by-auto statute that employed the term 'carelessly' has been amended to substitute the term 'recklessly': NJ Stat. Ann., § 2C:11–5 (West 1982). 'Heedlessly' has also been replaced by 'recklessly' in this statute: *ibid.* 'Wanton' has also been replaced by 'recklessly' in this statute: *ibid.* See also *ibid.*, § 2C:24–5 (defining 'willful' non-support). (While the Model Penal Code contains a provision establishing that the requirement of 'willfully' is satisfied by 'knowingly' unless a purpose to impose further requirements appears, see Model Penal Code, § 2.02(8) (Proposed Official Draft 1962), New Jersey has failed to adopt the provision.) 'Intent' is used in NJ Stat. Ann., § 2C:21–6(b)–(c) (West 1982). The use of undefined terms obviously undercuts the Model Penal Code's advances in clarity, consist-ency, and predictability, characteristics particularly important in a criminal code.

[92] The determination of the culpability requirements called for by an offence definition can be complex and sometimes confusing, as discussed in sects. D.3. and D.4. of this Ch.

[93] See Draft English Code, ¶ 18.

on a coffee break so he will not be killed. The essence of the narrow distinction between these two culpability levels is the presence or absence of a *positive desire* to cause the result; purpose requires a culpability beyond the knowledge of a result's near certainty. In the broader sense, this distinction divides the vague notion of 'callousness' from the more offensive 'maliciousness' or 'viciousness'. The latter may be simply an aggressively ruthless form of the former.

A person acts 'knowingly' with respect to a result if he is nearly certain that his conduct will cause the result. If he is aware only of a substantial risk, he acts 'recklessly' with respect to the result. The narrow distinction between knowledge and recklessness lies in the *degree of risk*—'practically certain' versus 'substantial risk'—of which the actor is aware. The distinction between recklessness (and lower levels of culpability) and the two higher levels of culpability (purposely and knowingly) is that we tend to scold a reckless actor for being 'careless', while an offender who falls within one of the higher culpability categories is condemned for 'intentional' conduct.

While knowing and reckless culpability focus upon the likelihood of causing the result—'practically certain' v. 'substantial risk'—purposeful culpability pays no regard to the likelihood of the result. This characteristic of the purpose requirement reflects an instinct that *trying* to cause the harm, whatever the likelihood, is more condemnable than acting with the belief that the harm will or might result without desiring it. The practical effect of this is that reckless conduct, as manifested in risk-taking, is elevated to purposeful conduct if the actor hopes that the risk will come to fruition. This characteristic of purpose also illustrates how specially demanding it is. A requirement of a particular belief is something a jury might logically deduce from other facts: the actor 'must have known' the certainty or the risk of harm if he knew this fact or that. A purpose requirement requires the jury to determine an actor's object or goal, a somewhat more complex psychological state. To find this, a jury may have to dig deeper into the actor's psyche, his general wants and motivations, to reach a conclusion. If a jury is conscientious in adhering to the proof-beyond-a-reasonable-doubt standard constitutionally required for offence elements, this may be a difficult conclusion to reach.

A person acts 'recklessly' with respect to a result if he consciously disregards a substantial risk that his conduct will cause the result; he acts only 'negligently' if he is unaware of the substantial risk but should have perceived it. The issue is not whether an actor should have been aware of the risk but whether in fact she was (and whether it was culpable for her to disregard the risk).

The narrow distinction between recklessness and negligence lies in the actor's *awareness of risk*. The distinction between negligence and the three higher levels of culpability is one of the most critical to criminal law. A person who acts purposely, knowingly, or recklessly is aware of the circumstances that make his conduct criminal or is aware that harmful consequences may result and is therefore both blameworthy and deterrable. A defendant who acts negligently, in contrast, is unaware of the circumstances or consequences, and therefore, some writers argue, is neither blameworthy nor deterrable.[94] While writers disagree over whether negligence is adequate to support criminal liability, it is agreed that negligence represents a lower level of culpability than, and is qualitatively different from, recklessness, in that the negligent actor fails to recognize rather than consciously disregards the risk. For this reason, recklessness is considered the norm for criminal culpability, while negligence is punished only in the exceptional situations, as where a death is caused.[95]

A person who fails to appreciate the risk that his conduct will cause a result is 'negligent' as to the result if the failure 'involves a gross deviation from the standard of care that a reasonable person would observe in the actor's situation'.[96] Thus, unless he grossly deviates from the standard of care that a reasonable person would observe, an actor is not negligent and, at least in the eyes of the criminal law, is without cognizable fault. Would a reasonable person in the actor's situation have been aware of the risk? Was her failure to perceive the risk a gross deviation from the attentiveness to the possibility of risk that the reasonable person in her situation would have had? These are the issues that the jury considers in assessing whether an actor was negligent. They are not factual but normative issues. The jury is asked to judge whether the failure to perceive the risk was, under the circumstances, a blameworthy failure.

3. ASYMMETRY IN THE DEFINITION OF CULPABILITY REQUIREMENTS

The description of culpability levels at the beginning of this section uses culpability as to causing a result to illustrate the differences between levels. In fact, Model Penal Code section 2.02(2) defines each of the four kinds of culpability in relation to each of the three kinds of objective elements: conduct, circumstance, and result. The following chart gives the section 2.02(2) definition for each variation.

---

[94] See e.g. Jerome Hall, *General Principles of Criminal Law* (2nd edn., Indianapolis, Indiana, 1960), 128.

[95] At least one jurisdiction does not punish negligently caused homicide: see NJ Stat. Ann., § 2C:11–2 (West 1982).

[96] Model Penal Code, § 2.02(2)(d). Parallel language appears in the definition of recklessness, in § 2.02(2)(c). In the context, however, the language concerns whether a 'law-abiding' person would have consciously disregarded the risk that the actor disregarded.

Type of Objective Element

		Result	Circumstance	Conduct
	Purposely	'it is his conscious object . . . to cause such a result'	'he is a aware of such circumstances or hopes that they exist'	'it is his conscious object to engage in conduct of that nature'
	Knowingly	'he is aware that it is practically certain that his conduct will cuase such a result'	'he is aware . . . that such circumstances exist'	'he is aware his conduct is of that nature'
Culpability Level	Recklessly	'he consciously disregards a substantial and unjustifiable risk that the material element . . . will result from his conduct'	'he consciously disregards a substantial and unjustifiable risk that the material element exists'	—
	Negligently	'he should be aware of a substantial and unjustifiable risk that the material element . . . will result from his conduct'	'he should be aware of a substantial and unjustifiable risk that the material element exists'	—

The Code's precision does much to bring clarity to what previously had been a troublesome area, but some peculiarities in the definitional scheme leave several ambiguities remaining. For example, note that the Code does not expressly define recklessness and negligence with respect to a conduct element. One explanation for this failure is that the drafters determined that, as a practical matter, neither recklessness nor negligence as to conduct is likely to arise. The Model Penal Code commentary notes that '[w]ith respect to each of [the] three types of elements, the draft attempts to define each of the kinds of culpability *that may arise*'.[97] Other sections

[97] Model Penal Code, § 2.02 comment 2 at 124 (Tent. Draft No 4, 1955) (emphasis added).

of the commentary, however, may be interpreted to suggest that the drafters did contemplate the possibility of recklessness or negligence as to conduct. Indeed, certain Code offences appear specifically to proscribe reckless conduct. For example, one who 'recklessly tampers with tangible property of another so as to endanger person or property' commits criminal mischief.[98] Similarly, one who 'purposely or recklessly . . . kills or injures any animal' is guilty of cruelty to animals.[99]

One can resolve this ambiguity in the Code's definitional scheme by reasoning that, because some culpability is required as to each element of an offence and 'recklessness' and 'negligence' as to conduct are not defined, 'knowledge'—the minimum culpability that is defined with respect to conduct—is required. This argument can be buttressed by referring to section 2.02(5), which states that: 'When recklessness suffices to establish an element, such element also is established if a person acts purposely or knowingly'. Some jurisdictions specifically provide that 'knowing' is required as to a conduct element.[100] Another approach is for a court to define 'recklessness' and 'negligence' with respect to conduct by extrapolating from the definition of those terms with respect to circumstance and result elements.

This ambiguity may be insignificant if 'conduct' elements are defined narrowly to include only literally the *conduct* (muscular movement) of the actor.[101] Under this approach, culpability as to an actor's 'conduct' is relevant in the rare case that he does not know that he is engaging in a muscular movement and these instances are likely to be exempt from liability under the involuntary act defence.[102] Culpability as to the *nature* of one's conduct, under this approach, is more accurately described as culpability as to the circumstances and the results of one's conduct. 'Recklessness' and 'negligence' are defined with regard to circumstance and result elements. This narrow interpretation of what constitutes a 'conduct' element not only gives a clear definition, without need for judicial extrapolation,

---

[98] Model Penal Code, § 220.3(1)(b). But see the alternative interpretation of such language discussed in Robinson, *Criminal Law*, n. 56 above, at § 4.2.

[99] Model Penal Code, § 250.11.

[100] See S 1437, 95th Cong, 2d Sess, §§ 302(c), 303(b)(1) (1978) (recklessness as to conduct undefined; minimum state of mind that must be proved with respect to conduct is knowledge); see also Alaska Stat., §§ 11.81.610(b), 900(a)(2)–(4) (Supp. 1984). The following jurisdictions also clearly exclude conduct from their definitions of recklessness and negligence, but they do not provide specifically that knowledge is required where no culpability as to conduct is specified in the offence definition. Ariz. Rev. Stat. Ann., § 13–105(6)(b)–(d) (Supp. 1988); Colo. Rev. Stat., § 18–1–501(3), (8) (1990); Ky. Rev. Stat. Ann., § 501.020(3)–(4) (Bobbs-Merrill 1975); Mo. Ann. Stat., § 562.016(4)–(5) (Vernon 1979); Ohio Rev. Code Ann., § 2901.22(c)–(d) (Page 1982); Or. Rev. Stat., § 161.085(9)–(10) (1981); Tex. Penal Code, § 6.03(c)–(d) (West 1992); Utah Code Ann., § 76–2–103(3)–(4) (1990).

[101] This interpretation is supported by Model Penal Code, section 1.13, which defines 'conduct' to mean an '*action* or omission' and defines 'action' to mean 'a bodily movement'. For discussion of related difficulties, see Robinson, *Criminal Law*, n. 56 above, at § 4.2.

[102] See sect. C.2. of this Ch.

but also has the important advantage of maximizing the legislature's ability to provide a different culpability level for different elements of a single offence. To consider 'conduct' as including the circumstances and results of one's conduct is to treat the conduct (narrow sense) and the circumstances and results of the conduct as a single element. This requires that a single culpability level must apply to all. To strip the circumstances and results of conduct from the 'conduct' element and to treat them as independent 'circumstance' and 'result' elements creates several elements and thereby allows different culpability as to different elements. These issues are discussed further in the next section.[103]

Another asymmetry revealed by the chart is the definition of 'purposely' with respect to a circumstance element. Recall that the hallmark of purposeful culpability in the context of result elements is the actor's *conscious object* to cause that result; 'knowing' as to a result requires only that the actor be aware that his conduct will cause the result, not that he desires or hopes that it will. 'Purposely' as to a conduct element has an analogous meaning: it must be the actor's conscious object to engage in conduct of that nature. It is not enough that he is aware that his conduct is of that nature ('knowing' as to conduct). In the context of circumstance elements, however, 'purposely' requires only that the actor 'is *aware* of such circumstances or hopes that they exist'. In other words, 'purpose' as to a circumstance can be shown by proving no more than is required to show 'knowing' as to a circumstance. The distinction between 'purposely' and 'knowingly' is thereby eliminated for circumstance elements.[104]

The absence of a specified culpability requirement in an offence definition does not mean that culpability is not required.[105] Modern codes permit strict liability in very limited instances, generally only for the least serious offences, such as traffic violations. Model Penal Code sections 2.02(1) and 2.05, similar provisions in American state codes, and Draft English Code clause 20(1), are meant to require culpability for all elements of all offences other than the most minor. In some jurisdictions, when the drafters intend that culpability is not required, a phrase such as 'in fact' is inserted at the appropriate place in the offence definition to signal the absence of a culpability requirement.[106]

---

[103] See sect. D.4. of this Ch.

[104] 'Knowledge that the requisite external circumstances exist is a common element of [purpose and knowledge]. But action is not purposive with respect to the nature or result of the actor's conduct unless it was his conscious object to perform an action of that nature or to cause such a result': Model Penal Code, § 2.02 comment 2 at 233 (1985).

[105] *Morrisette* v. *United States* (1952) 342 US 246, 263, 72 S Ct. 240, 96 L Ed. 288 (omission from statute, prohibiting illegal conversion of US property, of any mention of intent not to be construed as eliminating that element from the crime denounced).

[106] 'Having intercourse with a person who is in fact under 14 years of age' indicates that no culpability is required as to the fact that the sexual partner is under 14.

Where the offence definition does not explicitly provide a culpability requirement, Model Penal Code section 2.02(3) supplies one. Section 2.02(3) reads in 'recklessly' for all circumstance and result elements and, because of the Code's failure to define recklessness as to conduct, it is sometimes interpreted to read in 'knowingly' for all conduct elements.[107] Consider, for example, the Model Penal Code's indecent exposure offence:

A person commits a misdemeanor if, for the purpose of arousing or gratifying sexual desire ..., he exposes his genitals under circumstances in which he knows his conduct is likely to cause affront or alarm.[108]

An application of section 2.02(3) results in the following complete offence definition:

A person commits a misdemeanor if, for the *purpose* of arousing or gratifying sexual desire ..., he [*knowingly* engages in conduct by which he *recklessly* causes the exposure of what he is aware of a substantial risk are (i.e. *reckless*)] his genitals under circumstances in which he *knows* his conduct is likely to cause affront or alarm.

Obviously, such an explicit statement generates a grammatically awkward definition. A general provision that reads in a fixed level of culpability provides the necessary guidance yet leaves offence definitions readable.[109] Such a general read-in-reckless provision also is useful because recklessness is generally the minimum culpability required for criminal liability. Reading in 'recklessness' when no culpability is stated gives voice to this norm. Special circumstances may lead code drafters to use a higher or a lower level in particular instances but, absent special reasons, recklessness is the minimum culpability required. Thus, a general provision such as Model Penal Code section 2.02(3) at once provides a comprehensive statement of all culpability requirements, a readable offence definition, and recklessness as the standard minimum culpability.

Legislatures are free to deviate from the norm of recklessness in either of two ways. First, the legislature can explicitly provide a culpability requirement other than recklessness for a specific element of an offence definition. This is what the legislature has done in requiring 'a purpose to arouse' and 'knows ... likely to affront' in the indecent exposure offence. In addition, it can provide that a stated culpability requirement applies to more than a single element of the offence. This second alternative is provided in the Model Penal Code by section 2.02(4), which codifies a general rule of statutory construction requiring that a stated culpability term, which does not distinguish among the elements, be applied to all elements

---

[107] Cl. 20(1) of the Draft English Code has the same effect.

[108] Model Penal Code, § 213.5 (1980).

[109] The practice seems particularly appropriate given that the culpability requirements read in to complete an offence definition frequently are less significant—e.g. less frequently at issue—than are the explicitly stated culpability elements.

of the offence. Thus, where the offence of causing a suicide is defined to punish one who 'purposely causes such suicide by force',[110] the actor must be purposeful as to using force and as to the result of causing the suicide. Normal rules of statutory construction no doubt generate the same result.

4. DIFFICULTIES WITH MODERN AMERICAN CULPABILITY SCHEMES

As suggested at the beginning of this section, while the Model Penal Code's culpability scheme offers many advances, like most pioneering legislation, it creates its own special problems. Some of the ambiguities described above hint at the problems, which are here explored in greater detail.

The asymmetries in the Code's culpability definitions are a source of difficulties because of the Code's failure to define and distinguish between the three kinds of objective elements that it identifies. To act 'purposely' with respect to 'conduct' or in causing 'a result', an actor must have such conduct or result as his conscious object; but to act 'purposely' with respect to 'an attendant circumstance', an actor need only be aware of such circumstance. Recall also that 'recklessness' and 'negligence' are defined as to circumstance and result elements but not as to conduct elements. Thus, while a recklessness requirement as to a circumstance or result element will be applied as defined, if an element is a conduct element, there is some ambiguity as to what is required. Some jurisdictions require that 'knowing' be proven.[111] (The Draft English Code has its own asymmetries.[112])

Because of these asymmetries, the classification of an objective element is critical. The precise requirements of an offence cannot be determined until the objective elements of an offence definition are characterized as either 'conduct', 'an attendant circumstance', or 'a result'. Yet, the Model Penal Code does not define 'result' or 'circumstance'. (Nor does the Draft English Code.[113])

Consider the offence of theft by deception, which entails purposely obtaining property through deceit. A person 'deceives' if he purposely '[c]reates or reinforces a false impression [as to value]'.[114] One might argue that this requirement is a single elaborate conduct requirement: 'creates

---

[110] Model Penal Code, § 210.5(1).

[111] See e.g. Alaska Stat., § 11.81.610(b)(i); see 1 Robinson, *Criminal Law Defenses*, n. 32 above, at § 61(b), n. 104.

[112] For example, Draft English Code cl. 18(b) defines desiring a circumstance to exist or a result to occur is 'intentional'. Cl. 18(a), however, defines 'knowing' as to a circumstance—being aware of its existence—but provides no analogous definition as to a result.

[113] The Model Penal Code defines 'conduct', but uses seemingly contradictory forms of that term in different Code provisions. It previously has been suggested that one take a narrow view, such that 'conduct' simply refers to an actor's bodily movement. Model Penal Code, § 1.13(2) & (5). In other places however, especially where the phrase 'conduct constituting the offence' appears, 'conduct' seems to be used in a broad sense to mean bodily movement and all its relevant characteristics, such as the circumstances and results of the conduct.

[114] Model Penal Code, § 223.3(a).

or reinforces a false impression as to value.' Or, the prohibited conduct element might be 'creates' or 'reinforces' and the proscribed result might be interpreted as either (a) a false impression as to value (with no 'attendant circumstance'), (b) a false impression (with value as a 'circumstance'), or (c) an impression (with both falsity and value as 'circumstances'). To select the proper interpretation requires a definition of what constitutes a 'conduct', 'circumstance', or 'result'. And the interpretation selected will determine the culpability required.

Assume that a court applies section 2.02(4) to require that the stated culpability requirement, 'purposely', applies to all elements of the offence of theft by deception. The actor's *conscious object* must then encompass all conduct and results, but because of the way 'purposeful' as to a circumstance is defined, the actor need only be *aware* of the existence of a circumstance element. If the court applies interpretation (a) described above, the actor's *conscious object* need encompass every element of the offence because all elements are either conduct or results. If interpretation (b) is applied, however, the actor's *conscious object* must encompass only 'creating' and a 'false impression'; it need not be the actor's conscious object or hope—he need only be aware—that the false impression concerns 'value'. Finally, if the court applies interpretation (c), the actor's *conscious object* need only encompass 'creating an impression'; he need only be *aware* of the fact that the impression is 'false' and concerns 'value'. These differences create the potential to manipulate improperly a defendant's liability by altering the content of the categories 'conduct', 'result', and 'circumstance', thereby altering the applicable culpability requirement.

Consider a statute that forbids 'recklessly obstructing any highway'.[115] What culpability should be required as to 'obstructing'? A court might take any of three approaches. Because 'obstructing' appears to be a conduct element and 'recklessly' is not defined with respect to conduct, the court might determine that 'knowing' is the appropriate culpability as to 'obstructing' because it is the minimum culpability defined with respect to conduct. Instead, a court might attempt to define recklessness as to conduct and require that newly-defined culpability. Given the enactment of a comprehensive culpability scheme, such definition seems a legislative task. A third, and perhaps the best, approach is for a court to observe that the verb 'obstructing' is a combination of separate conduct and result elements. The term 'obstructs' means to '*render impassable* without unreasonable inconvenience or hazard'.[116] In essence, the offence imposes liability when an actor engages in conduct by which he causes— i.e. 'renders'—any highway impassable. The culpability term 'recklessly', under this approach, can be meaningfully read to apply to the result element of causing the highway to be impassable. The separate conduct

---

[115] See e.g. Model Penal Code, § 250.7.   [116] *Ibid.*

element can be interpreted as requiring 'knowing' conduct because that is the minimum culpability defined as to conduct.

The difficulties with the Model Penal Code scheme—the failure to define the categories of objective elements and the use of terms that combine elements of different categories—can be avoided with a few revisions, most of which may be done through judicial interpretation of existing provisions. With revision, the Code's scheme can be made workable and can realize the full benefits of the insights and advances of the drafters. Here are some of the reforms that would be helpful, many of which were signalled at the beginning of this Chapter, in the discussion of the objective elements of conduct, circumstance, and result.

First, define 'conduct' elements literally, that is, narrowly, to mean pure conduct: bodily movement of the actor, as Model Penal Code section 1.13 defines it. Thus, objective elements of an offence definition that might otherwise be classified as conduct elements, but which actually describe *characteristics* of the conduct, are treated as circumstance or result elements. For example, the definition of harassment makes it an offence if an actor 'insults . . . another in a manner likely to provoke violent . . . response'. Under a narrow view of the conduct element the required conduct is the simple act of speaking. The conduct's characteristics—its insulting character, its likelihood of provoking a violent response—are treated as circumstance or result elements. Under this narrow view of conduct, the conduct element emerges as a relatively unspecific and unimportant aspect of an offence definition. In homicide, for example, the particular conduct that the actor engages in to cause the death of another human being does not matter. What matters is that the actor's conduct, of whatever nature, did cause the prohibited result. The most significant elements of an offence definition, then, typically are the circumstance and result elements.

Such a narrowly defined conduct element continues adequately to serve the important purposes of the act requirement: to distinguish fantasising from intention and to exclude from liability intentions too irresolute ever to be carried out, to provide some minimal objective evidence confirming mens rea, to set a minimal objective limit on the government's criminalization power, and to give a point of reference for enforcement of the concurrence requirement and for the statute of limitations and jurisdiction and venue.[117] Moreover, because it provides a more definite and specific point of reference, this narrow definition of conduct, which excludes results of the conduct, more clearly satisfies those purposes that require identification of a single time and place of the offence than does a broader definition of conduct.

As a corollary to this first revision, whenever a single verb compounds a conduct element with a result element or a conduct element with a

---

[117] See sect. C.1. of this Ch.

circumstance element, the legislature should redraft the language of the stat-ute or, absent such redrafting, courts should distinguish the two aspects of the element in determining the culpability requirements. By more clearly identifying the existence of a result element, this approach also more clearly identifies where the special requirements of causation apply.[118]

As noted, the Model Penal Code provides no definition to distinguish circumstance elements from result elements. Is causing the 'obstruction of a public highway' a single result element? Or is it a result element of causing an 'obstruction' and a circumstance element of 'a public highway'? To resolve such problems, the third proposal defines a result as a *circum-stance changed by the actor*. All elements that do not fit this definition are independent circumstance elements. In the hypothetical above, the actor creates only the obstruction; he cannot create or alter the road's legal sta-tus as a 'public highway'. Thus, causing the 'obstruction' is a result ele-ment and 'public highway' is a circumstance element. To summarize, in each offence, the conduct element, although perhaps linguistically merged with other elements, is distinguished. It simply performs the function of the act requirement. Result elements are easy to identify, as circumstances changed by the actor. All other elements are circumstance elements.

Another corollary to the narrow scope of the conduct element is to give the culpability requirement accompanying the conduct element a similarly narrow meaning. If the conduct element encompasses only an actor's act, not the characteristics of the accompanying circumstances or the results of the act, the required culpability as to the conduct encompasses only the actor's mental state as to engaging in the bare act itself and not his mental state as to the circumstances or results of the conduct. On behalf of this proposal, and indirectly on behalf of the narrow conduct proposal, one can note that a broader interpretation of conduct makes the culpab-ility as to the conduct element all-encompassing. A requirement of 'know-ing' as to conduct, which is most frequently required, sets 'knowing' as the required culpability as to the pertinent attendant circumstances and the pertinent results of his conduct. But to assume that the culpability requirement as to 'conduct' controls as well the culpability as to the circumstances and results of the conduct, as the broader interpretation of conduct does, undermines element analysis generally. Such an approach short-circuits the Code's attempt to allow separate and sometimes dif-ferent culpability requirements for the circumstances and results of one's conduct.

Under the narrow definition, an actor's culpability as to his conduct—e.g. being aware of the nature of one's conduct—rarely is a matter of dis-pute; his culpability as to the circumstances and result of his conduct is

---

[118] It also better identifies the other instances where the presence of a 'result' element has special implications. See sect. B.1. of this Ch.

of primary practical importance. Indeed, the Draft English Code defines its culpability terms only with regard to circumstance and result elements.[119] Culpability as to conduct simply requires, for example, that an actor be aware that he is moving his trigger finger or swinging his arm. The only cases that present an issue under the narrowly-defined conduct element involve an actor suffering a considerable and abnormal disability. Such abnormalities typically are given more detailed consideration under provisions such as those governing the voluntariness requirement or excuse defences. The culpability requirements of an offence definition, in contrast, operate primarily to assess the culpability of normal persons. The normal person typically desires to move his body in the way that he moves it, thus satisfies the narrow culpability-as-to-conduct requirement. The narrow interpretation of conduct is consistent with and avoids the problems inherent in the drafters' failure to define recklessness and negligence as to conduct. An actor who is only 'aware of a substantial risk' or is 'unaware of a substantial risk' that he is moving his trigger finger or arm is an actor who will have an excuse defence. Thus, no definitions of recklessness or negligence as to conduct are needed.

One final but important difficulty with the Model Penal Code scheme is found in too broad a reading of section 2.02(4), which provides:

Prescribed Culpability Requirement Applies to All Material Elements. When the law defining an offence prescribes the kind of culpability that is sufficient for the commission of an offence, without distinguishing among the material elements thereof, such provision shall apply to all the material elements of the offence, unless a contrary purpose plainly appears.

The commentary describes this provision as one that embodies the most probable legislative intent.[120] The provision may well go too far, however, in allowing what may be an exceptional culpability requirement, such as purposeful, which is meant by the legislature to apply only to one element of the offence, to govern the culpability requirements of all other offence elements. In other instances, the provision may have the equally undesirable effect of having an unusually low culpability requirement, such as negligence, apply to all elements, when it was meant only to apply to one.

Consider, for example, the offence of burglary. An actor commits burglary when he 'enters a building or occupied structure . . . with purpose to commit a crime therein, unless the premises are at the time open to the public or the actor is licensed or privileged to enter'.[121] As 'purpose' is the only culpability element prescribed and as no contrary legislative purpose plainly appears, a provision like Model Penal Code section 2.02(4) can be interpreted to require that, to be liable for burglary, an actor must

---

[119] See Draft English Code, ¶ 18.
[120] Model Penal Code, § 2.02 comment 6 at 129 (Tent. Draft No 4, 1955).
[121] Model Penal Code, § 221.1.

act purposely with respect to each element. In other words, the actor must be aware of or believe or hope that *all the circumstance* elements exist. He will escape liability if he thought it likely, but was not certain and did not necessarily hope, that he is not 'licensed or privileged to enter' or that he is entering a 'building or occupied structure'.[122] But burglary typically is understood to require purpose only as to the 'intent to commit a crime therein'. 'Purpose' is an unusually stringent culpability requirement.[123] There are few areas where legislatures want so demanding a requirement. Too broad a reading of section 2.02(4) allows the exceptional case, where purpose becomes the standard for all elements of the offence. An analogous difficulty arises with the use of negligence. Where only negligence is required as to an offence element, strict application of section 2.02(4) applies this stated culpability term to all elements, although recklessness is normally the minimum culpability required.[124]

A better reading of section 2.02(4) applies its rule only to that part of the offence definition within the minimal grammatical clause in which the stated term appears. This is consistent with the provision's direction that the rule applies only where the offence definition prescribes culpability, 'without distinguishing among the material elements thereof'. That is, grammatical structure may provide such distinction among elements. In the context of burglary, this interpretation applies 'purpose' only to 'to commit a crime therein'. The other elements of the offence are governed by the other rules of construction; the culpability requirements are derived either from other stated culpability terms or from section 2.02(3) reading in the standard 'recklessness'.

This discussion suggests rules for how Model Penal Code sections 2.02(3) and 2.02(4) ought to interact. Consider the definition of harassment: 'A person commits a petty misdemeanor if, with purpose to harass another, he . . . insults . . . another in a manner likely to provoke violent or disorderly response'.[125] Model Penal Code section 2.02(3) requires recklessness whenever an offence definition fails to specify the culpability with respect to a particular element. On the other hand, when the offence definition specifies a culpability element, without distinguishing among elements, section 2.02(4) requires that the stated culpability apply to all elements, unless a contrary purpose appears.

If section 2.02(4) were applied to require the stated culpability of 'purpose' as to all elements, even those outside its minimal grammatical clause,

---

[122] 'Purposely' as to a circumstance requires either a hope or awareness, as required for 'knowingly'. See sect. D.2. of this Ch. Thus, 'knowledge' as to a circumstance element— 'aware of high probability of its existence' § 2.02(7)—satisfies the requirement but 'recklessness'—'aware of a substantial risk' § 2.02(2)(c)—does not.

[123] 'Acting knowingly is ordinarily sufficient': Model Penal Code, § 2.02 comment 3 at 125 (Tent. Draft No 4, 1955).

[124] This is the point of having a section like Model Penal Code, section 2.02(3) read in recklessness where no culpability is stated.   [125] Model Penal Code, § 250.4(2).

the actor has to be purposeful with respect to all elements—e.g. it must be his conscious object to 'insult another' and his conscious object that the insult be 'likely to provoke violent or disorderly response'. Yet, as noted above, purpose is a special and a very demanding culpability requirement, while recklessness is well-established as the 'norm' for criminal liability. If section 2.02(3) is applied to all elements outside the grammatical clause in which 'purpose' appears, the defendant must be purposeful only as to harassing another, and need be only reckless with respect to all other elements. The section 2.02(3) recklessness requirement should be preferred. Section 2.02(4) admittedly should apply the stated culpability requirement to the entire grammatical clause in which it appears but should apply said requirement outside that clause only when the placement and effect of the stated culpability term suggest that it is intended to govern culpability requirements outside of the clause.

The better interpretation of section 2.02(4), as noted above, views it as requiring that a stated culpability term should apply to the minimal grammatical clause in which it appears unless the context demonstrates that it is intended to apply to other, subsequent clauses as well. Section 2.02(3) is best interpreted as supplying the culpability requirements to any elements to which section 2.02(4) does not apply. For example, in the absence of legislative direction to the contrary, recklessness is required as to the circumstance element of 'an unlicensed or unprivileged entry' in burglary. This interpretation of section 2.02(4) is not inconsistent with its language, which says the stated culpability applies only when such culpability is provided 'without distinguishing among the material elements thereof'. The interpretation rests upon an assumption that, when a stated culpability is placed within a grammatical clause, such placement distinguishes the elements within the clause from those outside. The use of section 2.02(3) here, to fill in any gaps after application of section 2.02(4), is consistent with the Model Penal Code's view that the culpability level of recklessness should be applied when the required culpability is unstated, a view that is supported by the fact that recklessness generally is accepted as the appropriate norm for imposing criminal liability.

In many offences, section 2.02(3) has no application. In the context of homicide, for example, this interpretation of section 2.02(4) means that the culpability level as to the victim being a 'human being' is the same as the culpability as to causing death. 'A person is guilty of criminal homicide if he purposely, knowingly, recklessly or negligently causes the death of another human being.' The different degrees of homicide are then identified as dependent upon the actor's level of culpability: purposefully or knowingly causing the death is murder, recklessly is manslaughter, and negligently is negligent homicide.[126] Because the offence is defined in a

---

[126] See Model Penal Code, §§ 210.2, 210.3, 210.4.

single clause, the stated culpability requirement applies to all elements of the offence, including the circumstance element of 'human being'.[127] Thus, if 'human being' is defined for homicide purposes to include a 'viable foetus', the doctor who purposely kills a foetus and is reckless as to it being a viable foetus, is liable for manslaughter but not murder.[128]

Note that the interpretations proposed here are not designed either to raise or to lower the culpability requirements of offence definitions. They are, rather, designed to create a system in which the legislature can effectively, easily, and clearly define the culpability requirements as it desires. If a culpability requirement other than recklessness is to apply to a particular element, the legislature need only state such culpability requirement in the offence definition. If the legislature desires the stated requirement to apply to more than one element, it can achieve this by its choice of placement of the stated culpability term within the offence definition. The legislature can provide an explicit culpability requirement to apply to particular elements (those within the clause) without fear that the requirement will be interpreted to apply more broadly than intended.[129]

To conclude, other codes may avoid these problems of the Model Penal Code, but any culpability scheme will likely have its own set of problems. A code drafter cannot expect to avoid all problems. The gap between the complexity of human feeling and the limitations of human language insures that this goal can never be reached. A realistic goal is to reduce the size and importance of the problems so that the system gives a close enough approximation to proper results to maintain its moral credibility.

[127] That this is the intended reading of the homicide statute is supported by Model Penal Code, section 2.02(10), which provides that where the grade or degree of an offence depends upon its culpability level, the grade or degree shall be that for the lowest culpability for any element. Thus, if section 2.02(3) were applied to require reckless as to 'human being' in homicide, one could be purposeful as to the killing and reckless as to 'human being' yet still be liable only for manslaughter, under section 2.02(10).

[128] One might argue that, while this application of section 2.02(4) is not inappropriate in homicide, it generates improper results in other instances. Under Model Penal Code, section 211.1(1)(b), for example, it is an assault if the actor 'negligently causes bodily injury to another with a deadly weapon'. Is it clear that the negligence requirement ought to apply both to 'causing bodily injury' and to 'with a deadly weapon'? Should an actor be liable for assault if he has no awareness of even a risk that what he has is a 'deadly weapon'?

[129] The conflict between sections 2.02(3) and 2.02(4) mirrors the two competing forms of the definition of offences—element analysis and offence analysis—described in the previous section. In providing that any stated culpability level applies to all elements of the offence, section 2.02(4) is characteristic of an offence analysis model of offence definition. Section 2.02(3), on the other hand, reflects the element analysis approach adopted in sections 2.02(1) and 2.02(2), which allow and facilitate the application of different culpability requirements to different elements of the same offence. Section 2.02(3) of course is central to the implementation of element analysis. It assures that each objective element has an accompanying culpability requirement, but does not assume that such culpability is the same for each element of an offence.

4

Principles of Imputation

Chapters 3 and 5 each take up a recognized conceptual grouping of doctrines, the definitions of offences and general defences, respectively, show flaws in the way each is conceptualized and suggest refinements to avoid the noted problems. This Chapter has a more difficult task. It attempts to establish that a conceptual grouping of equal importance to the definition of offences and general defences should be recognized: doctrines of imputation.

Typically, an actor is liable for an offence if and only if she satisfies the elements of an offence definition. There exist two kinds of exceptions to this paradigm of equivalence between satisfying an offence definition and criminal liability. An actor *escapes liability* even though she *does* satisfy the elements of an offence if she satisfies the conditions of a *general defence*. This well known group of doctrines is the subject of Chapter 5.

A second, and reverse, exception is what may be called doctrines of imputation. An actor may be *liable* for an offence even though she does *not* satisfy the offence elements, if a rule or doctrine *imputes* the missing element. This conceptual group is as basic and important as general defences, yet the current conceptualization of criminal law essentially ignores its existence. This Chapter describes the doctrines that make up this group and demonstrates their shared operation in imputing a required offence element. It also shows that, beyond the shared operational character, these doctrines share common theories and rationales.

A. The Process of Imputation

Some writers have suggested that the imposition of liability absent a required element of the offence is illogical and immoral. In *Director of Public Prosecutions* v. *Majewski*,[1] for example, the defendant argued that it is both illogical and unethical to impute to a defendant a culpable state of mind (for assault) that he in fact did not have (because he was voluntarily intoxicated). The defendant relies upon a passage from Lord Hailsham in *Director of Prosecutions* v. *Morgan*:

[1] [1977] AC 443.

[O]nce it be accepted that an intent of whatever description is an ingredient essential to the guilt of the accused I cannot myself see that any other direction [than requiring proof of the intent] can be logically acceptable. Otherwise a jury would in effect be told to find an intent where none existed or where none was proved to have existed. I cannot myself reconcile it with my conscience to sanction as part of the English law what I regard as logical impossibility, and, if there were any authority which, if accepted, would compel me to do so, I would feel constrained to declare that it was not to be followed.[2]

But, just as many general defences commonly are recognized, which exculpate despite satisfaction of the paradigm elements of the offence, many doctrines of imputation are common and well-established. That is, many traditional doctrines inculpate an actor despite the absence of a 'required' element of the offence definition. If, for example, an actor causes another person to engage in illegal conduct, the actor may be liable for an offence defined to require such conduct although in fact he has not performed the conduct that the offence requires. He is held liable despite this absent element because the conduct of the other person is imputed to him under the doctrine of complicity or causing crime by an innocent.[3] Similarly, a requisite culpable state of mind commonly is imputed to an actor if he would have had the culpable state of mind but for his voluntary intoxication.[4] These familiar results follow from special rules governing complicity and voluntary intoxication. There is no suggestion that the actor in fact satisfies the required element. In each instance, the special conditions required by the doctrine of imputation are said to justify treating the actor as if he satisfies the imputed element.

A legislature could conceivably include inculpatory (and exculpatory) exceptions to the offence paradigm within the offence definition.[5] They typically do not, because of both drafting ease and theoretical clarity. Like

---

[2] *Morgan* [1976] AC 182.

[3] See e.g. Model Penal Code, § 2.06(3), Draft English Code, ¶¶ 25–9.

[4] See e.g. Model Penal Code, § 2.08(2), Draft English Code, ¶ 22.

[5] Arson, for example, is defined in Tennessee to include complicity in arson '[a]ny person who willfully and maliciously sets fire to or burns, causes to be burned, *or who aids, counsels or procures* the burning of any house . . . shall be guilty of arson': Tenn. Code Ann., § 39-3-202 (1982) (emphasis added); see also W Va. Code, § 61-3-1 (1977) (arson committed by one who burns or aids, counsels, or procures burning of a house). Similarly, definitions of an offence sometimes incorporate the rules governing voluntary intoxication, and impose liability even though intoxication may negate an otherwise required culpable state of mind. See e.g. Tex. Penal Code Ann., § 19.059(a) (Vernon 1974) (emphasis added). The paradigm of liability for arson under the Tennessee statute generally requires proof that the actor set fire to or burnt the house. If the actor aids, counsels, or procures another to do the burning, however, that act is imputed. Similarly, the paradigm for manslaughter under the Texas statute includes recklessness, but this element is imputed if the actor causes death if driving while intoxicated. In either case, a required element of the offence is eliminated, and liability instead is supported by a combination of the remaining elements of the paradigm and the special requirements of the doctrines of complicity (for arson) or intoxication (for manslaughter).

the general defences, such as insanity, duress, and law enforcement authority, which are separate and apart from any offence definition, the rules of
imputation represent principles of liability independent of any offence. Also
like general defences, most of the doctrines of imputed liability, at least
theoretically, apply to all offences; that is, they can impute a required element of any offence.[6] The use of general imputation provisions is not only
logical, given their theoretical independence from any particular offence,
it is also efficient. A general provision can be stated once, in as much detail
as is needed, yet can be applied to all offences. Some doctrines of imputation tend to apply to certain recurring factual situations: transferred intent
appears most commonly in bad-aim murder cases. But this is a factual
rather than a theoretical limitation of the principle.

It is not the mechanism of imputation that deserves criticism, but rather
those doctrines of imputation in which the special conditions required do
not fully justify the imputation called for, that is, do not justify treating
the actor the same as if he satisfied the missing element. Defences—exceptions to the offence paradigm that redound to the defendant's benefit
—typically are supported by articulable, rational explanations. Can one
articulate sound theoretical and practical reasons to support each inculpat-
ing exception? In the description of imputation doctrines that follow, many
have a sound justification. In some doctrines, however, the justification
for the imputation seems weak or unpersuasive.[7] The crucial theoretical
issue in each instance is: does the satisfaction of the special conditions of
the doctrine justify treating the actor as if he or she satisfies the missing
element?

B. THE DOCTRINES OF IMPUTATION

Criminal law permits the imputation of both objective and culpability elements of an offence. While the most obvious and common instances of
imputing objective elements are found in the rules governing complicity,

---

[6] Certain rules can normally be applied regardless of the offence; those governing complicity, causing crime by an innocent, voluntary intoxication and omissions, the doctrines
of transferred intent, of transferred actus reus, of substituted objective elements and of substituted mental elements, the suspension of the concurrence requirement, the *Pinkerton* doctrine, the natural and probable consequence rule, vicarious liability, and the rules governing
liability of officials within an organization. While some presumptions apply to a variety of
defences, see *Sandstrom* v. *Montana* (1979) 442 US 510 (presumption that persons intend
natural and probable consequences of their acts), many presumptions apply only to a particular offence.

[7] For an example of a doctrine that in many formulations serves to impute an unsatisfied
element without rational justification, see Paul H. Robinson, *Criminal Law* (Boston, 1997),
§ 4.5 (discussing the formulations of the diminished capacity 'defence' that bar the introduction of mental illness evidence that negates a required culpability element) (hereinafter
Criminal Law).

such rules are only one of several doctrines that impose liability even though the defendant has not satisfied all of the objective elements of an offence. Where an actor exercises control over an innocent person's actions, the latter's satisfaction of an objective element of an offence may be imputed to the former as an instance of 'causing crime by an innocent'.[8] Similarly, various statutory and judicial presumptions permit the imposition of liability even though the evidence adduced at trial does not establish all the objective elements of the offence.[9] On occasion, the doctrines of 'substituted culpability' and 'transferred mens rea'[10] have been formulated in reverse, to operate as doctrines of 'substituted objective elements'[11] and 'transferred actus reus',[12] to impute a missing objective element and thereby hold the actor liable for the offence intended (rather than imputing the missing culpability element to hold him liable for the offence actually committed). Thus, an actor who commits statutory rape but who, because of his mistake as to the true identity of his partner, believes he is instead committing incest, for example, can be held liable for the offence he thought he was committing, incest. Finally, the rules imposing liability

---

[8] See e.g. Model Penal Code, § 2.06(2)(a); Draft English Code, ¶ 26(c). Some cases of this sort will be analysed as raising only a causation issue, but that has the effect of short-circuiting the special requirements of the causing-crime-by-an-innocent doctrine.

[9] See e.g. Tenn. Code Ann., § 39–1–507 (1982) (presumption of manufacture of moonshine from assembly of still); NY Penal Law, § 265.15 (McKinney 1975) (every passenger of automobile in which firearm discovered presumptively guilty of possession of firearm); NC Gen. Stat., § 14–113.12 (1981) (presumption of forgery of financial transaction cards from fraudulent possession of such cards); SC Code Ann., § 16–17–230 (Law Co-op 1976) (presumption of defacing flag from possession of defaced flag). The doctrine of constructive possession also imputes objective elements. See generally Charles H. Whitebread and Ronald Stevens, 'Constructive Possession in Narcotics Cases: To Have and Have Not' (1972) 58 *Virginia LR* 751 at 761–2 (describing constructive possession as 'a legal fiction used by courts to find possession in situations where it does not in fact exist'). Similarly, the rule of joint possession may render the issue of actual possession immaterial by imputing possession to all persons found in the proximity of contraband, i.e. in a room or a car. Comment, 'Possession of Narcotics in Pennsylvania: "Joint" Possession' (1972) 76 *Dickinson LR* 499 at 508 (describing Pennsylvania cases on joint possession as reaching same result as New York presumption of possession of weapon in vehicle).

[10] For a discussion of these, see Robinson, *Criminal Law* n. 7 above, at §§ 5.1 (discussing transferred mens rea), 5.2 (discussing substituted objective elements).

[11] Let me give an illustration of 'substituted objective elements'. If an actor believes he is burgling a store when he in fact burgles a dwelling (a different offence), he may be convicted of the offence of burgling a store even though an element of the offence, 'store', is not satisfied. The existence of a comparable objective element in the actual offence, 'dwelling', is used as a justification for imputing the required objective element of the offence charged. This was the approach originally adopted and later rejected by the drafters of the Model Penal Code: Model Penal Code, § 2.04(2), comment 2, at 137 (Tent. Draft No 4, 1955). Kentucky and West Virginia have adopted this approach: see Ky. Rev. Stat. Ann., § 511.030(1); W Va. Code, (p) § 61–3–11(b).

[12] Where A shoots at B but hits C, the objective element of the death of C may be 'transferred' to justify holding A liable for the intentional homicide of B, at whom he was shooting. See *Mayweather* v. *State* (1926) 29 Ariz. 460 at 462, 242 P 864 at 865. Such 'transferred actus reus' is an alternative, and uncommon, method for dealing with cases typically analysed in terms of 'transferred intent'.

for omissions, when the offence charged is defined only in terms of affirmative conduct, also may be viewed as instances of imputed conduct.[13]

Just as a variety of rules and doctrines imputes an unsatisfied objective element of the offence charged, another group of doctrines imputes a required culpability element. The most common of these doctrines shapes the law governing voluntary intoxication. Also imputing a culpable state of mind, the doctrine of 'transferred intent' imputes the required culpability to an actor who intends to harm one person but actually harms another.[14] Imputation also is accomplished through a device that may be termed 'substituted culpability'.[15] This doctrine uses an actor's culpability for the offence he thought he was committing as the basis for imputing to him the intention required for the offence that he in fact committed. Courts that permit suspension of the requirement of concurrence between act and intent make a similar imputation: an actor's earlier intention to commit an act that he believes is the offence is relied upon to impute to him the required intention during his later conduct that actually constitutes the offence.[16] Finally, as with objective elements, a variety of statutory and judicial presumptions effectively impute culpability elements, upon proof of a logically related fact.[17]

Other rules impute both objective and culpability elements. If A and B conspire to rob a bank and B purposely kills a guard, both the killing and the purposeful culpability as to killing may be imputed to A under the *Pinkerton* doctrine.[18] The 'natural and probable consequence' rule in complicity law analogously expands the liability of accomplices.[19] Similarly,

---

[13] See generally Robinson, *Criminal Law*, n. 7 above, at § 3.4.

[14] See e.g. Model Penal Code, § 2.03(2)–(4); Draft English Code, ¶ 24(1).

[15] See e.g. Model Penal Code, § 2.04(2).

[16] See e.g. *Thabo Meli and Others* v. *The Queen* [1954] 1 WLR 228, [1954] 1 ALL ER 373. See also *Regina* v. *Church* [1965] 2 WLR 1220 (defendant knocked victim unconscious, then threw her into river, thinking she was dead).

[17] Some presumption statutes that impute objective elements also impute mental elements. For example, possession of a still has been used to presume both the manufacture (or attempt to manufacture) and the required intention to manufacture whiskey: Tenn. Code Ann., § 39–1–507 (1982) (presuming manufacture from assembly of still). Commonly, however, presumptions impute only required mental elements. For example, proof of unlawful entry into a building may trigger a rebuttable presumption of the intent to commit larceny required for burglary: Nev. Rev. Stat., § 205.065 (1981). Dissemination or possession of obscene material in the course of business may trigger a presumption of the knowing or reckless possession for sale or dissemination required for conviction: Model Penal Code, § 251.4(2) (1980). Judicially created presumptions are also common.

[18] See *Pinkerton* v. *United States* (1946) 328 US 640, 66 S Ct 1180, 90 L Ed 1489.

[19] Under this rule, 'an accessory is liable for any criminal act which in the ordinary course of things was the natural or probable consequence of the crime that he advised or commanded, although such consequence may not have been intended by him': (1961) 22 *CJS Criminal Law*, § 92. The natural and probable consequence rule is codified in several jurisdictions: see Wis. Stat. Ann., § 939.05(2)(c) (West 1982); cf. Iowa Code Ann., § 703.2 (West 1979) (accomplice liable for acts of co-felon unless accomplice 'could not reasonably expect [act] to be done' in furtherance of initial offence); Kan. Stat. Ann., § 21–3205 (1981) (liable if act reasonably foreseeable consequence of crime); Me. Rev. Stat. Ann., tit. 17-A,

the complicity aspect of the felony-murder rule in the United States imputes both objective and culpability elements to the accomplice. Finally, vicarious liability, and its special subclass governing the liability of officials of organizations, can impute offence elements to an actor because of his relationship to another in the United States and in England and Wales.[20] This is not an exhaustive list of the criminal law's instances of imputation.

There are at least four instances of substantive if not formal imputation: the aggravation of culpability in felony murder, possession offences, status offences, and strict liability offences. These are not formal instances of imputation because each offence is defined so that it does not formally require the 'imputed' element. That is, liability is imposed only upon proof of all the elements of the formal definition of the offence. There is reason to believe, however, that the statutory definition itself embraces principles of imputation rather than a complete statement of the paradigm conditions for liability in such cases.

Murder generally requires either an intentional or knowing killing or recklessness 'manifesting extreme indifference to the value of human life'. But if an accidental (even unavoidable) killing occurs in the course of a bank robbery, the felony-murder rule can aggravate the actor's culpability and allow conviction for murder. Such a killing does not satisfy the 'normal' (i.e. paradigm) requirements for murder as expressed in the murder definition. It does, however, satisfy the formal definition of the offence of 'felony murder', because that offence requires only that the actor cause a death during commission of a felony. Thus, in a formal sense, there is no imputation. But one can view the formal definition of felony murder as codification of a principle that imputes the culpable state of mind required for murder whenever the actor causes a death in the course of a felony. A similar analysis applies to the misdemeanor-manslaughter rule.[21]

---

§ 57.3 (1983) ('reasonably foreseeable consequence' of 'conduct'). Even without statutory authority, courts have employed the natural and probable consequence rule to impute both mental and objective elements: see e.g. *United States* v. *Clayborne* (DC Cir. 1974), 509 F (2d) 473 at 475, 481 (murder by defendant Clayborne in course of chase was natural and probable consequence of defendant Brown's participation in criminal venture; proof that Brown shared Clayborne's intention to kill therefore not required); *Johnson* v. *United States* (DC Cir. 1978) 386 A (2d) 710 at 713 (defendant liable for natural and probable consequence of initial fight with victim regardless of intent regarding result). The Model Penal Code's complicity provision and those patterned after it, however, reject the natural and probable consequence rule, and impose liability for confederate's offence only when the normal complicity requirements are met: see Model Penal Code, § 2.06(3).

[20] See e.g. Draft English Code, ¶¶ 29, 31.

[21] The Model Penal Code's treatment of felony murder is instructive. After conceding that 'principled argument in . . . defence [of felony murder] is hard to find' (Model Penal Code, § 210.2 comment 37 (1980)), the drafters nonetheless have retained an ameliorated form of the doctrine, which facilitates classifying as murder an accidental killing during a felony. This 'reasonable substitute for the felony-murder rule' (*ibid.*, comment 29 (Tent. Draft No 9, 1959)) provides that a death caused during the commission of certain specified felonies creates a rebuttable presumption that the defendant caused the death recklessly under

Possession offences may present the clearest case of codified imputed liability. Again, to be held liable for possession, one must satisfy all the elements of the definition of the offence. But, as with felony murder, the definition of the offence does not truly represent the paradigm—it does not fully and accurately describe the harm or evil the offence seeks to punish. Possession offences seek to prohibit and punish not possession itself, but harmful conduct, past or future, that is facilitated and evidenced by the possession. The possession of trace amounts of narcotics, for example, suggests their past use or distribution. The possession of burglar's tools suggest a planned (or past) burglary.[22] Status offences are analogous to possession offences; the definition does not represent the true paradigm of the offence. Thus, vagrancy statutes, common before they were subject to constitutional challenge, punish the conduct and culpability of attempted theft.[23]

Strict liability offences are a fourth instance of codified imputed liability, although the characterization is more tenuous here. While the definition of a strict liability offence does not formally contain a culpable state-of-mind

circumstances manifesting extreme indifference to the value of human life, as required for murder. Such a revision invites characterization of the traditional felony-murder rule as an irrebuttable presumption of the culpability required for murder.

[22] In addition to punishing possession of narcotics and burglar's tools, many jurisdictions punish possession of counterfeiting dyes, dangerous weapons, motor vehicle master keys, or drug paraphernalia. E.g. Me. Rev. Stat. Ann., tit. 17-A, § 403 (1983); 18 USC § 474 (1982), Model Penal Code, § 5.06 (Proposed Official Draft 1962); *People* v. *Stinson* (1970) 8 Cal. App. (3d) 497, 87 Cal. Rptr. 537 (conviction for possession of sawn-off shotgun); NJ Stat. Ann., § 2C:5–6 (West 1982); Cal. Health & Safety Code, § 11364 (West Supp. 1983) (possession of paraphernalia used for unlawfully injecting or smoking controlled substance); accord NJ Stat. Ann., §§ 24:21–47 to 48 (West Supp. 1983). (Often these statutes are patterned after the Model Drug Paraphernalia Act of the Drug Enforcement Administration of the United States Department of Justice.) In each instance, one can readily identify the actual harm or evil that is of concern, and it is this harm and the accompanying elements of culpability that more appropriately comprise the paradigm of the offence. In relation to this *true* paradigm, there is indeed imputation. The objective and culpability requirements of the paradigm are imputed upon proof of possession.

[23] For example, in 1547 the preamble to the Slavery Act, a vagrancy statute, noted: 'Idleness and vagabondry is the mother and root of all thefts, robberies, and all evil acts, and other mischiefs'. An Act for the Punishment of Vagabonds, 1547, 1 Edw. 6, ch. 3; see Model Penal Code, § 250.12 comment (Tent. Draft No 13, 1961); Forrest W. Lacey, 'Vagrancy and Other Crimes of Personal Condition' (1953) 66 *Harvard LR* 1203; Arthur H. Sherry, 'Vagrants, Rogues and Vagabonds—Old Concepts in Need of Revision' (1960) 48 *California LR* 557. Vagrancy was at one time an offence in every American jurisdiction. Caleb Foote, 'Vagrancy-Type Law and its Administration' (1956) 104 *University of Pennsylvania LR* 603 at 609 and n. 7. See generally Note, 'The Vagrancy Concept Reconsidered: Problems and Abuses of Status Criminality' (1964) 37 *New York ULR* 102 at 108–14 (discussing vagrancy statutes from 48 jurisdictions). They frequently have been replaced by 'loitering or prowling' offences, which are designed to prohibit and punish a variety of preparatory criminal conduct. The drafters of the Model Penal Code, for example, rejected the concept of status criminality and proposed instead a 'suspicious loitering' offence that punishes one whose conduct justifies suspicion that he is about to engage in criminal activity. Model Penal Code, § 250.12 (Tent. Draft No 13, 1961). Section 250.12 was subsequently modified to require justifiable 'alarm' for the safety of persons or property: Model Penal Code, § 250.6. Under loitering and prowling offences, elements of a preparatory offence are in effect imputed upon proof of loitering or prowling.

element, a vast literature supports the normative claim that culpability should be required in all offences.[24]

One may well challenge the claim that each of these four classes of offences is designed to punish criminal conduct other than that described in their formal definition and that the elements of the *true* paradigm are imputed upon proof of the conditions stated in the offence's formal definition. One may argue that the definitions do accurately represent a paradigm, one that simply rejects the traditional requirements of harmful or evil conduct and personal culpability that are typical of other offence definitions. This line of argument is more successful with some claimed codified forms than with others. It seems difficult to argue that possession alone really is the harm or evil sought to be prohibited and punished by possession offences. One may argue that pure status offences and strict liability offences define a punishable harm or evil, but this characterization is possible only if one is willing to reject the notions of act and culpability as universal requirements for criminal liability.[25] Many would be unwilling to do so. Slightly more defensible is the claim that felony murder represents an independent harm or evil in which the traditional culpability for murder really is not relevant.

C. The Theories of Imputation

Given the variety of rules and doctrines of imputed liability, one may reasonably question whether there is any similarity in their supporting rationales. Yet four theories can be identified that commonly are used to support imputed liability. Reflecting the tensions in criminal law generally, some of these justifications adhere closely to the requirement of personal blameworthiness as a prerequisite for criminal liability, while others rely on more practical concerns.[26]

---

[24] e.g. Jerome Hall, *General Principles of Criminal Law* (2nd edn., Indianapolis, Indiana, 1960), 70–1; Glanville Williams, *Criminal Law: The General Part* (2nd edn., London, 1961), 75–99; Rollin M. Perkins, 'The Civil Offense' (1952) 100 *University of Pennsylvania LR* 832; Francis Bowes Sayre, 'Mens Rea' (1932) 45 *Harvard LR* 974. See generally Model Penal Code, § 2.05, comments 1 and 2, at 140–6 (Tent. Draft No 4, 1955) (summarizing arguments and cataloguing literature). Evidence also suggests that, as a descriptive matter, culpability remains part of the general paradigm for all criminal offences. Every modern criminal code includes general provisions either requiring culpability or at least creating a presumption that the legislature intended to require culpability, as to each element of every offence that carries the stigma of the criminal sanction: see e.g. Model Penal Code, §§ 2.02(3), 2.05 (Proposed Official Draft 1962).

[25] Indeed, if one is willing to disregard the requirements of an act and culpability, one may be able to claim that many instances of clear *formal deviation*, such as complicity, are in fact instances of *substantive compliance* in which no imputation occurs. But this approach does not advance the inquiry. If, however, these offences are accepted as instances of substantive deviations from the paradigm, then a comparison of these offences to other instances of imputed liability may provide insight into the proper formulation of these offences.

[26] For a more detailed discussion, see Paul H. Robinson, 'Imputed Criminal Liability' (1984) 93 *Yale LJ* 609.

In many instances, an actor is held accountable despite the absence of a required element of culpability because he is causally responsible for the conduct of another or for the absence of a required state of mind in himself or another. In the case of objective conduct elements, the actor may have caused another to perform, or assisted another in performance of, the required conduct. In the case of mental elements, the actor may have caused the absence of the required mental state in himself or another by external means, such as intoxicants, or through simple 'deliberate blindness' to the circumstances or consequences of his own conduct or the conduct of another. This 'causal theory' generally corresponds well to our collective notions of blameworthiness.

In some instances, however, while there may be a community consensus that an element should be imputed because the actor is as blameworthy as if he had in fact satisfied the element, there is no analytic theory to support the consensus. Rather, the best one can do is to restate the conclusion: the actor is as blameworthy as one who satisfies the element. The doctrine of transferred intent is illustrative. The label itself, cast in terms of transferring intention, somewhat deceptively suggests an analytic process, but the best explanation of why the intent to shoot the desired victim should be 'transferred' to the actual victim is that both intentions seem equally culpable. The theory is merely one of apparent equivalence. The Model Penal Code reveals its reliance upon such an 'equivalence theory' when it provides that '[a]lthough ignorance or mistake would otherwise afford a defence to the offence charged [i.e. would negative a required culpability element], the defence is not available if the defendant would be guilty of another offence had the situation been as he supposed'.[27] The rationale for imputing the absent state of mind is simply that the actor had the intention (or other level of culpability) to commit another offence and therefore is as blameworthy, and can properly be so treated, as if he had the required intention for the offence committed.

Both the causal and the equivalence theories correspond to our notions of blame and are consistent with a criminal law that seeks to distribute liability in proportion to blameworthiness. Under either theory, the requirements of the imputation doctrine together with the satisfied elements of the offence assure a degree of blameworthiness that approximates that of the offence charged. Because a causal theory both tracks blameworthiness and provides a clear analytic foundation for imputation, it may be the preferred justification for imputation.[28] Where a strong causal theory

---

[27] Model Penal Code, § 2.04(2). See also Draft English Code, ¶ 24(1).

[28] Because a causal theory leads to analysis of specific elements required by liability—i.e. culpability as to causing, the causal relationship, and culpability as to the substantive offence —it encourages the precise definition of the conditions that must be satisfied prior to imputation. The equivalence theory, however, merely asserts an equivalence and thus encourages imprecise definitions and may permit arbitrary results. Equivalence theories, in this sense, are akin to the early 'wickedness' notion of mens rea typical of 'offence analysis'; like 'offence

is available, no other rationale is necessary.[29] Because of analytical short-comings, an equivalence theory fails to provide a general principle for discovering and supporting analogous instances of imputation. Every claim of equivalence must be justified by an independent demonstration of consensus.

A third theory eschews strictly proportioning liability to blameworthiness, primarily because of practical problems of proof. Thus, doctrines of imputation supported by this theory may generate liability disproportionate to blame. It may sometimes (even frequently) be the case that proportionate blameworthiness does exist, but the prosecution need not prove requirements that would demonstrate such blame. Such proof requirements, it is argued, allow many culpable persons to escape conviction or make convictions too costly to obtain.[30] Such an 'evidentiary theory' for imputing a required element balances the competing interests of fairness and utility. As a result, the rules and doctrines supported by this theory are the subject of considerable controversy.

To accept an evidentiary rationale, one must be willing to accept potentially erroneous convictions in exchange for increased ease of prosecution. The latter interest goes beyond concern for the convenience of prosecutors. Difficulties in successful prosecutions permit dangerous criminals to escape conviction. The evidentiary advantage of such imputation will reduce the number of such dangerous acquittals. Rules relying upon evidentiary rationales are thus subject to the criticisms presented in the broader debate over evidentiary advantages for the prosecution generally. Evidentiary rationales comprise a specialized subgroup of non-culpability rationales. Rather than rejecting the validity of the blameworthiness principle, such evidentiary theories seek to approximate the desired results of the principle as closely as the problems of proof permit.

Finally, in still other instances of imputation, proportionality between liability and blameworthiness is sacrificed on utilitarian grounds to other important societal interests, most commonly crime control. Such a 'crime control theory' for imputing required objective and mental elements often

---

analysis', equivalency theories should be replaced whenever possible with a theory more compatible with the modern 'element analysis' approach to culpability.

[29] In *Moore* v. *State*, for example, the court rejected defendant's contention that he was not guilty of burglary since he did not 'break' into the victim's residence: Because the victim unlocked the door at gun point, defendant 'was *as guilty of breaking as if* he had taken the keys from her hand and unlocked the door himself': (1977) 267 Ind 270 at 369, NE (2d) 628 (emphasis added). The causal argument for this type of causing crime by an innocent is so compelling that the court need not have relied upon the more vague equivalence rationale that the quoted language suggests. The actor is as culpable as if he had engaged in the prohibited conduct himself, because he caused the element to be satisfied by another.

[30] The evidentiary theory is most often employed to support imputation of mental rather than objective elements. One would expect such a pattern of application since the evidentiary rationale responds to problems of proof, and proof of mental elements is more difficult than proof of objective elements.

supports strict liability rules and doctrines, for example. In each instance the need to reduce future crime is offered as the justification for imputing a required element even though the conditions of imputation do not suggest that the actor is (or even probably is) as blameworthy as the resulting liability normally would require. Typically, this is done because the actor, although not so blameworthy, is seen as dangerous or is seen as an effective example by which others can be deterred.

Crime control rationales are the most susceptible to criticism and should be the least favoured in supporting imputation. Such rationales must justify not simply the creation of an evidentiary shortcut to proving the presence of required offence elements, as in evidentiary rationales; they also must justify the injustice of liability disproportionate to blame. Crime control rationales therefore implicate the broader debate over whether criminal law should serve a utilitarian crime-control purpose or should punish only according to the degree of an actor's personal blameworthiness.

These four theories—causal, equivalence, evidentiary, and crime control —do not provide categories of imputation doctrines but rather are explanations or justifications for imputing an absent element of an offence definition. It is possible, even likely, that more than one theory may justify some doctrines, while only a combination of two or more theories or rationales can adequately explain others. In each instance, examination of the underlying rationale provides a basis for assessing the legitimacy and persuasiveness of the reasons for imputation.

To summarize the major points of this Chapter, the definition of an offence describes the elements normally required to hold an actor liable for the offence; it is that offence's paradigm for liability. Despite the absence of a required element of the definition, however, an actor may be held liable for the offence if a doctrine imputes the absent elements. Such a doctrine does not alter the definition of the offence, but rather provides an alternative means of establishing the required elements, or at least an alternative means of holding the defendant as if the required elements were satisfied. For the most part, the principles underlying imputation reflect concerns beyond those of the offence at hand; a single doctrine of imputation may apply to a range of offences or to all offences. As a group, instances of imputed liability play as significant a role in criminal law theory and practice as do general defences.

5

General Defences

The most common conceptualization of defences among modern codes is that reflected in the organization of the American Model Penal Code summarized in Chapter 1. The Code recognizes what it calls 'Justification' defences in Article 3, such as self-defence and law enforcement authority, and in Article 4, under the heading 'Responsibility', it collects such defences as insanity and immaturity. In addition to these two defence groups, the Code provides a variety of defences, such as mistake, intoxication, duress, consent, entrapment, sprinkled among the provisions of Article 2, entitled 'General Principles of Liability'. Still others, such as time limitations, former prosecution, are included in Article 1, entitled 'Preliminary'. It is unclear what degree of conceptual similarity the Code drafters think exists among the defences they collect in Article 1 or among those they collect in Article 2. Here, then, are the three groupings of defences most typical of modern American codes: justification defences, responsibility-related defences, and other defences (related to general principles of liability and other preliminary matters). The Draft English Code also has a three-part structure, but one that ignores the justification-excuse distinction. It recognizes two groups of defences under the headings 'Incapacity and Mental Disorder' and 'Defences', and includes other defences in a variety of places in the General Part.

This Chapter argues that current conceptualizations hide important fundamental distinctions between defences and between defence groups, and that this obscuration distorts the theories and formulation of defences. This Chapter argues that better conceptualization and a more accurate reflection of how current law actually operates would instead recognize five groups of defences. Chapter 2 sketched the proposed categories: two groups in which the 'defences' are conceptually tied to the definition of specific offences—absent element defences and offence modification defences—and three groups of general defences that theoretically apply to all offences—justifications, excuses, and non-exculpatory defences. Let me briefly remind the reader of the five categories and their interrelation, then highlight the conclusions of the Chapter with regard to each of the groups.

Some doctrines that are called defences are nothing more than the absence of a required offence element. When I take your umbrella believing it to be my own, I may claim a mistake defence. Yet my defence derives not from a special defence of mistake but rather from the elements of the theft offence. The definition of theft includes a requirement that the actor know that the property taken is property owned by another. If I mistakenly believe that the umbrella I take is my own, I do not satisfy the required element of knowledge. Such a mistake 'defence' may be called an absent element defence because it arises from the inability of the state to prove a required element. It is within accepted casual usage to call such claims 'defences', but they are simply another way of talking about the requirements of the offence definition.

Some defences are formally independent of the offence elements but in fact concern criminalization issues closely related to the definition of the offence. They typically refine or qualify the definition of a particular offence or group of offences. Voluntary renunciation, for example, provides a defence in the United States to inchoate offences like attempt or conspiracy. Consent is recognized as a defence to some kinds of assault in the United States. Such a consent defence helps define what we mean by the offence of assault (an unconsented-to touching), just as renunciation helps refine the definition of inchoate offences (as extending only to unrenounced criminal plans). Indeed, assault frequently is formally defined as an unconsented-to touching; the absence of consent is included as an element of the offence. As the practice illustrates, the difference between absent element defences and offence modification defences, as they may be called, is one of form more than substance. An offence modification defence can as easily be drafted as a negative element of the offence.

Other defences, in contrast, have general application to all offences. Such general defences represent general principles of defence that are not dependent upon or related to the definition of any particular offence or group of offences. They exist to bar liability for a reason unrelated to the criminalization decision embodied in the offence definition. General defences are of three sorts: justifications, excuses, and non-exculpatory defences.

Justification defences, such as lesser evils, self-defence, and law enforcement authority, exculpate on a theory that the actor avoided a greater harm or evil. That is, while an actor satisfies the elements of an offence, his conduct should be tolerated or even encouraged because of the benefit it brings. An actor who burns a firebreak on another's land may thereby commit arson, but also may have a justification defence (of lesser evils) if by that burning he saves 100 innocent lives from an approaching forest fire.

Excuse defences, such as insanity and duress, exculpate under a different theory. The actor has admittedly caused a net societal harm or evil but he is excused because he cannot properly be held responsible for his conduct. Note the difference in focus between justifications and excuses. An actor's conduct is justified; an actor is excused.

Non-exculpatory defences, a final group of general defences, do not exculpate an actor but do provide exemption from liability. Even though the actor's conduct is criminal and unjustified and the actor is fully responsible for it, non-exculpatory defences are made available because they further important societal interests. Thus, diplomatic immunity may provide a defence, without regard to the guilt or innocence of the actor, because by forgoing trial and conviction of the offending diplomat our diplomats abroad are free from prosecution by their host countries.

There is a logical hierarchy among these three kinds of general defences. If an actor's conduct is justified, there is nothing to excuse. Thus, one might naturally make the justification inquiry before the excuse inquiry (or the non-exculpatory defence inquiry). If the conduct is not justified, an excuse defence may exculpate the defendant as blameless. If the actor is not excused, he nonetheless may qualify for a non-exculpatory defence. But such a defence does not exculpate the actor; it only exempts from liability and punishment.[1] (For pedagogical reasons, this Chapter takes up these groups of defences in reverse order: non-exculpatory defences, excuses, and then justifications.)

The remainder of the Chapter looks more closely at each of these groups: how each group differs from the other groups, the existence of distinguishable subgroups within a group, the shared theory and structure of the defences within the group, and a critique of current formulations. Let me briefly signal some of the highlights of these discussions.

The most important part of the discussion of non-exculpatory defences may be its identification of which defences it includes. Current law does much to hide a defence's membership in what ought to be seen as a disfavoured class. Diplomatic immunity may be an obvious member, but also a member is the entrapment defence, for example. Another important part of the discussion is the implication of recognizing a defence as non-exculpatory. Social science data increasingly suggest that openly exculpating blameworthy offenders undercuts the moral credibility of the criminal justice system and thereby reduces its effectiveness as a mechanism of behavioural control.[2] If this is true, it must be recognized that there is a social cost in every use of a non-exculpatory defence, and such use should be limited to those instances in which that societal cost brings a greater societal benefit.

The discussion of excuses demonstrates the emptiness of the current conceptualization. Insanity and immaturity, grouped together under current conceptualization as 'responsibility' defences, may have a similarity to one another in their potential long-term character, a characteristic that excuse defences, like duress and involuntary intoxication, do not share. But their

---

[1] See Paul H. Robinson, 'Criminal Law Defenses: A Systematic Analysis' (1982) 82 *Columbia LR* 199, 232; but see Douglas Husak, 'The Serial View of Criminal Law Defenses' (1992) 3 *Criminal L Forum* 369.

[2] See Paul H. Robinson and John M. Darley, 'The Utility of Desert' (1996) 91 *Northwestern ULR* (hereinafter 'Utility of Desert').

potential long-term characteristic is of little conceptual or practical significance. It is the effect of the actor's lack of ability to understand and control his or her conduct that is central to the actor's blameworthiness. On
that issue—effect on an actor's ability to understand and control—the four
defences are similar if not identical. As the discussion suggests, if there is
an important distinction between different excuses, it is between all of the
disability excuses, on the one hand, and the mistake excuses, on the other.
The discussion suggests a common internal structure among excuses and
among the excuses of these two subgroups.

The discussion of justification defences performs similar functions. It
shows the commonality among justifications that distinguishes them from
excuses and non-exculpatory defences. It also shows differences among them
that suggest three conceptually important subgroups: defensive force justifications, public authority justifications, and the general justification of
lesser evils. Within each of these groups a common internal structure among
the defences is identified.

The most important issue taken up in the discussion is the confusion
of current law concerning the fundamental nature and theory of justification defences. Justification defences are traditionally thought of as focusing
upon the actor's reasons for acting, hence the defence's use of subjective
'believes' criteria. I argue that a closer examination of how justification
defences operate suggests that they look, instead, to the nature of the
actor's deeds, and that they ought to be formulated objectively. Subjective
issues, such as the actor's belief, should be dealt with under the independent defence of mistake as to a justification, which is an excuse defence
and not a justification defence at all. Confusion on the point has led to
improper defence formulations that give improper liability results and prevent the law from clearly announcing its rules of lawful conduct.

A. Non-exculpatory Defences

In 1992 the actor robs, rapes, and beats an elderly woman. The crime
goes unsolved until 1997, when he is identified and arrested. Although
he has committed the offence, caused the harm sought to be prevented
by the statute, and has no claim that his conduct is justified or excused,
the actor nonetheless may have a defence. The statute of limitations bars
his conviction for robbery, rape, and assault in the United States, despite
his clear blameworthiness, because forgoing his conviction is said to further other public interests, interests more important than imposing liability on deserving offenders.

Other 'non-exculpatory defences', as they may be called, include diplomatic immunity, judicial, legislative, and executive immunities, immunity after
compelled testimony or pursuant to a plea agreement, and incompetence.
Each of these forms of immunity furthers an important societal interest:

reciprocal protection of our diplomats abroad, protection of governmental officials from personal liability arising from their official duties, the need to compel incriminating testimony from some offenders to prosecute others successfully, and the avoidance of the costs and risks of trials through inducement of plea agreements, respectively. The last defence, incompetence, is based primarily on concerns of fairness to the defendant. It prohibits trial unless the defendant has an adequate ability to consult with his lawyer and to understand the proceedings against him. Later in this section the discussion examines the characteristics of the entrapment defence that suggest it is non-exculpatory.

Compelling non-exculpatory public policy interests also serve as the basis for many constitutional defences. The prohibition against double jeopardy in the fifth amendment of the United States Constitution, for example, may foreclose the trial of a blameworthy and convictable offender by barring the state from making repeated attempts to convict him. (Statutory forms of the prohibition are found in sections 1.08 to 1.10 of the Model Penal Code and clause 11 of the Draft English Code.) Notions of procedural fairness demand that the prosecution not subject a defendant to the embarrassment, expense, and ordeal of trial more than once nor compel a defendant to live in a continuing state of anxiety and insecurity. Dismissals based on the operation of the exclusionary rule or upon prosecutorial misconduct also may be non-exculpatory in nature, where such dismissals are unrelated to the reliability of the evidence or of the fact-finding process. The public policies served by non-exculpatory defences may be as broad as protecting all members of society from unlawful searches, or they may focus on assuring fairness in the treatment of the particular defendant, only indirectly conferring a benefit on society at large.

The balancing of competing interests that underlie non-exculpatory defences should be distinguished from the balancing that occurs in justification defences. In the latter, the harm done by defendant's conduct is weighed against the harm avoided or the benefit gained from that conduct. The actor whose conduct causes no net societal harm or evil is judged blameless and given a justification defence.[3] In non-exculpatory defences, the defendant's conduct neither creates a societal benefit nor avoids a societal harm; the defendant may well be fully blameworthy. The societal benefit from the defence arises not from the actor's conduct but from forgoing the actor's conviction. A defendant with a non-exculpatory defence may escape conviction in spite of his or her blameworthiness.

1. Minimizing the Societal Costs of Non-exculpatory Defences

While non-exculpatory defences yield identifiable societal benefits, it also is true that the criminal justice system incurs a cost each time a non-

---

[3] See generally sect. C of this Ch.

exculpatory defence is permitted. Permitting such defences undermines the purposes for which criminal liability is imposed. Acquitting culpable offenders, who admittedly have caused the harm or evil prohibited by the criminal law, undercuts the aims of special and general deterrence. The offender's acquittal shows others (and the actor him- or herself) that it is possible to violate the criminal law without suffering the threatened sanctions. In addition, the criminal justice system is deprived of authority to incapacitate or rehabilitate such offenders, thereby increasing the likelihood of future offences. Utilitarian concerns aside, non-exculpatory defences permit blameworthy offenders to escape the punishment they deserve.

In addition to these traditional arguments in support of a desert distribution of liability and punishment which necessarily stand in opposition to non-exculpatory defences, social science findings suggest other arguments, utilitarian arguments other than deterrence, incapacitation, and rehabilitation, in favour of a desert distribution of liability and punishment. Recent empirical evidence suggests that criminal law's most effective mechanism of compliance is not the deterrent threat (of punishment or condemnation) but rather is law's capacity to gain moral credibility with the people. Further, and most importantly, the compliance power of the criminal law is directly proportional to its moral credibility.[4] If the criminal law is seen as unjust in one instance, its moral credibility and its concomitant power to gain future compliance is incrementally reduced.[5]

Reforms to the current system could reduce the detrimental effects of non-exculpatory defences without abolishing the defences. For example, while permitting an acquittal, the system nonetheless could make clear its condemnation of the conduct and the actor through a special verdict of 'guilty but not punishable'. Certainly, the present verdict of 'not guilty'

---

[4] See e.g. Tom Tyler, *Why People Obey the Law* (New Haven, Connecticut, 1990); Austin Sarat, 'Studying American Legal Cultures: An Assessment of Survey Evidence' (1977) 11 *Law and Society R* 427; Robinson and Darley, 'Utility of Desert' 216–19, above.

[5] See generally Paul H. Robinson and John M. Darley, Justice, *Liability, and Blame: Community Views and the Criminal Law* (Oxford, 1995), ch. 7, 201–3; Robinson and Darley, 'Utility of Desert' n. 1, above. In addition, the perceived 'justice' of the system is crucial to gaining the co-operation and acquiescence of those persons involved in the process (offenders, potential offenders, witnesses, jurors, etc.). Greatest co-operation will be elicited where the criminal law's liability rules and the community's views of justice generate identical results. Conflict between the two undercuts the moral credibility of the system and thereby engenders resistance and subversion. See e.g. Louis Michael Seidman, 'Soldiers, Martyrs, and Criminals: Utilitarian Theory and the Problem of Crime Control' (1984) 94 *Yale LJ* 315 at 319; S. M. Kassin and L. S. Wrightsman, *The American Jury on Trial* (New York, 1988) 158–9; Alan W. Scheflin and Jon Van Dyke, 'Jury Nullification: The Contours of a Controversy' (1980) 43 *Law and Contemporary Problems* 52 at 71–5; M. R. Kadish and Stanford H. Kadish, *Discretion to Disobey* (Stanford, California, 1973), 32–3. In addition, moral condemnation is an inexpensive yet powerful form of deterrent threat. It demands none of the costs that attend imprisonment or even supervised probation, yet, for many persons, it is a sanction to be very much avoided. The more important social acceptance is to the person, the more terrible this threatened sanction. This marvellously cost-efficient sanction is available, however, only if the system retains its moral credibility. Each time the system is seen to convict where no community condemnation is appropriate, the condemnation for subsequent convictions is weakened.

exacerbates the detrimental effects of non-exculpatory acquittals, for it misleads the public into thinking that the system thinks no wrong was done and no blame is due.[6] Successfully minimizing the detrimental effects of non-exculpatory acquittals depends in part upon public awarness of the special nature of non-exculpatory defences, yet at present there is little public appreciation for their special nature and still less awareness of which defences are of this sort.

The special nature of non-exculpatory defences also suggests that less strict adherence to the legality principle is in order. The legality principle is meant to ensure, among other things, that an actor has the opportunity for notice of the rules governing liability.[7] Such potential for notice is desirable because an actor cannot conform his or her conduct to the requirements of law if those requirements are not known. In the case of non-exculpatory defences, the actor's conduct may be deplored and sought to be deterred. In these instances, vagueness and ambiguity in defining the scope of the defence may have the effect of deterring undesirable conduct.

This deterrence must be distinguished from the undesirable 'chilling effect' of vague offence definitions. There is every reason to maintain clarity in defining prohibited conduct; only the limits of the non-exculpatory defence may tolerate greater vagueness. The immune foreign embassy attaché may behave himself if he is unsure whether he is covered by diplomatic immunity. The corrupt congressman may decline to exercise improper influence if he is unsure whether his legislative immunity extends to such impropriety.[8] One can argue that such offenders have few grounds to complain of the vagueness or ambiguity of the defence or to insist on a favorable construction, for they are blameworthy offenders and the conduct at issue has been announced as prohibited and condemnable.[9]

Given the nature of non-exculpatory defences, there is also little reason to provide a defence to an actor who calculates his conduct to take advantage of a non-exculpatory defence, but who is mistaken, even reasonably mistaken, as to the conditions of the defence. A better rule provides that

---

[6] It is an advantage, in this respect, that most nonexculpatory defences are determined by the judge before trial. But see the entrapment defence discussed later in this sect., at text accompanying note 29.

[7] See generally Paul H. Robinson, *Criminal Law* (Boston, 1997), § 2.2 (hereinafter *Criminal Law*).

[8] In contrast, it remains important that the law clearly define for legislators what is and is not improper influence.

[9] Similarly, even if judicial creation of offences is limited or common law offences abolished to promote fair notice, judicial revocation of a non-exculpatory defence should be permitted. The defendant has been afforded notice of all elements describing the proscribed conduct, and despite such notice has committed the offence. It seems proper to hold that in such instances an actor commits an offence at his own peril. When the Supreme Court reduces the availability of a constitutionally-based non-exculpatory defence, it commonly applies the reduced scope to the case at hand, in other words, without prior notice. See e.g. *United States* v. *Salvucci* (1980) 448 US 83, 100 S Ct. 2547, 65 L Ed. (2d) 619 (abolishing automatic standing rule and applying more limited standing rule to case at bar).

an actor who acts under a belief that he has a non-exculpatory defence acts at his peril. If the requirements for the defence in fact are not satisfied —the attaché is not immune, legislative immunity does not cover the condemnable conduct—then the public policy interests that normally support the defence are not served and no defence ought to be permitted.

Another implication of the nature of non-exculpatory defences is the status that such a defence gives an actor in a conflict with others. Defensive force justification defences give an actor a right to resist physical aggression against the actor's person or property and to interfere when aggression is directed against another's person or property. But this right to resist or to interfere with aggression exists only if the aggression itself is unlawful. If the aggression is not unlawful, if it is an officer making a lawful arrest, for example, generally there is not and should be no right to resist or interfere.[10] When the aggressor's conduct is not unlawful because the aggressor has a non-exculpatory defence, however, resistance and interference should be permitted, even encouraged. The immune diplomat may escape conviction for an unjustified and unexcused attack, but it hardly follows that the intended victim is bound to submit or the observer to acquiesce.[11]

One final implication of the nature of non-exculpatory defences concerns the consequences that attach to a non-exculpatory acquittal. Conviction for a criminal offence typically risks not only punishment, as through imprisonment, fine, or probation, but also a host of other civil disabilities. An offender may forfeit basic rights and privileges: citizenship; employment opportunities in licensed and unlicensed occupations; the capacity to litigate, to testify, and to serve as a juror or as a court-appointed fiduciary; voting, parental, and marital rights; and the rights to hold public office, to carry a firearm, to inherit, and to receive insurance, pension, and workmen's compensation benefits.[12] The offender also may incur forfeiture, civil restraint and injunction, civil liability, and civil commitment.[13] Further, the

---

[10] See sect. C.5.1(1) of this Ch.

[11] Properly interpreted, the Model Penal Code reaches this conclusion. See *ibid*.

[12] See e.g. *Schanuel* v. *Anderson* (7th Cir. 1983) 708 F (2d) 316 (statute prohibiting ex-felon from obtaining employment as a detective held constitutional); Ariz. Rev. Stat. Ann., § 13–3410 (Cum. Supp. 1983) (upon conviction of certain drug offences, licensing authority may revoke a professional license); Mo. Ann. Stat., § 222.010 (Vernon 1962) (all civil rights are terminated during a term of imprisonment, and a person sentenced is thereafter deemed 'civilly dead') (§ 222.010 is now repealed and replaced by *ibid*., §§ 561.016 to 561.026 (Vernon 1979 and Vernon Cum. Supp. 1983) (loss of privileges reasonably related to the conviction; temporary loss of voting rights; cannot serve as a juror)); Minn. Stat. Ann., § 609.165 (West Cum. Supp. 1983) (governs restoration of civil rights lost due to conviction); ND Cent. Code, § 12.1–33–01 (Cum. Supp. 1983) (civil rights are lost during incarceration). See generally Eric E. Younger, 'Not Completely Dead—But Seriously Injured; Collateral Consequences of Misdemeanor Arrest and Conviction' (1976) 52 *Los Angeles Bar* J 50.

[13] See e.g. Mich. 2d Proposed Rev. § 1255 (1979); NJ Stat. Ann., § 2C:13–12.1 (West Cum. Supp. 1983–84); ND Cent. Code, § 12.1–33–01 to 12.1–33–02.1 (Cum. Supp. 1983). See generally Special Project, 'The Collateral Consequences of a Criminal Conviction' (1970)

conviction may be used to impeach an offender in a subsequent trial where the offender is a witness or a defendant-witness,[14] and to aggravate the sentence for a subsequent offence.[15]

Given the disfavoured nature of non-exculpatory defences, some of these collateral consequences may appropriately be retained, despite acquittal, if the acquittal rests exclusively upon a non-exculpatory defence. Even if the offender is not punished for his past violation, ought not society be able to protect itself from new violations? Some precedent exists for this. The immune diplomat may escape liability, but nonetheless may be expelled from the country. The incompetent defendant may escape immediate trial, but nonetheless may be incarcerated until his trial is possible. (Other precedent is found in the fact that collateral consequences frequently are retained when an offender is pardoned.[16]) In current practice, however, most offenders acquitted under a non-exculpatory defence escape all penalties and disabilities.

Assume a guilty defendant's case is dismissed because of police or prosecutorial misconduct, for example. The rationale for the non-exculpatory defence may rest upon the conclusion that allowing such an acquittal— forgoing the condemnation of conviction and the restraint of imprisonment or supervision—is an acceptable cost to suffer in order to further the societal interest in deterring official misconduct. But is it equally clear that the interest in deterring such official misconduct also outweighs the

---

23 *Vanderbilt LR* 929; President's Commission on Law Enforcement and Administration of Justice, 'Task Force Report: Corrections' (1967), 88–92; Model Penal Code, §§ 6.04, 6.13.

[14] See e.g. Fed. R Evid. 404, 609. See *United States* v. *Keller* (3rd Cir. 1980) 624 F (2d) 1154 (government sought to introduce evidence of a prior prosecution for drug dealing that resulted in acquittal on the basis of entrapment; entrapment was defence in instant case; evidence held inadmissible); Note, 'Excluding Evidence of Prior Crimes When Trial Resulted in Acquittal—*State* v. *Wakefield*' (1980) 6 *William Mitchell LR* 455 (describing as the minority position the exclusion of evidence of a prior crime that resulted in acquittal). In some cases, the evidence may be admissible as substantive proof of intent, motive, scheme, or identity: see Annotation (1980) 2 ALR (4th) 330.

[15] Many states have enacted habitual or persistent offenders statutes: e.g. Conn. Gen. Stat. Ann., § 53a–40 (West Cum. Supp. 1983–84); Del. Code Ann., tit. 11, § 4214 (1979); NC Gen. Stat., § 14–7.1 (1981); NJ Stat. Ann., § 2C:44–3(a) (West 1982). Other states aggravate penalties for recidivists: e.g. Hawaii Rev. Stat., § 706–606.5 (Cum. Supp. 1982); PR Laws Ann., tit. 33, § 3302 (Cum. Supp. 1981). See generally Annotation (1980) 2 ALR (4th) 618 (discussing the validity of statutes authorizing imprisonment of habitual or repeated traffic offenders). Some of these collateral consequences may occur even if a defendant successfully presents a defence to criminal conviction. Civil commitment, civil restraint or injunction, forfeiture, civil liability, and expulsion from the country do not depend upon a conviction. But most other collateral penalties and disabilities cannot now be imposed if the defendant is not convicted: see Robinson, *Criminal Law*, n. 6 above, at § 10.2.

[16] See e.g. Fed. R Evid. 609 (impeachment by prior conviction permitted even though defendant was subsequently pardoned); *State* v. *Clark* (La. 1981) 402 So. (2d) 684 (pardon for previous convictions did not prevent their use to impeach defendant's credibility); cf. *Hozer* v. *State Police & Firemans Pension Fund* (App. Div. 1967) 95 NJ Super. 196, 201–4, 230 A (2d) 508 at 511–2 (pardon did not erase moral stain of the offence and pardoned policeman was not entitled to a pension provided for 'honorable service').

benefits of all collateral consequences that might have attached to the conviction? Should the corrupt official be able to keep his public office? Should the child molester retain his licence to drive a school bus? Should the rapist be permitted to escape sentencing as a repeat offender after a subsequent rape? Should the con-man escape impeachment as a prosecution witness in a subsequent capital offence trial?

The non-exculpatory acquittee may by all standards be blameworthy, and there may be nothing in the actor's character or conduct to suggest that the actor deserves to escape conviction. Rather, it is the *societal* interests that justify an acquittal under a non-exculpatory defence. And, as society may choose to adopt a non-exculpatory defence because of the balance of competing societal interests, so too may it properly choose to modify the defence or its consequences as it sees fit. Thus, a non-exculpatory defence may result in exemption from custodial or supervisory sanctions, yet permit the imposition of collateral consequences that are, on balance, too important to society's protection to be ignored. Collateral consequences often provide the most critical protections for society, sometimes with modest infringement upon an offender's interests. In other words, the public policy nature of non-exculpatory defences means that the scope and effect of the defence should be a matter of balancing the competing public interests. Because the interests supporting a non-exculpatory defence are enough to permit the offender to escape conviction itself, it does not follow that the interests are enough to support the offender escaping all collateral consequences that might accompany conviction.

The greatest practical hurdle to maintaining collateral consequences of conviction upon a non-exculpatory acquittal is identifying the cases of non-exculpatory acquittal of blameworthy offenders. Many non-exculpatory defences bar prosecution, thus no authoritative determination of blameworthiness is readily available. Double jeopardy, diplomatic immunity, and incompetence by their terms bar trial of the defendant. Other non-exculpatory defences, such as the statute of limitations and the immunities (judicial, legislative, executive, testimonial, and plea-bargaining) often are litigated before trial. This difficulty can be solved easily enough by a change in procedural rules. If the prosecution intends to seek the imposition of collateral consequences upon a non-exculpatory dismissal, and if the defendant wishes to object, the guilt determination process goes forward. Alternatively, the issues of blameworthiness could be litigated specially at a proceeding for imposition of collateral consequences. Whether the additional expenditure of resources would be worth the effort may depend upon how great a threat the defendant would continue to present if no collateral consequences were imposed.[17]

---

[17] In each instance, of course, if such collateral sanctions are contemplated, an actor must be given the opportunity to rely instead upon an exculpatory defence if such is available to him.

2. THE NATURE OF THE ENTRAPMENT DEFENCE

A useful exercise to illustrate the character and implications of non-exculpatory defences is to analyse a defence whose status is unclear. The entrapment defence is a good candidate, for it has some characteristics that suggest a non-exculpatory nature and others that do not.

Where a police officer or agent induces or triggers an actor's commission of an offence, the actor may be entitled to an entrapment defence.[18] The United States is one of the few countries in the world that recognizes such a defence, and, within the United States, jurisdictions disagree over how the defence should be formulated. The two most common forms of the defence might be called the 'objective' or 'police misconduct' formulation and the 'subjective' or 'predisposition' formulation. The apparent disagreement between these two formulations concerns how much the defence should focus on the *police* conduct and how much it should focus on the effect of the police conduct on the *defendant*. Which of the two general approaches is preferable depends on what we seek to achieve by recognizing an entrapment defence.

'Objective' formulations of the entrapment defence focus on the impropriety of the police conduct. Under the Utah statute, for example, entrapment is any police conduct that 'creat[es] a substantial risk that the offence would be committed by one not otherwise ready to commit it'.[19] The defence does not require that *the defendant* be 'not otherwise ready to commit it'. The defence is available, without regard to the *defendant's* predisposition, if the police conduct is such that it might cause an offence by 'one not otherwise ready to commit it'. In *State* v. *Taylor*, for example, the defendant's ex-girlfriend, Stubbs, acting as an undercover agent for police, uses the defendant's feeling of affection for her to induce him to [purchase] illegal drugs.[20] Taylor is given an entrapment defence even though he had been an addict in the past and had procured drugs for others. On this occasion, the police conduct in inducing the offence was viewed as inappropriate because it played upon the defendant's feelings of love and affection for Stubbs. The defendant was given a defence despite his predisposition to commit the offence.

Model Penal Code section 2.13 adopts an even more objective form than the Utah statute. It requires only that the defendant's conduct be 'in response to' the police conduct,[21] not even requiring, as Utah does, that

---

[18] See authorities collected at 2 Paul H. Robinson, *Criminal Law Defenses* (St Paul, Minnesota, 1984), ii, § 209, n. 1 (hereinafter *Criminal Law Defenses*).

[19] Utah Code Ann., § 76–2–303.   [20] (1979) 599 P (2d) 496.

[21] Model Penal Code, § 2.13(2). Under the Code, entrapping conduct includes not only conduct that 'creates a substantial risk that such an offence will be committed by persons other than those who are ready to commit it': Model Penal Code, § 2.13(1)(b). An officer also entraps if he: '[makes] knowingly false representations designed to induce the belief that such conduct is not prohibited': Model Penal Code, § 2.13(1)(a).

the defendant be 'induced' by the police conduct.[22] Thus, even if Taylor were unmoved by Stubbs' requests, he has a defence under the Model Penal Code once the police conduct is judged to be improper inducement. Under the Code, the propriety of the police conduct is the only issue.

'Subjective' formulations of the entrapment defence focus on the degree to which the entrapping conduct rather than the actor's own choice is responsible for commission of the offence. The Delaware statute, for example, permits an entrapment defence only if the defendant is 'induced' to commit an offence that he (the defendant) 'is not otherwise disposed' to commit.[23] The defence is given, under this formulation, 'because the wrongdoing of the officer originates the idea of the crime and then induces the other person to [commit the offence] when the other person is not otherwise disposed to do so'.[24]

Evidence of predisposition is not necessarily limited to the defendant's conduct *prior* to the entrapping conduct. In *Harrison* v. *State*, for example, the defendant, a prison guard, agrees to smuggle in marijuana for a prisoner, who is acting as an agent for the police.[25] The defendant is denied an entrapment defence, although it is clear that she had never smuggled drugs into prison before and would not have done so on this occasion but for the inducement of the police. The court notes that evidence of the defendant's predisposition to commit the offence may come from how the defendant responds to the police inducement. In *Harrison*, once the defendant was approached, she took an active role in planning the smuggling, failing to take any of several opportunities to withdraw, and committed two offences a month apart.

An objective formulation of the entrapment defence is clearly a non-exculpatory defence. It uses the threat of acquittal of the defendant as a means of deterring improper police conduct; the blameworthiness of the defendant is not relevant. A subjective ('predisposition') formulation might appear at first glance to be an excuse, similar to duress, that exculpates the defendant because he or she is coerced to commit an offence. More careful analysis, however, suggests that such a characterization is doubtful. The subjective formulation of the entrapment defence does not satisfy the traditional requirements for an excuse. The 'induced' requirement in entrapment is analogous to the coercion requirement in duress. But a duress defence is not given simply because an actor was subject to coercion, just as an insanity defence is not given simply because the actor has some

---

[22] It can be argued, however, that Model Penal Code section 2.13(1) requires actual inducement; the section defines unlawful entrapment as conduct by which an officer 'induces or encourages another person' to commit an offence, through certain defined means. But this interpretation seems inconsistent with the use of 'in response to' (rather than 'is induced') in section 2.13(1). One might conclude that, under the Code, it is enough that the officer *thought* he was inducing the defendant, even though no inducement in fact was needed.

[23] Del. Code Ann., tit. 11, § 432.   [24] *Id.*

[25] (Del. 1982) 442 A (2d) 1377, 1379–80.

mental illness. An excuse requires that the disability be sufficiently strong in its effects that we could not reasonably have expected the actor to have avoided the violation.

In the context of duress, an excuse is permitted only if the coercion was such that 'a person of reasonable firmness would have been unable to resist'.[26] As will become clear in the discussion of excuses in the next section, a disability, such as mental illness or involuntary intoxication, can be the 'but for' cause of an offence, yet not necessarily provide a defence.[27] The disability must not only contribute to the offence, it must be sufficiently strong as to render the actor blameless for the offence conduct. Nothing in the entrapment defence, even in the subjective formulation, ensures that such a degree of coercion is present. The subjective formulation at most requires a showing that the actor would not have committed the offence *but for* the officer's inducement. As the law of insanity and involuntary intoxication teaches, this is not enough to render the actor blameless.

If the subjective formulation represented a true excuse, because the pressure brought to bear on the actor rendered the actor blameless, there would be no reason to limit the defence to cases of inducement by government agents. If private citizens induced an offence using the same pressure, such private entrapment also logically should be recognized as a defence. In fact, private entrapment is not a defence. In *United States v. Perl*,[28] for example, defendant Dr Perl was induced by a private citizen to commit minor acts of terrorism to help the plight of Soviet Jews. The private citizen then turned Dr Perl in to the police. The court denied an entrapment defence, a result consistent with entrapment's non-exculpatory rationale. Dr Perl may well have been induced by another to commit the offence, but unless the inducement rose to the level of a duress excuse, he remained blameworthy for the offence, and, as a matter of non-exculpatory public policy interests, forgoing his conviction would do nothing toward deterring improper police conduct. One must conclude that the subjective formulation of entrapment, like the objective formulation, operates as a non-exculpatory defence. The primary difference between the two is that the subjective formulation lets off fewer offenders. By excluding predisposed offenders, it allows conviction of these more dangerous offenders but continues to provide some deterrence to improper police conduct.

The non-exculpatory public policies underlying the entrapment defence also manifest themselves in the defence's specific exclusion of certain serious offences. The Model Penal Code, for example, makes its entrapment defence 'unavailable' for offences in which 'causing or threatening bodily injury is an element'.[29] A true excuse would not exclude a defence for cer-

---

[26] See e.g. Model Penal Code, § 2.09.   [27] See sect. B.1.3. of this Ch.
[28] (1978) 584 F (2d) 1316.
[29] Model Penal Code, § 2.13(3). As the Code drafters explain:

   'It will not seem generally unfair to punish someone who has caused or threatened bodily injury to another, even though he was induced to his action by law enforcement

tain classes of offences. The duress defence, for example, remains available for offences that cause or threaten bodily injury. But, in attempting to deter improper police conduct, it is reasonable for a jurisdiction to conclude that acquitting violent offenders is too high a price to pay for deterrence.

To summarize, some reduced blameworthiness may be present where an actor is induced by another to commit an offence, at least where the actor is not otherwise predisposed to do so. But such inducement alone, without a showing that the actor could not reasonably have been expected to avoid the violation, is insufficient to justify an excuse. Nor is the limitation of the entrapment defence to cases of inducement by police officers or agents consistent with the notion of entrapment as an excuse. In reality, the primary reasons for the entrapment defence are deterrence and estoppel: deterrence of improper police inducement and avoiding the apparent unfairness of allowing the government to induce an offence and then prosecute it. Given its non-exculpatory status, the entrapment defence is best determined by the judge before trial, rather than by a jury at trial (as is sometimes done[30]). Further, as with all non-exculpatory defences, a 'not guilty' verdict for entrapment is misleading in that it suggests a lack of blameworthiness.

B. Excuses

Like non-exculpatory defences, excuses are general defences in that they apply to all offences; they are available even though the actor satisfies the elements of an offence. Excuses admit that the deed is wrong, but, unlike non-exculpatory offences, they exculpate the actor because the actor's characteristics or situation suggest that the actor should not be blamed for the violation. Blame arises not from engaging in conduct that in fact constitutes a criminal harm or evil, but rather from choosing to engage in such conduct. Absent meaningful choice there can be no blame and ought to be no liability or punishment.[31]

officials. It is unlikely that a law-abiding person could be persuaded by any tactics to engage in such behavior, and a person who can be persuaded to cause such injury presents a danger that the public cannot safely disregard': Model Penal Code, § 2.13 comment 420 (1985).

[30] See e.g. *United States* v. *Russell* (1973) 411 US 423, 93 S Ct. 1637, 36 L Ed. (2d) 366 (Court reversing Ninth Circuit's decision to overturn jury finding of no entrapment). The Model Penal Code takes the better course of having the defence decided by the court: see Model Penal Code, § 2.13(2).

[31] Not all writers agree that the best explanation of excuses is an actor's absence of a choice to act in a way that violates the law. Some have suggested that excuses recognize an actor's 'unfairly limited opportunity' to conform his conduct to law: see Sanford H. Kadish, 'Excusing Crime', in S. Kadish (ed.), *Blame and Punishment* (New York, 1987), at 81; Michael S. Moore, 'Choice, Character, and Excuse', in E. Paul, F. Miller, and J. Paul (eds.), *Crime, Culpability and Remedy* (Oxford, 1990), at 29 (hereinafter 'Choice, Character, and Excuse'). Others have suggested that excuses key primarily upon an actor's character. See

Justifications and excuses are similar, in that both are general defences and both exculpate an actor because of blamelessness. A distinction between the two was of practical importance at early common law,[32] but fell into disuse when both kinds of defences came to acquit a defendant in the same fashion. The distinction remains one of conceptual importance, however. Justified conduct adheres to the criminal law's rules of conduct. It is behaviour that is to be encouraged (or at least tolerated) in the future. In determining whether conduct is justified, the focus is on the *act* and its circumstances, not the actor. An excuse, in contrast, represents a legal conclusion that the conduct is wrong, undesirable, that the conduct ought not to be encouraged or tolerated and should be avoided in the future, even in the same situation. Criminal liability nonetheless is inappropriate in cases of excuse because some characteristic of the actor or the actor's situation vitiates the actor's blameworthiness. Excuses do not suggest the absence of net harm, as do justifications, but rather shift blame for the harm from the actor to the disability or other cause of the excusing conditions. The focus in excuses is on the *actor*. Acts are justified; actors are excused.

Not every distributive principle for criminal liability necessarily recognizes excuses. A distributive principle based upon just desert supports the recognition of excuses in order to exculpate blameless offenders. One also might argue that a utilitarian distributive principle based exclusively on special deterrence similarly supports the recognition of excuses. That is, there is little special deterrent value in sanctioning an offender if the offender is unable to appreciate the criminality of his conduct or to conform it to the requirements of law. On the other hand, there may well be *general* deterrent value—the deterrence of other potential offenders who do not have an excuse—in sanctioning such blameless offenders. Punishing a blameless offender may be particularly effective at signalling to the general public that the law is serious about punishing such violations. Persons contemplating such an offence ought not even to hope to be excused. Such an extreme form of strict liability, it might be argued, increases the motivation to avoid such a violation. A distributive principle that looks only to incapacitation or rehabilitation of dangerous offenders similarly may deny an excuse to a blameless offender, at least where the source of the excuse continues or is likely to recur. In these cases, the criminal law would want to take jurisdiction over such offenders in order to administer

---

Pete Arenella, 'Character, Choice, and Moral Agency', in E. Paul, F. Miller, and J. Paul (eds.), *Crime, Culpability, and Remedy* (Oxford, 1990), at 59; David Hume, *An Enquiry Concerning Human Understanding* (1949), 108; George Vouso, 'Background, Responsibility and Excuse' (1987) 96 *Yale LJ* 1661.

[32] The excused defendant was acquitted, but his property nonetheless was forfeited to the crown. See N. Hurnard, *The King's Pardon for Homicide Before A.D. 1307* (London, 1969), x–xi.

required incapacitation or rehabilitation.[33] That excuses are in fact recognized by current doctrine suggests that in this instance desert and possibly special deterrence are the guiding distributive principles rather than general deterrence, incapacitation, or rehabilitation.[34]

Excuse defences are of two sorts: disability excuses and mistake excuses. The disability excuses include insanity, immaturity, involuntary intoxication, duress, a number of kinds of involuntary conduct such as convulsion, and some forms of impaired consciousness such as somnambulism and hypnotism. Mistake as a defence was discussed in earlier, in Chapter 3.D., in the context of mistake negating an offence element; the issue here is mistake as an excuse defence, where it does not negate an offence element. The mistake excuses include defences for reliance upon official misstatement of law, unavailable law, and mistake as to a justification. (The next section, concerning justifications, will have more to say about this last mistake excuse.)

1. THE INTERNAL STRUCTURE OF EXCUSE DEFENCES

The common rationale of excuses—to exculpate blameless defendants —gives rise to common requirements: a *disability* or *reasonable mistake* must cause an *excusing condition*. Under each defence doctrine, an actor is excused if, because of the special conditions, the actor could not reasonably have been expected to avoid the violation.

A conclusion of blamelessness may derive from either of two kinds of explanations. In the disability excuses, the actor can point to abnormal circumstances or abnormal characteristics that make it too difficult for the actor to appreciate the criminality or wrongfulness of his or her conduct or too difficult to conform his or her conduct to the requirements of law. In the mistake excuses, no disabling abnormality exists, but the actor can claim that, because of a reasonable mistake, he or she did not realize the conduct violated the law. Disability and mistake excuses generate the same conclusion of blamelessness in markedly different ways. In the disability excuses, the disabling abnormality sets the actor apart from the general population. The mistake excuses do the opposite: they argue that the actor should not be punished because in fact he or she has acted in a way that anyone else would have acted in the same situation. That is, the actor's mistake is reasonable; any reasonable person would have made the same mistake.

However, this latter route to blamelessness creates potential problems in giving an acquittal, for mistake excuses have no useful disabling abnormality on which to shift the blame for the offence harm. Nor is there a disabling

---

[33] See generally H. L. A. Hart, *Punishment and Responsibility* (New York, 1973), 28–53.

[34] Some writers have sought to argue that the recognition of excuses is not inconsistent with these utilitarian goals. See R. A. Posner, *Economic Analysis of Law* (3rd edn., Boston, 1986), 201; Steven Shavell, 'Criminal Law and the Optimal Use of Nonmonetary Sanctions as a Deterrent' (1985) 85 *Columbia LR* 1232 at 1255–9.

abnormality to help distinguish the actor from the general population, making apparent why this actor is not being punished for the violation. This absence of a distinguishing feature has the potential to weaken the law's continuing prohibition of the actor's conduct, for the acquittal is more easily mistaken for a toleration of the conduct itself. Indeed, the absence of a disabling abnormality in mistake excuses may explain why the law is·more hesitant to recognize mistake excuses and, when they are recognized, why it severely restricts their reach.

Objective appearances aside, however, the two mechanisms of excuse in fact are analogous. Both rely upon a conclusion that the actor could not reasonably have been expected to avoid the violation. Where a disabling abnormality exists, the claim of excuse is essentially a claim that the reasonable person suffering a similar disability similarly would have been unable to avoid a violation.

1.1 The Disability Requirement

By *disability* is meant an abnormal condition of the actor at the time of the offence, such as insanity, intoxication, subnormality, or immaturity.[35] Each such disability is a real-world condition with a variety of observable manifestations apart from the conduct constituting the offence. It may be a long-term or even permanent condition, such as subnormality, or a temporary state like intoxication, somnambulism, automatism, or hypnotism. Its cause may be internal, as in the insanity defence, or external, as in coercion from another person in the duress defence. The disability requirement serves to distinguish the actor from the general population; it provides an object to which the blame may be shifted, and it allows the law to acquit the actor because he is different, while continuing to condemn and prohibit the conduct for others. The existence of a disability also provides some evidence that a resulting excusing condition does in fact exist. These purposes of the disability requirement confirm the need for a legal disability to have confirmable manifestations beyond the criminal conduct at hand.[36] The Model Penal Code intoxication defence, for example, requires 'a disturbance of mental or physical capacities resulting from the introduction of substances into the body'.[37] The Draft English Code refers to things that 'impair awareness or control'.[38]

---

[35] In a few limited instances, a mistake may substitute for the disability. See text accompanying notes 42–4 in this Ch.

[36] Such manifestations signal the actor's abnormality to others and provide some factual support for the conclusion that the actor's conduct is not a meaningful exercise of free will.

[37] Model Penal Code, § 2.08(5). Mental disease or defect has been defined as 'any normal condition of the mind which substantially impairs behavior controls': *McDonald* v. *United States* (DC Cir. 1962) 312 F (2d) 847 at 851. The Model Penal Code formulation gives no independent definition of a 'mental disease or defect'. It is not uncommon for courts to look to such authorities as American Psychiatric Association, *Diagnostic and Statistical Manual of Mental Disorders* (3rd edn., Washington, DC, 1980).

[38] English Draft Code, ¶ 22(5)(a).

Having a recognized disability does not itself qualify an actor for an excuse, for it is not the disability that is central to the reason for exculpating the actor. An actor is not excused because he or she is intoxicated, but rather because the *effect* of the intoxication in the instant situation is to create a condition that renders the actor blameless for the conduct constituting the offence. The requirement of an *excusing condition*, then, is not an element separate from the actor's disability, but rather is a requirement that the actor's disability cause a particular result, a particular exculpating mental, emotional, or physical condition in relation to the conduct constituting the offence.

1.2 Four Kinds of Excusing Conditions and Their Implications

Society generally is willing to excuse an actor under any of four types of conditions. In descending order of severity, they include:

(1) when the conduct constituting the offence is simply not the product of the actor's voluntary effort or determination (e.g. the actor is having a seizure);

(2) when the conduct is the product of the actor's voluntary effort or determination, but the actor does not accurately perceive the physical nature or consequences of the conduct (e.g. the actor hallucinates that what in fact is a gun is a paint brush, or accurately perceives the physical characteristics of the gun but does not know that guns can shoot bullets that injure people) and therefore does not know that the conduct is wrong or criminal;

(3) when the actor accurately perceives and understands the physical nature of the conduct and its consequences, but does not know that the conduct is wrong or criminal (e.g. the actor thinks God has ordered him to sacrifice a neighbour for the good of mankind or believes, because of paranoid delusions, that the man waiting for a bus is about to assault him); or

(4) when the actor accurately perceives the nature and consequences of the conduct and knows its wrongfulness and criminality, but lacks the ability to control his or her conduct (e.g. because of an insane compulsion or duress) to such an extent that the actor can no longer reasonably be expected to conform his or her conduct to the requirements of law.

The first excusing condition occurs where the conduct constituting an offence does not include a volitional act. Cases of this sort include 'conduct' via reflex action or convulsion. This first excusing condition presents the clearest case of blamelessness. The absence of volition in a criminal act is only a step above the absence of a muscular contraction. Nearly any disability causing the excusing condition is recognized as adequate for a defence; the resulting dysfunction apparently is sufficiently gross that it establishes its own abnormality. Traditionally, such conditions bar conviction because they prevent satisfaction of the voluntary act that is said to be an element of all offences.[39] However, there may be advantages to treating such cases as providing a general excuse defence rather than as negating a required element, as signalled in Chapter 3 and discussed in greater detail in Chapter 8 (section B).

In an excusing condition of the second sort there is, admittedly, a voluntary act but the actor is exculpated because he or she is unaware of the nature of the act, that is, unaware of its physical nature or its common immediate consequences. Such is the case of an actor who, suffering from a delusion that he is squeezing an orange, strangles his wife. The defect typically is one of perception.[40] When this second excusing condition is relied upon, the law limits the excuse to specific disabilities. The dysfunction must be caused by involuntary intoxication, insanity, or one of a few unusual sources of dysfunction, such as automatism or somnambulism.[41]

In the third category of excusing condition, the actor engages in conduct voluntarily and knows the nature of the conduct, but does not know that the conduct is wrong or criminal. The defect is one of knowledge rather than perception. It can result from a simple lack of information, or from a lack of the intelligence or cognitive function necessary to use available information to determine wrongfulness or criminality. The law seems more suspicious of these claims for excuse. A normal person's plea for excuse based on ignorance of the law proscribing the conduct generally is rejected. Because normal people can make such mistakes, presence of the excusing condition alone does little to distinguish the actor from the general population. Instances of this third excusing condition thus are more selectively excused, generally requiring either a disability with persuasive indications of abnormality or special circumstances of mistake compelling a conclusion of blamelessness. This basis for exculpating an actor underlies the disability excuses of insanity, subnormality, involuntary intoxication, and immaturity.[42] Certain instances of mistake also are in this third group.

Four types of mistakes are permitted by some jurisdictions to provide a general excuse defence (in contrast to mistakes that provide an 'absent element' defence, by negating an element of the offence). Reliance upon

---

[39] See the discussion of this in Ch. 3. Such defences are found, for example, in Model Penal Code, § 2.01(2)(a)&(d) and Draft English Code, ¶ 33(a)(i).

[40] However, where the excusing condition concerns ignorance of the probable *consequences* of the actor's conduct, it can be the result of a severe defect in knowledge rather than a defect in perception.

[41] See e.g. Model Penal Code, §§ 2.01(2) (involuntary act), 2.08(4) (involuntary intoxication), 4.01(1) (insanity); Draft English Code, ¶¶ 33(a)(ii) (physical incapacity), 35–40 (mental disorder).

[42] See e.g. Model Penal Code, §§ 2.08(4) (involuntary intoxication), 4.01(1) (insanity), 4.10 (immaturity); Draft English Code, ¶¶ 32 (immaturity), 35–40 (mental disorder).

an official misstatement of law and mistake due to the unavailability of a law are two such general mistake excuses.[43] A mistake as to whether one's conduct is justified also is commonly recognized as an excuse.[44] In such cases the actor does not know his conduct is wrong or criminal because, under the circumstances as the actor perceives and understands them to be, the conduct is justified. A fourth commonly recognized mistake excuse, reliance on unlawful military orders, is essentially a special subclass of a mistake as to a justification excuse, where the justification is the public authority of lawful military orders.[45]

In instances of the fourth excusing condition, the actor engages in conduct voluntarily, correctly perceives the nature of the conduct, and is aware that it is wrong. The actor is exculpated because he or she lacks the capacity to control his or her conduct, and thus cannot fairly be held accountable for it. For this fourth excusing condition, the law generally is unwilling to excuse unless there is a clear and confirmable disability that distinguishes the actor from others, explains the criminal conduct, and takes responsibility for it. A loaded .357 Magnum pointed at the actor's head, for example, may provide the objective, confirmable criteria necessary to distinguish the actor's ability to control his conduct from that of the general population. Insanity and intoxication can cause this excusing condition, as they can cause the previous two excusing conditions. The duress defence is based solely on this defect in control.[46] Hypnotism sometimes is recognized as an excuse because it may cause this fourth excusing condition, although it often is incorrectly listed as an example of the involuntary act defence, the first excusing condition.[47]

To say that one of these excusing conditions must be satisfied is to say that a disability, by itself, will not excuse. It is not enough that the actor is intoxicated or subject to duress; the intoxication or duress must cause an excusing condition. This may seem rudimentary, especially in the case of duress or intoxication, but the implications for other excuses are dramatic. The inadequacy of a disability by itself to excuse means that there ought to be no such thing as 'status excuses', which the common law recognized and which some modern theorists appear to support.[48] Being mentally ill

---

[43] See e.g. Model Penal Code, § 2.04(3) (mistake excuse for unavailable law and for reliance upon official misstatement of law); Draft English Code, ¶ 46 (unavailable law only).

[44] This typically is provided by justification statutes providing that 'an actor is justified if he believes' that justifying circumstances exist. See sect. C.5.1. of this Ch.

[45] The excuse and the justification of lawful military orders commonly are treated together under the 'defence of military orders': see e.g. Model Penal Code, § 2.10.

[46] See e.g. Model Penal Code, § 2.09; Draft English Code, ¶¶ 42 (duress by threats), 43 (duress of circumstances).

[47] See Robinson, *Criminal Law*, n. 6 above, at § 9.2.

[48] Common law recognition of 'status excuses' is exemplified by Blackstone: 'In criminal cases, therefore, idiots and lunatics are not chargeable for their own acts, if committed when under these incapacities': 4 W. Blackstone, *Commentaries*, *24. Hawkins would appear to be in agreement: 'As to the first point it is to be observed, that those who are under a natural

is not itself enough. There is no class of mentally ill persons who are free of criminal responsibility for whatever they might do. Rather, the insanity defence requires that the actor's mental illness be such that on this occason it is of such a nature and effect that it excuses the offence at hand. One might well be mentally ill yet be liable for an offence, if the mental illness does not play a sufficient role in the offence. In other words, the disability must cause an excusing condition *for the conduct constituting the offence charged.* If the actor, while preparing a knowingly false income tax return, hallucinates that a neighbour's barking dog has turned into an attacking tiger, he may be considered insane at the time of filing the false return, but he does not merit an insanity excuse if his hallucination plays no part in the preparation and filing of the return. If he kills the dog/ tiger in perceived self-defence, of course, he may be excused for the killing. In both cases, the actor may be suffering from insanity. Only in the case of the killing, however, can the disability be said to have created an excusing condition (type two and type three) that undercuts his responsibility for the offence.[49]

1.3 Objective Limitations on Excusing Conditions

Perhaps the most important implication of the excusing condition requirement is this: a disability is insufficient for an excuse even if the disability is a 'but for' cause of the offence.[50] The effect of this principle can be dramatic. Assume an elderly male, with no prior record of child abuse, is given a drug while in the hospital. While under the influence of the drug, he goes to another room in the hospital and molests a young girl.[51]

---

disability of distinguishing between Good and Evil, as infants under the Age of Discretion, Idiots and Lunatics, are not punishable by any Criminal Prosecution whatsoever': W. Hawkins, *Pleas of the Crown* (London, 1973) (1716), i, 2. Similarly, some modern theorists support such excuses, arguing that '[One] category of excuses consists of those excuses in which it is unclear whether moral norms were violated or not. These I call the status excuses, because it is the general condition of the agent (his status) that determines whether or not he is excused. Infancy, insanity, diminished capacity, and intoxication are the main examples': Moore, 'Choice, Character, and Excuse', n. 30 above, at 31.

[49] In the insanity defence, most modern codes make clear that a causal connection must exist between the mental illness and the charged offence: see e.g. Model Penal Code, § 4.01(1) ('as a result of mental disease or defect he lacks'); Draft English Code, ¶ 35(2) (allowing rebuttal of a presumption of causal connection). Immaturity commonly is formulated as a 'status excuse' in many jurisdictions. That is, the defence requirements look only to whether the actor fits a defined class, without regard for whether he satisfies the excusing conditions for the offence at hand: see e.g. Model Penal Code, § 4.10; cf. English Draft Code, ¶ 32.

[50] In other words, no excuse is permitted even if the actor would not have committed the offence but for the disability. For further discussion of the 'but for' cause requirement, see Ch. 3, sect. B.2.

[51] The facts are similar to those in *State* v. *Mriglot* (1976) 15 Wash. App. 446, 550 P (2d) 17, where the appellate court approved the trial court's denial of the defendant's requested instruction that he should be excused if the jury found that he had been 'involuntarily *under the influence* or *affected* by the use of liquor or drugs' (emphasis by the appellate court).

Assume further that the evidence shows conclusively that the actor would not have committed this offence if he had not been given the drug. Should he be excused? One can appreciate the appeal of the defendant's claim that it was the drug, not his own free choice, that caused the offence. He would not have committed the offence 'but for' having been given the drug. Yet, under most modern excuse formulations, a jury could properly deny a defence. To be held blameless, it is not enough that the drug created an impulse that would not otherwise have existed or that it eroded a restraint that otherwise would have existed. Current excuses require that the compulsion be sufficiently overwhelming or that the actor's capacity to resist be sufficiently impaired that he could not reasonably have been expected to have avoided the offence.[52] It is the excusing condition requirement that implements the normative judgement of the adequacy of the compulsion or incapacity.

The result of the principle may be to place a greater burden on one actor than on others. And the greater burden may be one for which the actor is not responsible, as is the case with the molester in the hospital. But, then, many people no doubt have naturally occurring greater burdens than others in conforming their conduct to the requirements of law, either because of the kind of place in which they live or grew up or the kind of genes and physiology that they have. The law generally does not take account of such differences in burden to conform, unless the burden reaches a level of severity that is gross and abnormal. When this occurs—when an actor's circumstances or internal make-up cause an abnormally severe burden to conform—an excuse defence generally is available. Such abnormality frequently manifests itself in ways that suggest mental disease or defect or some other observable disabling abnormality. Absent such clear abnormality, however, each actor is obliged to resist the compulsions and overcome the incapacities tending toward crime. Thus, despite the fact that the elderly man in the hospital would not have committed the molestation but for the drug, he will not be given a defence unless the jury is persuaded that the effect of the drug was sufficiently strong that he could not have been expected to have avoided the violation.

To judge whether a person has resisted enough to avoid a violation, the law introduces objective standards into excuse formulations. While we may tend to think of excuses as being very subjective, the fact is that in principle all modern excuses hold an actor to some form of objective standard in judging the actor's efforts to remain law-abiding. Several excuses have explicit objective standards as part of their criteria. Mistake

---

[52] This was the point of the District of Columbia Circuit Court of Appeals in *United States* v. *Brawner* (1972) 471 F (2d) 969 when it overruled its earlier adoption of the 'product test' in *Durham* v. *United States* (1954) 214 F (2d) 862. That the offence was the 'product' of the actor's mental disease is not in itself enough to show that the actor is blameless and worthy of excuse.

excuses (as opposed to 'absent element' mistake defences) require that the actor's mistake be reasonable (non-negligent)—that is, that the mistake meet the objective reasonable person standard. The Model Penal Code duress defence, for example, requires that the actor meet the standard of resistance of 'the person of reasonable firmness'.[53] The Draft English Code requires that the circumstances are such that the actor 'cannot reasonably be expected to act otherwise'.[54] Other excuses, like insanity and involuntary intoxication, have broad criteria that invite a general normative assessment by the jury and, in this fashion, introduce what is essentially an objective standard.

Such objective limitations are what one would expect, given the fact that excuses serve a normative blaming-excusing function. It simply is not the case that we intuitively excuse every person who can show pressure or temptation or disadvantage in resisting the same. Our blaming and excusing judgements are more complex. We want to know: how strong was the pressure or temptation? How difficult was it for the actor to resist? Inevitably, we try to put ourselves in the actor's situation and imagine whether we would have been able to resist the violation in similar circumstances.

Not every excuse includes in its legal formulation an objective standard. Involuntary act, insanity, and involuntary intoxication have no apparent requirement of this sort. It would be a mistake, however, to assume that these defences excuse without regard for whether the actor has met our collective normative expectations for efforts to avoid a violation. These defences assure compliance with our normative expectations by limiting each defence in other ways that assure that the excused actor could not have been expected to have avoided the violation. In the involuntary act defence, for example, the required dysfunction is sufficiently great that it ensures that the actor's burden of compliance must have been unattainable. The act constituting the offence was not the product of the actor's effort or determination. No express objective standard is required to measure whether the actor should have tried harder to avoid the violation.

The formulations of the insanity and involuntary intoxication defences must take a somewhat different approach. A person is excused if, as a result of either disability, 'he lacks *substantial* capacity either to appreciate the criminality [wrongfulness] of his conduct or to conform his conduct to the requirements of law'.[55] The formulation leaves it to the jury to determine whether the loss of capacity was sufficiently 'substantial' to hold the actor blameless. Instead of explicitly providing an individualized objective standard that calls for a normative assessment, the formulation uses the openly vague term 'substantial', knowing, indeed intending,[56] that

---

[53] Model Penal Code, § 2.09(1).   [54] Draft English Code, ¶ 43(2)(b).

[55] Model Penal Code, §§ 2.08(4) & 4.01(1) (emphasis added).

[56] 'It was recognized, of course, that "substantial" is an open-ended concept, but its quantitative connotation was believed to be sufficiently precise for practical administration. The

the jury will use their collective intuitive judgements in deciding whether the loss of capacity was substantial enough to excuse.[57] It seems likely that the analysis and the result will be the same as under the individual-ized reasonable person test used in the mistake and duress excuses. That is, an actor's loss of capacity to control his conduct will be judged 'sub-stantial' only if 'the reasonable person in the actor's situation' could not reasonably have been expected to have avoided the offence.

Mistaken belief that one satisfies the conditions of an excuse is not itself an excuse. Believing you are insane, even if it is a reasonable belief, ought not give one an insanity defence.[58] An actor who makes a reason-able mistake as to a justification, in contrast, can claim that from his per-spective he reasonably believed that his conduct was justified, desirable, and therefore at least should be excused as blameless.[59] The actor who is mistaken as to his excuse can make no similar claim: even if he were cor-rect in his belief that excusing conditions existed, neither his conduct nor his apparent motivation is desirable, unlike a case of reasonable mistake as to a justification. Excused conduct is wrongful conduct that is con-demned and ought to be avoided.[60]

The objective standard of excuses employed by modern codes is not entirely fixed or strictly objective. In both the definition of reasonable mis-takes and the duress defence in the Model Penal Code, for example, the actor's conduct is to be measured against that of the reasonable person 'in the actor's situation'.[61] The phrase is meant to allow, indeed to en-courage, the decision-maker to take account of any special circumstances

law is full of instances in which courts and juries are explicitly authorized to confront an issue of degree. Such an approach was deemed to be no less essential and appropriate in dealing with this issue': Model Penal Code, § 4.01 comment 3 (1985).

[57] In the Draft English Code, the drafters portray the issue as a nearly scientific inquiry into whether a given abnormality exists or does not. Cl. 34 gives a specific definition of what will constitute a 'severe mental illness', the existence of which is the criterion for the defence. It appears not to require normative judgement. It seems clear, however, that no matter how drafters try to hide the fact (for what reason they try is unclear), the judge-ment called for by juries is one that is, should be, and will be normative rather than sci-entific in nature. See, for example, the discussion in the commentary to Model Penal Code, § 4.01.

[58] A literal reading of Draft English Code cl. 41(1) would seem to give a defence in such a case, but this seems clearly improper, and seems unlikely to have been intended by the drafters. In some cases, of course, a belief that one is mentally ill could be a symptom of mental illness which, together with other symptoms, might lead to such a finding. But noth-ing suggests that such a belief is itself conclusive proof of mental illness.

[59] See sect. C.5.1. of this Ch.

[60] For a further discussion of the issue of mistake as to an excuse, see Paul H. Robinson, *Criminal Law* (Boston, 1997), § 9.1, 'Mistake as to Excuse'.

[61] See Model Penal Code, §§ 1.13(16) (defining 'reasonably believes' and 'reasonable be-lief' as 'designat[ing]' a belief which the actor is not reckless or negligent in holding'); 2.09(2) (providing that duress defense may be unavailable if the actor recklessly or negligently 'placed himself in a situation in which it was probable that he would be subjected to duress'); 2.02(2)(c)&(d) (requiring comparison to reasonable person 'in the actor's situation' in deter-mination of recklessness or negligence with respect to offence element).

or characteristics of the actor that might alter our assessment of the actor's blameworthiness.[62] Current criminal law theory is unable to articulate the kinds of factors that ought to be taken into account and the kinds that ought not. This invitation to individualize authorizes decision-makers to decide *ad hoc* the factors that will and will not be taken into account. The hope is that the accumulated experience of the practice, together with continuing development by theorists, will lead to clearer guidance for decision-makers in the future.

2. A DISABILITY-ORGANIZED SYSTEM OF EXCUSES AND THE PROBLEM OF MULTIPLE EXCUSES

Most excuses are defined and distinguished according to the disabilities to which they apply. Where a mental disease or defect is the cause of the excusing condition, the insanity defence is applicable. Even where the results of the defendant's disability are identical to those that result from insanity—distortion in perception, ignorance of criminality, or impairment of ability to control one's conduct—if the disability is other than mental disease or defect, a defendant will be considered under another excuse. Thus, it is the *cause* of the excusing conditions—be it intoxication, immaturity, subnormality, hypnotism, duress, or some other disability—rather than the results, that determines which excuse defence is applicable.

This disability-organized system of defining excuses may have evolved because the disability is an independently observable phenomenon. Such a system has practical value because, as with justification defences, it frequently is appropriate to attach special rules to particular disabilities. For example, it may be more of a concern that a defendant voluntarily intoxicated himself than that he caused himself to become insane. Thus, special rules of the intoxication excuse are appropriate to account for the self-caused possibility, although otherwise the insanity and intoxication excuses are identical in formulation. On the other hand, as a theoretical matter, it seems the same principles should apply to both (all) excuses. It may be an unusual problem, but if an actor commits an offence during a psychotic episode brought on by his decision not to take his antipsychotic medication, then the actor's insanity defence ought to be limited in a way analogous to self-intoxication. If it is appropriate to take account of an actor's causing his own disability, there is no reason why

---

[62] If the actor were blind or if he had just suffered a blow or experienced a heart attack, these would certainly be facts to be considered in a judgement involving criminal liability, as they would be under traditional law. But the heredity, intelligence or temperament of the actor would not be held material in judging negligence, and could not be without depriving the criterion of all its objectivity. The Code is not intended to displace discriminations of this kind, but rather leave the issue to the courts: Model Penal Code, § 2.02 comment 4 (1985).

the principle should not apply to all disabilities, whether the defendant causes his own intoxication, hypnotism, duress, or insanity.[63]

The description of the four kinds of excusing conditions earlier in the Chapter revealed that a single disability may cause more than one kind of excusing condition. Insanity and intoxication, for example, may cause excusing conditions of the second, third, and fourth kinds. That is, the defects in the mental processes which come from mental illness or intoxication can cause defects either in the perception of the nature of the act, in the evaluation of its wrongfulness or criminality, or in an actor's ability to resist performing an act known to be wrong and criminal. A mental disease or defect also may cause two or more of these defects at one time.[64] Where this occurs, the actor nonetheless presents a single excuse defence, according to the disability present. (A single disability also may give rise to both a disability excuse and a mistake excuse, by having the disability adequately explain an otherwise unreasonable and unexcused mistake, for example. Thus, a mentally ill actor who has an insanity defence also may have a defence for a mistake as to a justification that would be denied to other actors because of the unreasonableness of the mistake, if his mental illness adequately explains the mistake.)

Just as a single disability can cause multiple excusing conditions, multiple disabilities can contribute to a single excusing condition. A slightly mentally ill offender may become involuntarily intoxicated when his medication unexpectedly interacts with a common cold remedy he buys over the counter. The mental illness and the involuntary intoxication each may cause a degree of impairment of the actor's ability .to control his conduct. Even if the degree of impairment from either by itself would be inadequate to excuse the actor, the cumulative effect of the two sources of impairment may rise to a level suggesting blamelessness for the offence conduct. If each of the disabilities is legally recognized and if together they cause a legally adequate excusing condition, there seems little basis on which to deny an excuse.

Unfortunately, current excuse defence doctrine typically assumes that only a single disability is at work in a given case. That is, to get an excuse, an actor must satisfy the requirements of at least one excuse defence and, in a disability-organized system of excuses, recall, each defence addresses

[63] For a discussion of the problem and a proposed solution, see Paul H. Robinson, 'Causing the Conditions of One's Own Defense' (1985) 71 *Virginia LR* n. 59 above, at 30–9.

[64] Specific kinds of mental illness may have a specific kind of effect. A congenital mental defect resulting in severely limited intelligence sometimes is given its own label, 'subnormality', but is more often, in present practice, simply grouped with forms of mental illness under 'insanity'. But that particular aspect of insanity would seem to cause conditions primarily of the third group and not the second, since there is no defect in perception inherent in low intelligence. Similarly, immaturity, or 'infancy', as it is often called, can be the cause of the failure to appreciate the wrongfulness or criminality of one's acts, but it cannot be said to distort one's perceptions of conduct.

a different disability. To use the example above, both the insanity defence and the involuntary intoxication defence require that the necessary level of dysfunction 'result from' mental illness or from involuntary intoxication, respectively.[65] No provision in modern codes allows an excusing condition to be satisfied by more than one disability, thus there is no opportunity to recognize the cumulative effect of multiple disabilities.[66]

Although perhaps not intended for this use, one can achieve some ability to recognize such 'combined excuses' through the individualized objective person tests. Under the Model Penal Code's duress provision, for example, an actor is excused if 'a person of reasonable firmness in his situation would have been unable to resist'.[67] One might properly argue that the effects of other disabilities ought to be taken into account as part of 'the actor's situation'. This technique also is available whenever a defence formulation uses the term 'reasonable' in its criteria, at least when that term is defined with an individualized objective standard. The Model Penal Code defines 'reasonable' to mean non-negligent;[68] and 'negligence', in turn, is defined by an objective standard but with the potential for individualizing that objective standard with some characteristics of the defendant that are relevant in assessing his blameworthiness.[69] The Draft English Code has no definition of 'reasonable', although the term is frequently used. In determining whether a mistaken reliance upon an official misstatement was 'reasonable' or in determining whether there is a 'reasonable' explanation for an actor's extreme emotional disturbance, a court is to look to what is reasonable for a person 'in the actor's situation'.[70] In each instance, this permits the decision-maker to take account, as part of 'the actor's situation', of duress, mental disease, involuntary intoxication, or other disabilities. This means of accounting for cumulative excuses does not provide a general solution but only a patchwork remedy with less than comprehensive coverage. A comprehensive approach that covers the cumulative effects of all excuses requires a general provision.[71]

[65] The required excusing condition—'lacks substantial capacity'—must 'result from' the mental illness, in § 4.01(1), or from the involuntary intoxication, in § 2.08(4). Neither defence is satisfied if the excusing condition cannot be attributed to one but rather is the cumulative effect of the two.

[66] A general excuse defence, embodying a legally recognized disability, would avoid the problems of combined excuses, but the rarity of these problems cannot alone justify a change.

[67] Model Penal Code, § 2.09(1).   [68] See Model Penal Code, § 1.13(16).

[69] See Model Penal Code, § 2.02(2)(d).

[70] See Model Penal Code, §§ 1.13(16), 2.02(2)(c)&(d).

[71] A principle of cumulative excuses might be codified as follows:

'Multiple Excuses. If an actor satisfies the requirements of more than one excuse, all such excuses shall be permitted as defences. If an actor suffers from more than one disability that is recognized as the potential basis for an excuse, but does not satisfy the requirements of the required effects [i.e. the excusing condition element] of any one excuse defence, the actor nonetheless shall be excused if the cumulative effect of the multiple disabilities satisfies the requirements of the required effects of any one of the relevant excuse defences.'

C. Justifications

Every jurisdiction recognizes that special circumstances can justify conduct that otherwise would be an offence. Unlawful aggression by another can trigger a right to use force in self-defence or in defence of another or of property. Aggressive force by a police officer is authorized to make an arrest. Even bus drivers may have a right to use some force to maintain order and safety on their vehicles. Beyond the use of force, a person can be justified in taking food from another's forest cabin to avoid dying of starvation, or in tying up to another's private dock to avoid the danger of a storm.

In each of these instances, a societal interest[72] is injured or endangered and the elements of an offence are satisfied. Yet, in each instance, whether it is defensive or aggressive force, a trespass, or some other normally criminal conduct, a defence is given under the common theory of all justification defences: although the conduct ordinarily constitutes an offence, when the justifying circumstances exist we are content to have the conduct performed. The existence of the justifying circumstances means that, while the harm prohibited by the offence does occur, it is outweighed by the avoidance of a greater harm or by the advancement of a greater good. In other words, there is no *net* societal harm.

This characteristic of justification defences is made explicit in the Model Penal Code's general justification defence, which gives a defence if 'the harm or evil sought to be avoided by such conduct is greater than that sought to be prevented by the law defining the offence charged'.[73] English law has no such general defence but each justification defence reflects the principle. Force in self-defence may injure the aggressor, but the injury is outweighed by the societal value of the defensive force—in avoiding the threatened harm to the victim and in condemning and deterring unjustified aggression generally. Force used to effect an arrest may injure the arrestee, but the harm is outweighed by the societal interest in effective criminal justice, which requires an effective arrest power.

Unlike absent element defences (for example, mistake and intoxication negating an offence element) and offence modification defences (for example, extreme emotional disturbance and renunciation), justification defences are not statements or alterations of the statutory definition of the harm sought to be prevented or punished by an offence. The harm caused by the justified behaviour remains a legally recognized harm that is to be avoided whenever possible. Under the special justifying circumstances, however, that harm is outweighed by the need to avoid an even greater harm or to further a greater societal interest.

---

[72] By 'societal interest' I mean to include any interest recognized by the society, whether that interest is individual, collective, institutional, tangible, or intangible.

[73] Model Penal Code, § 3.02(1).

Justifications also are distinguishable from excuses, of which insanity, duress, and immaturity are examples. As the previous section discusses, there is no claim in an excuse defence that the conduct is right or that it furthers a societal interest. On the contrary, the claim of excuse is an admission that the conduct is wrong but a plea that, because of special conditions that leave the actor blameless for performing conduct, the actor ought not be criminally liable for it. Unlike justified conduct, excused conduct is to be avoided whenever possible, even when the excusing conditions exist. We are content to have the police officer use force in making an arrest but, in contrast, we wish to restrain the insane attacker. We make it an offence to resist an arrest, but we hope the intended victim can successfully resist the insane attacker. We encourage others to assist the officer, but discourage with criminal liability anyone assisting the insane attacker.

While we can say all this about justification defences, their underlying theory remains ambiguous in a most important respect, as will become clear later in this section: is a justification defence given because an actor has committed what would otherwise be an offence *for the right reason*, or is it given because the actor's conduct does not cause a net societal harm, because it is *the right deed* given the situation? An analysis of this foundational issue will occupy much of this section. Before beginning it, the section summarizes what more can be said about the conceptualization of justifications.

1. THREE KINDS OF JUSTIFICATION DEFENCES

The three major conceptual groups of justification defences include the lesser evils defence, public authority justifications, and defensive force justifications. The defensive force justifications include self-defence, defence of others, defence of property, and defence of habitation. The public authority justifications include law enforcement authority, authority to maintain order and safety, parental authority, benevolent custodial authority, medical authority, authority to prevent a suicide, judicial authority, military authority, and general public authority.[74]

A forest fire rages toward a town of 1,000 unsuspecting inhabitants. The actor burns a field of corn located between the fire and the town; the burned field serves as a firebreak, saving 1,000 lives. The actor has satisfied all elements of the offence of arson by setting fire to the crop with the purpose of destroying it. The immediate harm he has caused—the destruction of the crop—is precisely the harm that the statute seeks to prevent and punish. Yet the actor is likely to have a complete defence, because

---

[74] For illustrations and authorities for each defence and for a discussion of the relations among the five defence groups, see Paul H. Robinson, 'Criminal Law Defenses: A Systematic Analysis' (1982) 82 *Columbia LR* 199 at 213–6 (hereinafter 'Systematic Analysis').

his conduct and its harmful consequences are justified.[75] His conduct is tolerated, even encouraged, by society.

The forest fire case provides an example of the 'lesser evils' or 'choice of evils' justification (sometimes called 'necessity' when the threat of greater harm stems from natural forces). This justification defence, though the least common in American criminal codes,[76] most clearly reflects the general principle of justification defences. In such lesser evils cases, the competing harms are readily apparent and more easily compared than in other justifications. The interests involved in 'defensive force' and 'public authority' justifications are more subtle and abstract, and the relative value of the interests more obscure.

A prowler attempts to steal chickens from a chicken coop. May the owner use physical force against the prowler to prevent the theft? Some limited degree of force is commonly permitted if it is necessary to protect property. It is not that society deems injury to a person less significant than property; rather, in weighing the interests at stake, the law considers not only the immediate physical harms—loss of a chicken versus personal injury—but also the societal interest in maintaining a right to hold personal property. The threatened theft endangers not only the rightful possession by this owner, but also the general stability and vitality of the rule of private possession. To state it negatively, society generally abhors unjustified aggressive takings. Society therefore is tolerant of the injury that must be inflicted to stop the aggressor. The same reasoning applies when the aggression is toward the defender himself or toward other persons. Society's interest in maintaining a right to bodily integrity, when combined with the physical harm threatened, outweighs the harm inflicted to stop the aggression.

The defensive force justifications are distinguished from one another by the interest that is threatened. Legislatures often wish to make special alterations or exceptions to the basic principle of defensive force justifications depending on the interest threatened to be protected. They may add a special provision to defence of property, for example, excluding the use of deadly force. They might permit the use of force to defend another person only if such other person would be justified in using such force. Thus, self-defence, defence of others, and defence of property are often defined separately.[77] But this need not be the case. Their shared function

---

[75] See e.g. Model Penal Code, § 3.02. The Draft English Code, cl. 43, would give a defence in these circumstances, but the Code's defence is formulated by analogy to duress; he is exculpated because 'he cannot reasonably be expected to act otherwise'. Thus, if the actor were not a terribly nice person and could have just as easily let the town burn as burn the field as a firebreak, he presumably would not be entitled to the defence. Such is not only an absurd result, but also inconsistent with English cases that give a lesser evils defence akin to that of the Model Penal Code formulation. See sect. C.5. of this Ch.

[76] See authorities collected in Robinson, *Criminal Law Defenses*, ii, n. 17 above, at § 124(e), n. 31.

[77] See e.g. Model Penal Code, §§ 3.04–3.06.

and underlying principle means that one could formulate a single defensive force provision, as the Draft English Code does.[78]

A third category of justifications, *public authority defences*, similarly reflects a balancing of harms.[79] When a deputy sheriff uses force in the execution of a judicial search warrant, his conduct may satisfy all the elements of assault. But his use of force furthers effective criminal justice, as well as the effective exercise of judicial authority. These intangible societal interests are thought to justify the harm that the deputy causes in executing the warrant.

Unlike defensive force justifications, public authority defences need not be triggered by a threat. The actor need only be protecting or furthering a legally recognized interest. On the other hand, where defensive force justifications are generally available to all citizens, the use of public authority justifications often is limited to certain persons, whose position or training makes them particularly appropriate protectors of the interest at stake. The interests to be furthered or protected may be personal or societal. They include criminal law enforcement, child-rearing and education, safety and order on public transportation vehicles or in institutions, life or health (as in medical emergencies and suicide prevention), military operations, and effective exercise of judicial authority, to name the most prominent. In each instance, the interest gives rise to an authority for the appropriate persons to act in a way that otherwise is criminal if it furthers or protects the interest. Like defensive force justifications, different public authority justifications are distinguished from one another according to the interest protected. Legislatures may refine the basic principle to provide a suitably limited justification defence for each interest and authority. The restrictions on law enforcement officers in making an arrest may be different from the restrictions on a bus driver in maintaining safety and decorum.

2. The Internal Structure of Justification Defences

The balancing of interests common to all justification defences is part of the internal structure of each defence. Justifications share other characteristics as well; all have the following internal structure: *Triggering conditions* permit a *necessary* and *proportional response*. Each of these requirements plays a role in ensuring that the conduct justified by the offence is indeed conduct that society encourages or at least tolerates.

---

[78] See Draft English Code, ¶ 44.

[79] See e.g. Model Penal Code, §§ 3.03, 3.07, 3.08. The Draft English Code apparently has no public authority justification defences, except the authority implicitly given to public officials under the defensive force provision, cl. 44, to react to a crime or breach of the peace. Presumably such public authority is to be granted in provisions outside the Code. Also cll. 45(c) and 4(4) of the Draft Code retain common law defences.

Triggering conditions are the circumstances that must exist before an actor is eligible to act under a justification. Defensive force justifications are triggered when an aggressor threatens unjustified force against the protected interest, as by attempting to burn the defendant's chicken coop. Public authority justifications are triggered when the circumstances evoke the use of the public authority given to the actor. A conductor's authority to maintain order and safety on a train may be triggered by a passenger who refuses to stop smoking, turn down his radio, or pay for his ticket. The general justification defence, lesser evils, has the broadest triggering condition. In its purest form, the defence is available whenever any legally protected interest is threatened and the harm or evil can be avoided by defensive or offensive action.

The triggering conditions of a justification defence do not give the actor the privilege to act without restriction. To be justified, the responsive conduct must satisfy two requirements: (1) it must be *necessary* to protect or further the interest at stake; and (2) it must cause only a harm that is *proportional* or reasonable in relation to the harm threatened or the interest furthered.

The *necessity requirement* demands that the defendant act only when and to the extent necessary to protect or further the interest at stake. Thus, where an aggressor announces his intention to assault the actor at noon the next day, the threat provides the triggering condition for self-defence. But if the actor is in no danger at the time, if he can just as effectively defend himself the next morning, he is not justified in immediately using physical force against the aggressor. In addition, when an actor is threatened and must act immediately, he is privileged to use only the degree of force that is necessary for self-protection. Even if most persons would find it necessary to use greater force, the force used is not justified if the individual actor could protect himself as effectively with less. Assume the actor is a karate expert who, with no risk of harm to himself, can dislodge an attacker's weapon with a high kick. While the average person might be justified in shooting the armed attacker, this actor must use the less harmful karate available to him, since any greater force, such as shooting, is not necessary to protect himself.

The *proportionality requirement* places a maximum limit on the necessary harm that may be caused in protection or furtherance of an interest. It bars justification, even if the harm caused by the actor is necessary to protect or further the interest at stake, if the harm caused is too serious in relation to the value of the interest. Assume an actor has no other option but to use deadly force to prevent the theft of apples from her orchard. Most jurisdictions would deny a defence for use of deadly force. This is true even if she truly had no less harmful means of protecting her orchard. It should be no surprise that such rules are not without controversy. They require the actor stoically to sacrifice a legally-recognized interest, frequently for the protection of an aggressor. But such commitment to proportionality—as in the valuation of human life over property alone, even the life of a law-breaker—is the mark of a civilized society. It is under this same principle that deadly force is rarely if ever permitted against a non-aggressor, suggesting that an innocent's life is a near absolute interest that can almost never be outweighed.[80]

This structure of *triggering conditions* plus a *necessary* and *proportional response* is common to all justifications—defensive force, public authority, and lesser evils. In the lesser evils justification, the triggering conditions are broader but the proportionality requirement is more strict. It permits the justification only if the actor causes a harm that is not merely reasonably proportional to, but actually less than, the harm or evil threatened. The less demanding 'reasonably proportional' requirement embodied in other justifications, defensive force and public authority, may reflect the more abstract nature of the interests at stake in those defences. The intangibility of the interests makes precise balancing difficult. Indeed, it is true of all justifications that, while the competing interests can be identified, they rarely can be sufficiently quantified to permit an entirely precise comparison in the proportionality assessment.

3. COMPETING THEORIES OF JUSTIFICATION: DEEDS V. REASONS

As noted at the beginning of this section, the nature of justification defences remains ambiguous in an important respect. In a typical case, a person knows of the justifying circumstances and, because of them, undertakes the justified conduct. But it is not uncommon that a person believes that his or her conduct is justified—believes that it will produce a net societal benefit—when in fact it is not and will not. The club-wielding attacker, when dragged to the street light, turns out to be a jogger carrying a flashlight whose bulb is out. Whether beating the jogger-mistaken-for-an-attacker is justified depends on whether the justification defence is given (1) because the conduct in fact is justified, or (2) because the person acts for a justified reason. Or consider the less common situation in which the actor does not realize that his conduct is justified: he mugs a jogger, only to find out that the victim was a club-wielding attacker. Whether beating the attacker-thought-to-be-a-jogger is justified depends again on

---

[80] The opinion of Lord Coleridge in *Dudley and Stephens* might be read to suggest such a philosophy that the value of innocent human life is an absolute that cannot be sacrificed, even for the interest of saving a greater number of lives: see (1884) 14 QBD 273. This philosophy, consistent with Kantian theory, is a legitimate alternative to the more utilitarian approach to the balancing of innocent lives espoused in the commentary to the Model Penal Code, which mechanically values each innocent life equally and permits a net saving of lives: see Model Penal Code, § 3.02 comment 2 (1985).

whether it is the quality of the *deed* or the actor's *reasons* for it that provide the rationale for justification defences.

The 'reasons' theory of justification (often called the 'subjective' theory of justification[81]) is clearly dominant in the literature and the law. The standard formulation of justification defences provides that 'an actor is *justified* if he *believes* that the conduct is necessary to' defend against unlawful aggression, to make an arrest, to maintain order on the vehicle, and so on. Under the 'reasons' theory, a person will get a justification defence as long as he or she believes that the justifying circumstances exist. Whether they actually exist or not is irrelevant. The force used against the jogger-mistaken-for-an-attacker is justified because it was used for the purpose of self-defence. The actor's reason was right even if the conduct was wrong. It also follows that, if the justifying circumstances do exist but the actor is unaware of them and acts for a different purpose, the 'reasons' theory denies a justification defence. If what matters is the reason for the deed, not the deed itself, the force used against the attacker-thought-to-be-a-jogger is not justified. While it might have been the right deed, necessary for self-defence, it was for the wrong reason.

This section argues that a 'deeds' theory (often termed the 'objective' theory of justification) is a better way to conceptualize justification defences. The rationale for justification is properly whether or not the conduct was something that we are content to have the actor perform under the justifying circumstances and to have others perform under similar circumstances in the future. The test for justification ought to be whether, on balance, the conduct in fact avoided a net societal harm (in the broadest sense of harm). An actor's reasons may be relevant to the actor's ultimate liability but, if so, they are properly taken into account by other criminal law doctrines: a mistaken reasonable belief that the conduct was justified may exculpate under an excuse defence; a mistaken belief that the conduct was not justified may inculpate as an impossible attempt offence.[82]

The 'deeds' theory suggests different results from the 'reasons' theory at each of these two conflict points: where the actor mistakenly believes the conduct is justified and where the actor mistakenly believes that it is not. Under the 'deeds' theory, whether the deed is in fact objectively justified is what matters; the actor's reasons for acting are irrelevant to the justification defence (although they may be relevant to other doctrines of exculpation or inculpation).

[81] I have substituted the 'reasons–deeds' terminology for the 'subjective–objective' because the latter has so many other uses with other meanings in other contexts that its use would seem to invite confusion.

[82] I first made this argument in Paul H. Robinson, 'A Theory of Justification: Societal Harm as a Prerequisite to Criminal Liability' (1975) 23 UCLA LR 266. George Fletcher wrote a critical response, George P. Fletcher, 'The Right Deed for the Wrong Reason: A Reply to Mr. Robinson' (1975) 23 UCLA LR 293 (hereinafter 'Right Deed').

Specifically, under the 'deeds' theory, a person who mistakenly believes that the conduct is justified is not justified (although the person may gain an excuse defence if the mistake is reasonable or perhaps a mitigation even if it is not). Thus, the force used against the jogger-mistaken-for-an-attacker is not justified, although it may be excused if reasonable. In the second kind of case, where a person's conduct in fact avoids a greater societal harm but the person is unaware of this, the conduct is justified despite the actor's ignorance. However, the person's belief that the conduct is not justified may give rise to attempt liability, depending upon whether the jurisdiction imposes liability for legally impossible attempts. Thus, the use of force against the attacker-thought to-be-a-jogger is justified, although the actor may be liable for an attempt unjustifiably to assault another.

This, then, is the point of dispute in the theory of justification: is the justified nature of the deed central, as the 'deeds' theory would have it, or irrelevant, as the 'reasons' theory suggests?[83] Most writers have signed on in support of the 'reasons' theory and in opposition to the 'deeds' theory,[84] some suggesting that the latter is 'absurd',[85] unfair,[86] or unduly burdensome.[87]

This section argues that a 'deeds' theory of justification is better, in the following senses. First, it generates liability results that are more just and that better match our collective intuitions of what is just. Secondly, even if the competing theories generated identical liability results, a 'deeds'

---

[83] I consider the possibility of some form of hybrid deeds-reasons theory later in the Ch. See sect. C.7.

[84] See e.g. Michael Corrado, 'Notes on the Structure of a Theory of Excuses' (1991) 82 *Journal of Criminal Law and Criminology* 465 at 489 (arguing that state of mind is a necessity and that Robinson's externalist perception is impossible to accept); Kent Greenawalt, 'The Perplexing Borders of Justification and Excuse' (1984) 84 *Columbia LR* 144 (recognizing that most modern statutes require a subjective belief in justification and that Robinson's fully objective approach is an exception) (hereinafter 'Perplexing Borders'); Wayne R. LaFave and Austin W. Scott, *Substantive Criminal Law* (St Paul, Minnesota, 1986), 685 (claiming that in order to have the benefit of justification one must act for that particular purpose); J. C. Smith and Brian Hogan, *Criminal Law* (8th edn., London, 1996), [37] (requiring state of mind as well as state of fact for justification is certainly reasonable) (hereinafter *Criminal Law*).

[85] Brian Hogan, 'The Dadson Principle' (1989) *Criminal LR* 679 at 680: 'It seems to me absurd to say that I may justify or excuse my conduct, however callous it was in the circumstances known to me at the time, by showing that there existed other circumstances which, had I but known of them, would have justified or excused my conduct'. (emphasis in original).

[86] Arnold Loewy, 'Culpability, Dangerousness, and Harm: Balancing the Factors on which our Criminal Law is Predicated' (1988) 66 *North Carolina LR* 283 at 289 (arguing that, as a matter of fairness, the issue ought to be one solely of culpability rather than result).

[87] Kevin McMunigal, 'Disclosure and Accuracy in the Guilty Plea Process' (1989) 40 *Hastings LJ* 957 at 979: '[A] purely objective view of self-defence . . . is a more difficult factual question for the defendant to resolve than the question of her own subjective belief since calculation of the harm threatened involves a number of variables [which] are beyond the defendants ability to perceive' (emphasis in original).

conceptualization lays bare the distinctions that are relevant to determining liability in these cases, while a 'reasons' theory obscures those distinctions. The 'deeds' conceptualization allows a clearer analysis and a better perspective from which meaningfully to debate the competing issues. Finally, a 'deeds' theory of justification improves the criminal law's rule-articulation function.[88] That is, it allows the law better to communicate to the public the conduct rules that it commands they follow.

Current American law typically follows the Model Penal Code formulation quoted above: an actor is *justified* if he *believes* that the conduct is necessary for defence.[89] Current English law also appears to adopt the 'reasons' theory. Smith and Hogan, for example, conclude that the law 'is stated exclusively in terms of the defendant's belief',[90] citing *Gladstone Williams, Dadson,* and *Thain*.[91] Section 24 of the Police and Criminal Evidence Act 1984 appears to be an exception to the general rule, for it justifies an arrest even if the officer did not at the time know of or believe in the justifying circumstances.[92] Clauses 44 and 185 of the Draft English Code appear to broaden this exception to make it the general rule. That is, they adopt a 'deeds' theory. They provide a defence if the actor 'uses such force as, in the circumstances *which exist*', is immediately necessary and reasonable for defence.[93] Interestingly, the drafters claim that the provision codifies the common law of self-defence and defence of another.[94] They concede that it modifies the common law of defence of property, arguing that such is necessary to avoid an irrational inconsistency betwee the rules for the defence of property and person.[95] As will become apparent later in the section, American law too is somewhat ambiguous as to which theory of justification it actually adopts, despite the apparent clarity of first appearances.[96]

---

[88] Paul H. Robinson, 'A Functional Analysis of Criminal Law' (1994) 88 *Northwestern ULR* 857 at 880–2 (hereinafter 'Functional Analysis').

[89] See e.g. Model Penal Code, §§ 3.02(1), 3.03(3)(a), 3.04(1), 3.05(1)(b), 3.06(1), and 3.07(1).

[90] Smith and Hogan, *Criminal Law*, n. 84 above, at 245.

[91] *Gladstone Williams* (1984) 78 Cr. App. R 276; *Dadson* (1850) 4 Cox CC 358; *Thain* (1985) 11 NI 31.

[92] Police and Criminal Evidence Act 1984, s. 24(4)(a), (5)(a), (7)(a) (providing that a person may arrest without a warrant 'anyone who is guilty of the offence' or words to that effect).

[93] See Draft English Code, ¶¶ 44(1), 185(1). The proposed code also provides a defence if the actor 'uses such force as, in the circumstances . . . which he believes to exist', is immediately necessary and reasonable for defence. This does not make the provision one based upon a 'reasons' theory of justification. Nothing in the 'deeds' theory prohibits a defence for mistake as to a justification. On the contrary, it assumes that such a defence will be provided but will be understood to be an excuse. Note that the provision of the proposed code does not identify either defence as a justification or an excuse.

[94] The drafters explain: 'if his defence is that he was defending his person, or that of another, the test at common law is whether what he did was reasonable': The Law Commission, *A Criminal Code for England and Wales* (London, 1989), ii, ¶ 44 comment 12.25.

[95] *Ibid.*   [96] See sect. C.5. of this Ch.

4. Incompatibility Between 'Reasons' Rationale and Current Law's 'Believes' Formulations

Before diving into a full comparison of the competing theories, consider a few things that raise some initial puzzlement, if not suspicion, about the 'reasons' theory. As Greenawalt expresses the theory: '[J]ustified action is morally proper action. [T]o be justified is to have sound, good reasons for what one does'.[97] It is the actor's reasons or motive for the conduct that supports the defence. Yet, the typical justification formulation, requiring that the actor 'believe' in the justifying circumstances, does not fully mirror this rationale. One can have knowledge of justifying circumstances but be motivated entirely by other, perhaps malicious, concerns.

Consider this hypothetical. Alphonse wishes to pummel his enemy, Buford, but has not done so for fear of being caught and punished. Alphonse lives in a rough neighborhood. As he sits on his porch he has seen many people robbed and beaten but has never intervened on their behalf. One day, to his delight, he sees that Buford is one of several aggressors in a robbery. He immediately intervenes, beating attacker Buford. He is motivated not by a desire to protect the victim but rather by his desire to hurt Buford without risking liability. Does Alphonse deserve a justification defence under the rationale of the 'reasons' theory? Is his conduct 'morally proper'? Are his 'reasons' for pummelling Buford 'sound and good'? No. His reasons for acting are base indeed: his long-simmering hatred. Yet, he nonetheless has a defence under the typical 'believes' formulation of current law.

If current law is based upon a 'reasons' theory, as Greenawalt and other 'reasons' theorists would have us believe, it ought not give a defence on the bare 'belief' that justifying circumstances exist. To require a particular 'reason' for acting, in modern statutory culpability terms, is to require a particular 'purpose',[98] not simply a belief in certain circumstances. If the 'reasons' theory of justification truly lay at the root of present justification defences, those defences would require more than a belief in the justifying circumstances. They would require that the actor's purpose was the justificatory purpose. (Note that giving a justification defence to Alphonse, as current law does, is consistent with a 'deeds' theory of justification; his conduct is objectively justified.)

This discrepancy between the standard legal formulation and the 'reasons' theory seems to weaken the claim that current law embraces that theory and that the embrace demonstrates general preference for that theory's liability results. But let us set aside this discrepancy for a moment and compare the liability results for the two theories directly. And, as we do

---

[97] Greenawalt, 'Perplexing Borders', n. 84 above, at 1903.
[98] Model Penal Code, § 2.02(2)(a).

that, let us assume that every person who acts with knowledge of justifying circumstances in fact acts for the justificatory purpose raised by the circumstances.

5. 'DEEDS' V. 'REASONS': LIABILITY RESULTS

Where both the deed and the reason are right or where both are wrong, the two theories generate the same liability results: the right deed for the right reason is free of liability; the wrong deed for the wrong reason is subject to liability. It is only in the case of mistake as to a justification and the case of an unknowingly justified actor that the theories give different results.

5.1 Mistake as to a Justification

Recall the liability differences in mistaken justification cases. The 'reasons' theory gives a justification defence because the actor believes that the justifying circumstances exist. Whether they actually exist or not is irrelevant. The force used against the jogger-mistaken-for-an-attacker is justified because it was used for the purpose of self-defence. The actor's reason was justified; the actual nature of the deed is irrelevant.

Under the 'deeds' theory, in contrast, the actual nature of the deed is central. The person who mistakenly believes his conduct is justified is not in fact justified, although the person may gain an excuse defence if the mistake is reasonable (or a mitigation even if it is not). Thus, the force used against the jogger-mistaken-for-an-attacker is not justified, although it may be excused.

The availability of an excuse defence under the 'deeds' theory of justification suggests that the liability results under the two theories are not different. Only the labelling of the results differs. The mistake as to a justification is 'justified' under the 'reasons' theory but only 'excused' under the 'deeds' theory. Does this mean that there is no real difference in the liability results between the two theories in the adjudication of mistaken justification cases?

5.1(1) Liability for Resisting a Mistaken Justification

Before reaching such a conclusion, look more carefully at the operation of justification defences. Whether conduct is justified can affect liability in two ways. First, whether conduct is justified or not determines whether the actor gains a defence to liability based upon that conduct. But the justified nature of conduct also affects the liability of others for resisting it. As discussed above, it is lawful to use force to resist a robber or even an insane attacker but not a police officer making a justified arrest. Do the two theories give different liability results in this respect?

Recall that a 'reasons' theory of justification considers the actual justified nature of the deed irrelevant; only the actor's reason is relevant. Yet application of such a theory gives clearly improper results in defining the situations where we want persons to be able to use defensive force lawfully. We want people to be able to defend lawfully against others who only mistakenly believe they are justified, but we do not want people to be able to defend lawfully against people who actually are justified. As the 'deeds' theory insists, the deed's actual objectively justified nature cannot be ignored; by ignoring it, the 'reasons' theory misstates the defensive force rules.

In fact, even codes that at first appear to adopt the subjective 'reasons' formulations concede this point. Having packed both mistaken and actual justification into the same concept, 'justification', the codes eventually unpack them in order to define the instances in which defensive force lawfully may be used. The obscurity, complexity, and confusion with which this unpacking occurs demonstrates the weakness of the 'reasons' theory in conceptualizing justification.

Consider a hypothetical. Moro is behind in his payments to loanshark Snake. Snake gave Moro a severe beating last week, with a warning that, if Moro missed another payment, he would be killed. The payment is due today but Moro does not have the money. He borrows a gun and hangs out at Deffi's Deli, the neighbourhood grocery store, in the hope that Snake will leave him alone in public. He is shocked when Snake comes in and walks straight at him. 'I won't let you get me, Snake!' he says as he pulls out his gun and aims. Just as he pulls the trigger, Deffi, the proprietor, who is directly across the counter from him, leans over and punches him. 'That's not Snake. It's his brother, you moron.' Deffi has made a point of learning to tell the difference between the look-alike brothers. Deffi's punch deflects Moro's shot. Snake's brother is wounded but not killed. Moro is cleared of assault charges because of his reasonable belief that he was about to be killed. Moro then files assault charges against Deffi. Is Deffi criminally liable for striking Moro?

The proper result, of course, is no liability for Deffi. If Moro really had been defending himself and Deffi interfered, Deffi might well be liable. But, here, Moro only mistakenly believes that an attack is imminent. Yet, one can see the problem facing the Model Penal Code drafters: the Code includes both mistaken and actual justifications within the term 'justified'. Moro, although mistaken, is 'justified' in the Code's terminology. Having combined mistaken and actual justification, how can the Code authorize lawful intervention in a case of mistaken justification yet prohibit it in a case of actual justification?

5.1(2) Privileged v. Unprivileged Force

Here is the Code's solution. It analyses the case as follows: under the Model Penal Code, Deffi is not justified in interfering to defend Snake's brother unless Snake's brother would be justified in using the same force in defence of himself.[99] The use of force against Moro by Snake's brother in turn is justified only if Snake's brother satisfies the requirements of self-defence:

Use of Force in Self-Protection. [T]he use of force upon or toward another person is justifiable when the actor believes that such force is immediately necessary for the purpose of protecting himself against the use of unlawful force by such other person on the present occasion.[100]

Thus, Deffi and Snake's brother can lawfully resist the mistaken Moro only if Moro's force is 'unlawful'. One might normally assume that 'justified' force is not 'unlawful force'. If that were the case, then, because Moro's shooting of Snake's brother is 'justified', it would not be 'unlawful', and Deffi would have no right to interfere with the shooting. But the Code's definition of 'unlawful force' is somewhat complex and ultimately gives a different result; it includes some kinds of 'justified' force but excludes other kinds. Section 3.11(1) defines 'unlawful force' as:

force, including confinement, which is employed without the consent of the person against whom it is directed and the employment of which constitutes an offence or actionable tort or *would constitute such offence or tort except for a defence (such as the absence of intent, negligence, or mental capacity; duress; youth; or diplomatic status) not amounting to a privilege to use the force.*[101]

In other words, under the Model Penal Code's scheme, two kinds of 'justified' conduct exist: privileged and unprivileged. The former may not lawfully be resisted; the latter may. Unfortunately, the Code gives no definition of what it means by 'privileged'. A review of the commentary suggests that the term is borrowed from tort law and is intended to mean objectively justified,[102] that is, the 'deeds' theory of justification. Having defined their term 'justified' to include mistake as to a justification, the Code drafters no longer have an objective justification concept they can turn to. Instead, they must try to borrow a concept from tort law, and are left unable to provide defined boundaries for the borrowed concept.

If we assume that the drafters mean 'privileged' to reflect a 'deeds' theory of justification, then Moro's mistaken force is not 'privileged', and, therefore, it is 'unlawful force' and, therefore, Deffi can lawfully defend Snake's brother against it, the proper result.

All codes that define justifications subjectively, as requiring only a 'belief' in the justifying circumstances, must engage in some similar gyrations to allow defensive force against mistaken justifications while prohibiting it against actual, objective justifications. Note, for example, that by including

[99] See Model Penal Code, § 3.05(1).
[100] Model Penal Code, § 3.04(1) (emphasis added).
[101] Model Penal Code, § 3.11(1) (emphasis added).
[102] Model Penal Code, § 3.11(1) comment 159 (1985).

the defences for objective justification and mistaken justification in the same defence provision, the Draft English Code creates the same difficulty for itself. Having packed the two together, clause 44(3) must unpack them, using an artificial definition of 'unlawful' that attempts to include within that term conduct for which the actor is acquitted because:

(a) he was under ten years of age; or
(b) he lacked the fault required for the offence or believed that an exempting circumstance existed; or
(c) he acted in pursuance of a reasonable suspicion; or
(d) he acted under duress, whether by threats or of circumstances; or
(e) he was in a state of automatism or suffering from severe mental illness or severe mental handicap.[103]

As with the Model Penal Code, the Draft English Code reaches the right result, but only through a definitional scheme that can be confusing. No such scheme is needed if a code's terminology uses 'justified' to refer only to conduct justified under a 'deeds' theory.

This practice of the Model Penal Code of defining 'unlawful force' that lawfully may be resisted as 'privileged force', makes it difficult to describe that Code and the many like it as adopting a 'reasons' theory, as they first appeared to do. In the only instance in which the mistaken-justification liability results differ for the two theories, the law follows the 'deeds' theory's focus on the actual nature of the deed rather than the actor's reasons for the deed. This concedes the primary tenet of the 'deeds' theory of justification: that the *nature of the deed* must be taken as determinative, no matter what the actor's *reasons* for the deed. Perhaps current law's approach to mistake as to a justification ought to be termed one of only a 'reasons' *terminology* rather than a 'reasons' *theory*.

In a later section it is shown that even adopting 'reasons' terminology is bad policy with serious detrimental effects. But before taking up that issue, consider the liability differences between the two theories, if any, for the cases of the unknowingly justified actor—the case of the attacker-thought-to-be-a-jogger—as done above for cases of mistaken justification.

5.2 Unknowingly Justified Actor

Recall the differing results of the two theories in the case of the unknowingly justified actor. The 'reasons' theory gives no justification defence because the actor does not believe that the justifying circumstances exist. Whether they actually exist or not is irrelevant. The force used against the attacker-thought-to-be-a-jogger is not justified even though it was necessary for self-defence. The actor's reason was wrong; the actual nature of the deed is irrelevant. Under the 'deeds' theory, in contrast, the actual nature of

---

[103] Draft English Code, ¶ 44(3)(a)–(e).

the deed is central. The person whose conduct in fact is justified, although he does not realize it to be so at the time, does receive a justification defence. Thus, the force used against the attacker-thought-to-be-a-jogger is justified, although the actor nonetheless may be liable for an attempt. This, then, seems a clear difference in liability results between the two theories, although the difference is only one in grading: the 'reasons' theory assigns full liability (no defence), while the 'deeds' theory assigns attempt liability (a justification defence to the substantive offence but no defence to the attempt offence).

5.2(1) Disagreement over the Significance of Resulting Harm

This disagreement over the proper liability level for the unknowingly justified actor may be simply a manifestation of a larger dispute, going beyond the nature of justification. The grading disagreement may only be one more battleground for the dispute over the significance of resulting harm. Those who believe that the criminal law ought to focus on culpable state of mind alone, and that the fortuity of resulting harm ought not affect liability, naturally prefer the result of the 'reasons' theory. Their view is that only the actor's subjective state of mind is relevant to liability. That the unknowingly justified actor believes that his conduct is unjustified is enough to impose full liability, they would argue, just as the person who thinks he has bought illegal drugs or believes he has lit a fuse on dynamite sticks is fully liable, even if it turns out that the powder is talcum and the dynamite sticks are wooden. The Model Penal Code, for one, takes this view when it adopts a rule that generally punishes attempts to the same extent as the substantive offence.[104]

If this is the reason for support of a 'reasons' theory of justification, there is not much more to be said on the liability issue. Even if one were to adopt a 'deeds' theory, which gives only attempt liability, attempts would be graded the same as the substantive offence, erasing any difference in the liability results between the theories. But the next two sections of this Chapter argue that there are other important reasons for preferring the conceptual scheme and terminology of the 'deeds' theory. Nearly all pure subjectivists (i.e. those believing resulting harm ought to be irrelevant to liability) can skip to the next section.[105]

I do not want to be read as conceding to the pure subjectivists. The fact is, they are a breed that exists (and will probably always exist) only in academia. I know of no jurisdiction that actually takes such a view,

---

[104] Model Penal Code, § 5.05(1). In reality, however, the Code does not adopt a view that rejects the significance of resulting harm. See Paul H. Robinson, 'The Role of Harm and Evil in Criminal Law: A Study in Legislative Deception?' (1994) 5 *Journal of Contemporary Legal Issues* 299 (hereinafter 'Harm and Evil').

[105] Even the pure subjectivist will be interested in the liability analysis for resisting an unknowingly justified actor. See sect. C.5.2(3) of this Ch.

whatever the code drafters may say they prefer. Nearly all American jurisdictions, even many of those adopting the Model Penal Code, reject that
Code's notion that attempts should be punished the same as the substantive offence.[106]

Even the Code itself is ambiguous in its apparent commitment to a subjectivist view. It creates an exception for attempts to commit a first degree felony, such as murder, so that attempted murder is graded less than
murder.[107] More important, if the Code really embodied the subjectivist
view that resulting harm is irrelevant, it would simply drop all result elements from its offences. Instead, it retains the standard offence definitions with result elements.[108] Further, it selects the most demanding and
traditional definition of causation, the necessary cause ('but for') test.[109]
If it were truly and unabashedly subjectivist, it would at very least adopt
a weaker causation test, perhaps a sufficient cause test (as was proposed
during the ALI floor debate on the causation section[110]). If results ought to
be irrelevant but for some unpleasant reason we must keep result elements,
why not make it as easy as possible to satisfy those elements? It may be
that the Code drafters only grudgingly added result elements to offences
and adopted a necessary cause test of causation because they thought that
people would demand such.[111] But this only concedes that the subjectivist
view of criminal law is one that cannot be sold to those who are governed by that law.[112]

What theory of justification is preferable if we assume, as the world
we know does, that resulting harm increases liability? If people generally
think that resulting harm matters, why do so many nonetheless seem to
prefer the 'reasons' theory of justification? Is this simply the product of
an untidy world, where the minority subjectivist view is adopted in the
formulation of justification because the Model Code took the minority
view? Is it that the minority subjectivist view has not been rejected by
the state code drafters, who typically hold the majority objectivist view,
simply because they do not see the connection between the issues or the
inconsistency of rejecting the Model Code's equal grading of attempts but
not its subjective formulation of justification? In short, probably yes.

If a jurisdiction admits the significance of resulting harm in assessing liability, if resulting harm may give rise to greater liability than no resulting

---

[106] See authorities cited in Robinson, 'Harm and Evil', n. 104 above, at n. 18.
[107] *Ibid.*
[108] See e.g. Model Penal Code, §§ 210.1, Criminal Homicide ('causes the death'); 211.1
Assault ('causes bodily injury to another'); 220.2(1) Causing Catastrophe ('person who
causes a catastrophe').   [109] Model Penal Code, § 2.03(1)(a).
[110] ALI Floor Debate on Model Penal Code § 2.03(1)(a), *ALI Proceedings* (1962), 77–9,
135–9 (proposing that actor's conduct be only 'a substantial factor in producing the result').
[111] See e.g. Model Penal Code, § 2.03 comment 257 (1985) ('when severe sanctions are
involved . . . it cannot be expected that jurors will lightly return verdicts leading to severe
sentences in the absence of the resentment aroused by the infliction of serious injuries').
[112] See generally Robinson, 'Harm and Evil', n. 104 above.

harm, it is difficult to see how a jurisdiction can reject the 'deeds' theory of justification, which gives attempt liability to the unknowingly justified actor, in favour of the 'reasons' theory, which ignores the fact that the conduct in reality causes no net harm. The actor may have thought he or she was causing a net societal harm but be surprised to find that no such net harm occurs. If the unknowingly justified actor is held liable, the liability is analogous to that of the attempter who thinks he is committing an offence, only to be surprised to find out that he is not.

5.2(2) Unknowing Justification as a Legally Impossible Attempt

The propriety of viewing the unknowingly justified actor as an instance of impossible attempt is confirmed by the fact that such an actor clearly comes within the language of the Model Penal Code's attempt provision. Section 5.01(1)(a) provides: 'A person is guilty of an attempt to commit a crime if, acting with the kind of culpability otherwise required for commission of the crime, he purposely engages in conduct which would constitute the crime if the attendant circumstances were as he believes them to be'.[113] Under the circumstances as the unknowingly justified actor believes them to be, he is committing an offence.

To deny the analogy between the two situations creates a challenge for the 'reasons' theorists. They must argue that the fortuitous lack of harm that undercuts an offence element—when the victim bends down just as the trigger is squeezed—reduces the grading to that of an attempt, but that the fortuitous lack of a net harm in a justification—maliciously burning the neighbour's field in fact saves the nearby town—does not reduce the grade to that of an attempt. On what grounds could such a distinction be defended?

Fletcher argues that there is an important difference between violating an offence norm and violating a justification norm; this is the theme of his response to my paper of twenty years ago.[114] I concede that the two certainly are different. Fletcher's arguments in this respect are persuasive, but then most scholars would not disagree with the claim that offences are conceptually distinct from justification defences.[115] What Fletcher must show is why offence rules and justification rules are different in a way that drives us to deviate from our general rule that the presence of resulting harm increases liability over that of an unsuccessful attempt to cause it. I find nothing in his analysis that addresses this central point.

To put the offence-justification dispute in a factual context, consider the following two cases. The actor believes a windstorm is coming but ignores the risk and burns a field's harvest stubble (a common practice by farmers

---

[113] Model Penal Code, § 5.01(1)(a).

[114] Fletcher, 'Right Deed', n. 82 above, at 308–18.

[115] There are some important exceptions to this, however, at least among English writers. See e.g. Glanville Williams, *Textbook of Criminal Law* (2nd edn., London, 1983), 138.

as a low-cost way to increase the fertility of the ground) despite the likelihood that the windstorm will cause the fire to burn a nearby town. It turns
out that the actor is wrong about the windstorm. There never existed any
danger to the nearby town, at least no more than the usual no-wind-
storm stubbleburning creates. Is the actor guilty of reckless endangerment
because she mistakenly believed that she was creating an unlawful danger? I think most would say, no; reckless endangerment requires proof of
a real, not just an imagined, unreasonable risk of harm.[116] At most, she
could be liable for *attempted* reckless endangerment, if such an offence
were recognized.[117]

Now assume the same actor maliciously burns her neighbour's cornfield,
but it turns out that the burning serves as a firebreak to an oncoming
forest fire about which she did not know. The burning saves the nearby
town and is, therefore, justified on the objective facts. I can argue, by
analogy, that the actor not be held liable for the full offence—i.e. she
should get a justification defence—because no net harm occurred. She
could be held liable for an attempt unjustifiably to burn the field (there
is no justifying good that comes from her externalized *intention* to burn
the field unjustifiably). If the absence of real danger means the stubble-
burner can be punished only for her externalized culpable intention (as
an attempt), how, in the absence of any net harm, can the cornfield-burner
who saved the town be punished for more than her externalized culpable intention (as an attempt)?

Note that Fletcher's claim that the issue should be resolved differently
in the justification context from in the offence definition context runs into
practical difficulty in modern codes. The Model Penal Code defines recklessness (and negligence) in a way that incorporates the concept of justification: it is criminal to disregard a risk (or, in the case of negligence, to
be unaware of a risk of which a reasonable person would be aware) that
is 'substantial and *unjustified*'.[118] Thus, the application of statutes requiring recklessness or negligence requires an assessment of the justification
of the risk, making it impossible to isolate justifications for special treatment apart from offence definitions.[119]

[116] Model Penal Code, § 211.2, Reckless Endangerment, provides in part: 'A person commits a misdemeanor if he recklessly engages in conduct which places or may place another
person in danger of death or serious bodily injury'. Thus if an actor does not fully extin-
guish a campfire which in turn causes a forest fire to ignite and places a nearby town in
imminent danger, the actor will be found guilty of reckless endangerment.

[117] I have argued elsewhere that it should be. See Robinson, 'Functional Analysis', n. 88
above, at 889–96.

[118] Model Penal Code, § 2.02(2)(c)&(d) (emphasis added).

[119] They have elsewhere used the term 'justified' to mean 'belief' that the conduct is justified. But under that meaning, one could indeed be liable for an offence of recklessness without ever creating an improper risk. The farmer who mistakenly thinks a windstorm is coming
creates no unjustified risk in an objective sense yet, if 'justified' is defined subjectively, he
has created an 'unjustified risk' and could be liable for reckless endangerment even in the
absence of any real unjustified risk. Such a result might be appropriate for a jurisdiction that

5.2(3) Liability for Resisting an Unknowingly Justified Actor

Beyond liability for the actor who performs the justified conduct, the competing theories of justification may have implications for the lawfulness of resisting an unknowingly justified actor. Recall that we undertook an analogous inquiry with regard to liability for resisting mistaken justification.

Under the 'reasons' theory, the actual justified nature of the deed is irrelevant, thus the unknowingly justified actor can be lawfully resisted because he acts for the wrong reason. Yet logic tells us that here again the 'reasons' theory gives improper results. Whether the deed is or is not actually justified is central to whether the law should allow it to be resisted.

Consider a situation similar to that of Moro and Deffi in the earlier hypothetical. This time assume that the person entering the shop really is the loanshark, not his twin brother. He intends to kill the customer—let me call the customer in this variation Duncan—but Duncan does not know of the planned attack. Duncan draws a gun to shoot the loanshark, not because Duncan fears attack, but because he does not want to pay back his gambling debt. In other words, he is unknowingly justified. The shop owner—call him Box—knows of the loanshark's planned attack and is loyal to the loanshark. Can shop-owner Box lawfully interfere with Duncan's shooting? In other words, should one be able to lawfully resist a person that one knows is an unknowingly justified actor?

As before, whether Box can lawfully interfere with Duncan depends upon how we characterize Duncan's conduct. If only reasons count, and Duncan has a bad reason, his conduct is unjustified, and presumably we will permit Box to use force to resist it, the 'reasons' theory. If it is the nature of the deed that counts, the 'deeds' theory, Duncan's shooting is justified and cannot lawfully be resisted. Clearly the law must prefer the 'deeds' theory. It is the nature of the deed, not the reasons of the actor, that must determine whether one lawfully can resist it.

What is the result under the Model Penal Code? Because Duncan does not have the 'belief' required for a justification, his shooting, even though it is necessary for his self-defence, is not justified.[120] Box lawfully can interfere with conduct that is 'unlawful'.[121] Is Duncan's unjustified conduct 'unlawful'? Recall that Model Penal Code section 3.11(1) defines 'unlawful force' as: 'force . . . which . . . would constitute [an] offence . . . except for a defence . . . not amounting to a privilege to use the force'. Duncan has no defence to his shooting; he will in fact be held fully liable for it. Thus, his shooting is 'unlawful' and Box lawfully can resist it even though he (Box) knows of the justifying facts! In other words,

---

looks only to subjective state of mind, but such would be inappropriate in the jurisdiction about which we speak, in which it is recognized that the actual existence or non-existence of results does indeed make a difference to liability.

[120] Model Penal Code, § 3.02.   [121] Model Penal Code, § 3.06.

even the contorted definition of 'unlawful force' in section 3.11(1) does not save the Code from improper results. Thus, in the context of the unknowingly justified actor, the Code's 'reasons' approach has a real and detrimental effect. While its effect is likely inadvertent—it is hard to believe that the drafters actually intended such a result—it demonstrates the dangers of constructing a code using the 'reasons' approach.

Note that the Draft English Code avoids this error by providing an objective form of justification. Whether Box can lawfully interfere with Duncan's shooting under the proposed Code depends upon whether Duncan's shooting is 'unlawful', under clause 44(3). Duncan has a defence to his intended shooting under clause 44(1)(c); the circumstances exist that make his shooting necessary to protect himself, even though he does not know of those circumstances. But his defence is not one of those enumerated in clause 44(3), situations in which, despite resulting in an acquittal, the conduct nonetheless is held to be 'unlawful'. Duncan's defence is not that he thought his shooting was necessary, as would be relevant under clause 44(1)(c), for example, but rather that his shooting was in fact necessary. Therefore, his conduct is not 'unlawful' under clause 44(3), and, therefore, Box cannot lawfully resist it, the proper result.[122]

5.3 Summary of Liability Results

The discussion of the previous section is rather long. Let me summarize the liability results generated by the respective justification theories. In cases of mistake as to a justification, both theories generate the same result—they give defence (or mitigation) for a mistake—but label the defences differently: the 'reasons' theory calling such defence a 'justification'; the 'deeds' theory calling such defence an 'excuse'. Both theories also allow a person lawfully to resist a mistake as to a justification, although this result takes some complicated manœuvres for the 'reasons' theory because it must allow lawful resistance to what it has labeled as 'justified' conduct.

In cases of unknowing justification, the theories do give different results, for both an unknowingly justified actor and a person resisting such an actor. The 'reasons' theory gives no defence to an unknowingly justified actor, thus full liability. The 'deeds' theory gives a justification defence but the unknowingly justified actor nonetheless is liable for an impossible attempt in most modern jurisdictions. Of course, for the pure subjectivist, who believes that resulting harm ought to be ignored and therefore

---

[122] Duncan may be liable for an impossible attempt under cll. 49 and 50 of the Draft English Code and his conduct might be considered 'unlawful' for the purposes of cl. 44 on this ground, which gives the wrong result in allowing Box lawfully to intervene. But this difficulty with the Draft Code could be fixed with minor changes by making clear that the right to use force depends upon the 'unlawfulness' of the actual conduct, not the conduct mistakenly envisioned in the mind of the person being defended against. This kind of fix is easier to make in the simpler formulations of justification defences described in the text accompanying notes 129–33 in this Ch.

attempts ought to be punished the same as the substantive offence, there is again no difference in the liability results for the unknowingly justified actor. But for all others, the 'reasons' theory insists on greater liability for the unknowingly justified actor than that of an impossible attempter even though the former is simply an example of the latter.

The two theories also give different liability results for one who resists an unknowingly justified actor. The 'reasons' theory, having concluded that the unknowingly justified actor's conduct is unjustified, allows a person lawfully to resist the justified conduct. This is the result under the Model Penal Code, but surely it is the wrong result (and may not have been intended by the drafters) for it allows a person lawfully to engage in conduct that the person knows to be against society's interest. The 'deeds' theory, in contrast, properly denies a defence to one who knowingly resists an unknowingly justified actor. (If the resister were unaware of the justifying circumstances, of course, she may be entitled to an excuse for mistaken justification.)

6. 'DEEDS' v. 'REASONS': TERMINOLOGY AND CONCEPTUALIZATION

Even if the liability results of the 'reasons' theory were not objectionable, good reasons exist to prefer a 'deeds' theory: (1) it clarifies the relevant issues rather than obscures them as a 'reasons' conceptualization does, and (2) it better performs the criminal law's function of informing the members of the community of the rules the criminal law commands they follow.

6.1 Clarity of Conceptualization: 'Justification and Excuse' v. 'Privileged Justification, Unprivileged Justification, and Excuse'

As the previous discussion explains, the 'reasons' theory creates a three-part conceptual structure distinguishing 'privileged justifications', 'unprivileged justifications', and excuses. (I put the phrases 'privileged justification' and 'unprivileged justification' in quotes because they are concepts of special meaning created by the Model Penal Code drafters and, for reasons that will become apparent, have never been adopted by the literature or used in ordinary legal discourse.) What I have called objective or actual justifications are of the 'privileged justification' class. A mistaken belief as to a justification is of the 'unprivileged justification' class. These two kinds of 'justifications' are defined in Article 3 of the Code. The defences of the excuse class, defined in Articles 2 and 4 of the Code, include insanity, duress, involuntary intoxication, immaturity, reliance upon official misstatement, or unavailable law.[123]

---

[123] See Robinson, 'Systematic Analysis', n. 74 above.

What is odd and misleading about this conceptualization is that the second class, 'unprivileged justifications', includes a defence of only one type, a mistaken belief in a justification, which is identical in character to excuses, the third class. Labeling the mistake-as-to-a-justification defence an 'unprivileged *justification*', suggests that it is conceptually similar to the defences of the 'privileged *justification*' group, yet in fact it is conceptually analogous to, indeed, more than that, it is conceptually indistinguishable from, the defences of the excuses group, especially the mistake excuses.

There can be little dispute that a mistaken belief in a justification operates as an excuse. As with all excuses, the claim is: while what I did in fact violated the rules of conduct, I ought not be blamed for the violation. A reasonable person *in my situation* (insane, under duress, involuntarily intoxicated, etc.) similarly would have been unable to avoid the violation. We would have preferred that the excused offender not engage in the conduct. Although we do not hold the excused actor liable, we advise others not to engage in such conduct in the future. We allow others lawfully to resist excused conduct. We prohibit others from assisting excused conduct.

As noted, mistake as to a justification is particularly akin to the other mistake excuses, such as mistake due to reliance upon an official misstatement or due to unavailable law.[124] In each instance the claim is: a reasonable person in my situation would have made the same mistake that I made.[125]

It is possible to conceptualize current criminal law rules in any number of ways. Presumably, the preferred conceptualization is the one that best advances the reason for having a conceptual scheme, and that reason, I argue, is to help us think most clearly about the issues and to give us the greatest insight into their proper formulation and application. The usefulness of any conceptualization, then, is a function of how much it helps us to see the most meaningful similarities and differences among the rules at issue. The conceptualization inherent in the 'reasons' theory of justification—distinguishing 'privileged justifications', 'unprivileged justifications', and excuses—fails the usefulness test because, for the reasons described, it misleads rather than clarifies the relation among the relevant doctrines.[126]

---

[124] See e.g. Model Penal Code, § 2.04(3).

[125] See generally George P. Fletcher, *Rethinking Criminal Law* (Boston, 1978), 762–9.

[126] Not all would necessarily agree with my suggestion for a clarity-insight test of a conceptualization. Listen to Kent Greenawalt's explanation of why he prefers the 'reasons' theory of justification: 'Whatever may be true about analogous words in other languages, 'justified' is most definitely not a special legal term. In discussions of ethics, justified action is morally proper action. 'Justification' is also used in relation to the reasons one puts forward for one's choices; an action is 'justified' in this sense when one has defended it with sound arguments. An essentially similar sense is employed when people speak of opinion

The best illustration of the 'reasons' theory's potential to confuse is found in a well known article by Kent Greenawalt, 'The Perplexing Borders of Justification and Excuse'.[127] After insisting on viewing justifications under a 'reasons' theory, in which mistaken justifications are deemed 'justifications', the author reviews these 'justifications', compares them to excuses, and concludes that the justification–excuse distinction is problematic.[128] His premise, of course, assures his conclusion. The cat owner who begins with the premise that his beloved Siamese really is his child in every meaningful sense can then complain that the pet–child distinction is not nearly so clear as people think.

Rather than demonstrating the perplexing borders of justification and excuse, the 'Perplexing Borders' article persuasively demonstrates the potential for confusion in treating mistaken justification as 'justification'. '[Having] sound, good reasons for what one does',[129] as Greenawalt defines justification, certainly should be grounds for a defence, an excuse defence.

A 'deeds' theory conceptualization, in contrast, is both simpler than the 'reasons' theory conceptualization and clarifies rather than obscures. It is simpler in that it requires only a two-part conceptual scheme—justifications and excuses. It is clarifying because it highlights the conceptual and functional identity of mistake as to a justification with other excuses.

The practical benefit of a better conceptualization is the potential for cleaner and clearer code provisions. Specifically, under a 'deeds' theory formulation, justifications are defined in objective terms that describe the permitted conduct. A mistake as to a justification is defined as a separate excuse defence. In formulating the defensive force defences—self-defence, defence of others, defence of property, etc.—the force an actor lawfully may defend against need not be defined using the unwieldy and obscure definition of 'unlawful', described above, with its undefined terms such as 'privileged'. Instead, the defensive force defences need only provide that an actor may lawfully defend against 'unjustified' force, as defined by the justification defences.

At least one state uses this form,[130] following the lead of the proposed federal criminal code drafted by the Commission for Reform of Federal Criminal Law.[131] Under this approach, the self-defence provision need read

---

writing as a process of legal justification. In epistemology, reference is made to 'justified' belief—that is, a well founded belief about facts. What joins these various senses is the idea that to be justified is to have sound, good reasons for what one does or believes': Greenawalt, 'Perplexing Borders', n. 84 above, at 1903. Greenawalt apparently believes that usage of terms in other disciplines is a more sound ground for conceptualizing criminal law.

[127] *Ibid.* [128] *Ibid.* [129] *Ibid.* 1903.

[130] See e.g. North Dakota Century Code, §§ 12.1–05–03 to 12.1–05–08, quoted at n. 150 below.

[131] *Final Report of the National Commission on Reform of Federal Criminal Laws* (1971), 43–64 (commonly referred to as the 'Brown Commission', after its chairman, Edmund G. Brown, former Governor of California).

simply, 'A person is *justified* in using force upon another person *to defend himself against* danger of imminent unjustified bodily injury . . . by such other person'.[132] Conduct is *unjustified* if it is in violation of a substantive offence and is not justified under the (objectively defined) justification defences.[133]

The Draft English Code gets only part way toward this cleaner, clearer approach. It recognizes a defence for the unknowingly justified actor. But it does not segregate force that is necessary from force that the *actor only believes* is necessary. Thus, as with the Model Penal Code, it has no defined concept of objective justification that it can use easily to define the force that lawfully may be resisted. In clause 44(3), it resorts to a similarly complex and artificial definition of 'unlawful' to make its defensive force provisions work properly.

6.2 *Articulating the Criminal Law's Commands to Those Bound by Them*

The most objectionable aspect of the 'reasons' conceptualization may be its detrimental effect on the law's ability clearly to communicate its commands to those who are bound by them. The criminal law's rules of conduct include the prohibitions, duties, and permissions contained in the objective elements of offence definitions and justification defences.[134] Conduct that is actually, objectively justified—'privileged justification', in the terminology of the Model Penal Code—is consistent with the rules of conduct. The law wishes to tell others that they can engage in similar conduct in a similar situation in the future. Conduct that is not actually, objectively justified—mistaken justification or 'unprivileged justification' —violates the rules of conduct and should be avoided by others under similar circumstances in the future. The violator at hand is excused only because his reasonable mistake renders his improper conduct blameless.

When we give people directions about what they should and should not do, our commands are necessarily descriptions of the conduct that we want avoided under what circumstances. An actor's motive or beliefs may be relevant to an assessment of his blameworthiness but is unnecessary to a description of the rule of conduct. To say 'do not use force against another unless you think the other is attacking you' may sound like a rule of conduct but is simply a compression of two distinct points. The rule of conduct says 'do not use force unless another is attacking you'; but we understand that in application *you can only act on what you know or believe.* But that second issue, of belief, is not an issue that one must deal with in stating the rule of conduct; it only becomes relevant in

---

[132] North Dakota Century Code, § 12.1–05–03 (emphasis added).
[133] The limitation to 'in violation of a *substantive* offence' avoids the problem discussed in sect. C.5.2(3) of this Ch.
[134] Robinson, 'Functional Analysis', n. 88 above, at 876–89.

adjudicating failures to follow the rule (to satisfy the ideal).[135] By combining objective and mistaken justification within a single 'justification' defence, the Code assures that verdicts of acquittal under a 'justification' defence will always be ambiguous in the message they announce, frustrating rather than advancing the law's educative effect.

Acquittal in a case where a justification defence is offered can mean either: (1) the conduct is disapproved but the actor is excused for it, or (2) the conduct is approved. Nothing tells the listener which is the case, yet the two possibilities give opposite conclusions about whether the conduct is within the rules of conduct that others are to follow in the future. In each instance, the listener is left to guess: do the rules permit what the actor actually did, or just what he thought he was doing, or both? Each case of mistaken justification can be misinterpreted as a case of true justification, thereby approving conduct that ought to be prohibited. Each actual justification—that is, conduct within the rules of conduct for others in the future—can be misinterpreted as a mistaken justification, thereby improperly discouraging conduct within the rules.

Assume, for example, that the defendant police officer viciously beats a suspect while arresting him because the officer believes such force is necessary to effect the arrest. And assume the officer is tried and acquitted for the assault. What message does his acquittal carry? Does it tell other officers they can lawfully use such force in making such an arrest under similar circumstances in the future, or does it tell them they cannot use such force (that this officer was wrong to use such force but is acquitted only because his mistake was reasonable)?

The point is illustrated by the acquittal of the officers whose severe beating of Rodney King was caught on videotape. There is evidence that the jurors found the officers' force excessive but that they thought the officers were not criminally liable for it because they did not realize at the time that their force was excessive. The jury took account of the danger that the officers felt, the confusion and uncertainty of the situation from the officers' perspective, the emotion generated by the preceding high-speed chase, and the possibly inadequate training that the officers may have had for dealing with such situations.

In the words of defence attorney Michael Stone, their goal was to persuade jurors to view the incident 'not through the eye of the camera but through the eyes of the police officers'. . . . On the night in question, [the officers] confronted a 250-pound man who they believed—wrongly—to be intoxicated with the drug PCP, said to endow users with 'superhuman strength'.[136]

---

[135] See *ibid.*; and Paul H. Robinson, 'Rules of Conduct and Principles of Adjudication' (1990) 57 *University of Chicago LR* 729 (hereinafter 'Rules of Conduct').

[136] 'Jury Was Asked to See Events as Police Did; Defence Depicted Officers in Urban Jungle', *Washington Post*, 30 April 1992, at A25. Officer Powell explained to jurors: 'He had very powerful arms. This was a big man . . . I was completely in fear for my life, scared

After hearing the evidence at trial, one juror explained the verdict this way:

At one point, King lunged at and connected with Officer Powell. The cops were simply doing what they'd been instructed to do. They were afraid he was going to run or even attack them. He had not been searched, so they didn't know if he had a weapon. He kept going for his pants, so they thought he might be reaching for a gun . . . I have no regrets about the verdict. I'll sleep well tonight.[137]

Another juror emphasized the difficult circumstances in which the defendants found themselves which might underlie an excuse-oriented view of the acquittal: '[King] was obviously a dangerous person, massive size and threatening actions. . . . They're policemen. They're not angels. They're out there to do a lowdown dirty job. Would you want your husband doing it, or your son or your father?'[138]

If one assumes the jury found that the officers mistakenly believed their force was not excessive, the traditional 'reasons' terminology would describe the officers as 'justified'. But that description, 'justified', can easily be taken as condoning the officer's conduct. Indeed, many people found the acquittals outrageous specifically because they seemed to condone the use of excessive force:

[The verdict] sends out a message that whatever you saw on that tape was reasonable conduct.[139]

[The verdict] tells me that police can do what they want. Everyone in the world saw that man get whipped and I don't know what the jury was seeing.[140]

What does it take to prove they're guilty? They're saying, 'So what if you videotape me, I still can beat you up.'[141]

[I]t is an outrage that our system can't punish those—particularly police officers—who use the power and majesty of the state to beat some man senseless.[142]

to death that if the guy got up again he was going to take my gun and there would be a shooting, and I did everything I could to keep him down on the ground.'

[137] 'The Jury's View', *Washington Post*, 1 May 1992, at A33.   [138] *Ibid.*

[139] Los Angeles Deputy District Attorney Terry White, reported in 'The Police Verdict', *New York Times*, 30 April 1992, at A1, col. 1.

[140] David Green, 32-year-old Northeast Washington construction worker, reported in 'Case Casts Long Shadow', *Washington Post*, 1 May 1992, at A1.

[141] Hilda Whittington, a Chicago nutritionist, who is black, reported in 'Riots in Los Angeles', *New York Times*, 1 May 1992, at A23, col. 1. In the same vein: 'It sends a very scary message to me. I can be driving my car and fitting a description. I try to respect cops as much as I can. I feel they should do the same. I'm very scared that something like this could happen to me': Emilio Henry, a black senior at Texas Southern University, in *ibid*. Similarly: 'The verdict sends two messages. For those who wear the uniform of the law, the message is that anything goes; for those whose only badge is their skin color, the message is to expect no justice from the criminal justice system': Eddie Williams, president of the Joint Center for Political and Economic Studies, a black DC think tank, reported in 'A Case of Haunting Images and Perplexing Questions', *Washington Post*, 1 May 1992, at A29.

[142] Jerry Brown, former Governor of California, reported in 'Where's the Out From White America?', *Washington Post*, 1 May 1992, at A27.

If the officers' conduct had been described as 'unjustified' because it was excessive, and the grounds for acquittal laid upon excuse of admittedly mistaken conduct, the verdicts might not have inspired these kinds of reactions. Instead of creating outrage, the finding that the conduct was 'unjustified' could have helped assure citizens that the conduct they saw on tape was indeed disapproved. It might also have made it clearer to police officers that they are not authorized to engage in such conduct under similar circumstances in the future. Instead of clarifying and reinforcing the rules of acceptable conduct, the 'reasons' terminology undercuts and confuses an understanding of the rules.

Indeed, the 'reasons' conceptualization prevents the system from even properly judging whether conduct is or is not within the rules of conduct. For example, in the case of the beating of Rodney King, even the jurors may not have formed a shared assessment of the excessiveness of the officer's conduct. By packing both mistaken justification and actual justification into the same label, 'justification', different jurors may have come to different conclusions about whether the officers' conduct was proper. Some might have thought it proper, while others thought it improper but excused. It seems hopeless to think that the public adjudication of criminal cases will educate the public about the law's commands when the doctrine's conceptualization and terminology prevents even jurors from having to agree on whether the conduct at issue is within the rules of conduct.

What is needed is a verdict system that distinguishes a justification from an excuse,[143] and an objective, 'deeds' theory of justification that allows judges and juries to make such a distinction.

7. The Deeds–Reasons Dual Requirement Proposal

I noted above that current law may be viewed as adopting a 'deeds' theory with regard to mistaken justification (in outcome if not in terminology)[144] and a 'reasons' theory with regard to the unknowingly justified actor.[145] This pattern of liability may lead one to propose a dual requirement for justification: that the actor both perform the right deed and act for the right reason. Such a dual requirement both explains and derives support from current law, which justifies defensive force against the attacker who only mistakenly believes he is justified (wrong deed) but denies such justification for force against the attacker who actually, objectively, is justified

---

[143] For a discussion of such a proposal, see Robinson, 'Rules of Conduct', n. 135 above, at 766–7. A more detailed proposal is contained in Paul H. Robinson, Peter D. Greene, and Natasha R. Goldstein, 'Making Criminal Codes Functional' (1996) 86 *Journal of Criminal Law and Criminology* 304.

[144] See sect. C.5.2(3) of this Ch.   [145] See sect. C.5.1. of this Ch.

(right deed) and, at the same time, denies a defence to the unknowingly justified actor (wrong reason).

That said, I find such a dual requirement puzzling. I understand the theory behind the 'reasons' approach: a justification defence ought to depend upon whether the actor thought he was justified; many theorists believe that an actor's externalized culpable state of mind ought to be the sole criterion for criminal liability. I also understand, and support, the theory behind the 'deeds' approach: that the defence ought to depend upon the absence of a net resulting harm; no net harm renders the unknowingly justified actor an impossible attempter, who, like any attempter, deserves less liability than one who actually brings about the harm or evil of the substantive offence. I do not, however, understand the theory behind this dual-requirement approach. It seems internally inconsistent in its view of the significance of resulting harm and the sufficiency of culpability as grounds for full liability. How can one articulate the general theory of liability behind requiring both the right reason and the right deed? Is the absence of a net harm significant or not? Is externalized culpability sufficient for full substantive liability or not? Apparently the answer to these questions is different in different situations—mistakenly justified and unknowingly justified—but it is not apparent why the answers to such questions should depend on the factual situation.

Even if one could articulate a theory for the dual requirement, it would not necessarily answer my many objections to the 'belief' requirement, as described in my opposition to the 'reasons' theory. To review, first, current law's expression of the 'reasons' theory—that the actor *believe* that his conduct is justified—fails to implement that theory.[146] Acting for the right reason means having the right motivation. The 'belief' requirement of current law simply requires that the actor have certain knowledge when he acts. Why should we irrebuttably presume in every instance that the actor is motivated by this knowledge? A true 'reasons' theory gives a defence only if the actor acts for the justificatory purpose.[147]

Secondly, a 'reasons' theory denies the significance of the analogy between the unknowingly justified actor and the impossible attempter.[148] That is, by denying a defence to the unknowingly justified actor, it treats him as indistinguishable from the actor with a similarly culpable state of mind who is not objectively justified. This view understandably appeals to those theorists who oppose giving significance to resulting harm, but it is clear that this view does not reflect our shared intuitions in assessing blameworthiness, nor does it reflect current law's treatment of resulting

---

[146] See sect. C.4. of this Ch.

[147] At least one writer has argued that the *Thain* case might be interpreted to require not only knowledge of the justifying facts, but also a justificatory purpose. See G. R. Sullivan, 'Bad Thoughts and Bad Acts' (1990) *Criminal LR* 559 at 560–1.

[148] See sect. C.5.2(2) of this Ch.

harm. Every known criminal law system gives significance in grading to whether a resulting harm or evil occurs. There is no apparent reason why the significance of resulting harm or evil should be denied in the context of the unknowingly justified actor.

Finally, the 'reasons' theory, by denying a justification to the unknowingly justified actor, authorizes others to resist that objectively justified conduct. Thus, beause the unknowingly justified actor is treated as unjustified, even one who knows of the justifying circumstances can lawfully resist him.[149]

8. DEEDS V. REASONS: SUMMARY AND CONCLUSION

To summarize, current law adopts the terminology of a 'reasons' theory of justification: an actor is justified if the actor believes the conduct is justified; the actual nature of the deed is irrelevant. In reality, however, current law adopts a 'deeds' theory of justification in its treatment of mistaken justification, the most common kind of case on which the two theories give different results. In the case of an unknowingly justified actor, an unusual case, current codes do indeed follow the logic of the 'reasons' theory, but that logic gives bizarre and undesirable results. It allows an actor to interfere with conduct that is objectively justified, even if the interfering actor knows of the justifying circumstances. And it imposes full liability upon the unknowingly justified actor rather than the attempt liability that is appropriate for what is essentially an impossible attempt.

In addition to the 'reasons' theory's problematic performance with regard to liability results, that theory should be rejected on independent grounds because it obscures and confuses the analysis of justification cases. The 'deeds' theory is preferable because it makes the important distinction between mistaken and actual justification and highlights the conceptual and functional identity of mistaken justification as an excuse.

Making the distinction between actual and mistaken justification is particularly important to the law's obligation to communicate its rules of conduct to the public bound by those rules. By including both mistaken and actual justification within the single term 'justified', a 'reasons' conceptualization invites the public to misconstrue a finding of 'justified' due to a mistaken belief in justification to mean that the conduct is truly justified in the sense of being within the rules of proper conduct to be condoned here and in the future. The reverse confusion also can occur. A finding of 'justified' based upon a conclusion that conduct is proper and condoned may be misinterpreted as a finding that the conduct actually is disapproved but the actor is excused. A 'deeds' theory, in contrast, uses every case adjudication to tell the community which conduct is approved

---

[149] See sect. C.5.2(3) of this Ch.

('justified') and which conduct is disapproved even though the offender at hand may not be punished for it ('excused').

The 'deeds' theory of justification, then, is preferred because only that theory gives proper liability results, only its conceptualization accurately describes the important similarities and differences between the doctrines, and only it educates the public as to the proper rules of conduct.[150]

[150] Objectively defined justifications might look something like the following.

'*Section 12.1–05–03. Self-Defence* A person is justified in using force upon another person to defend himself against danger of imminent unlawful bodily injury . . . by such other person.'

'*Section 12.1–05–04. Defence of Others* A person is justified in using force upon another person in order to defend anyone else if:

1. The person defended would be justified in defending himself; and
2. The person coming to the defence has not, by provocation or otherwise, forfeited the right of self-defence.'

'*Section 12.1–05–07. Limitations on the Use of Force—Excessive Force* A person is not justified in using more force than is necessary and appropriate under the circumstances.'

'*Section 12.1–05–08. Excuse* A person's conduct is excused if he believes that the facts are such that his conduct is necessary and appropriate for any of the purposes which would establish a justification . . . under this chapter, even though his belief is mistaken. However, if his belief is negligently or recklessly held, it is not an excuse in a prosecution for an offence for which negligence or recklessness, as the case may be, suffices to establish culpability'.

'*Section 12.1–05–12. Definitions* In this Article, unless a different meaning plainly is required: . . . 'Unlawful' force or threat means conduct that satisfies the objective elements of an offence, even if the actor has a defence, but does not include justified conduct.'

These provisions are from the North Dakota Century Code. That Code does not contain the definition of 'unlawful' force given in section 12.1–05–12 but, given its treatment of mistake as to a justification as an excuse, it might logically intend such a definition.

Part III

A Functional Structure

This Part critiques the current operational structure of criminal law as developed in Part II, and suggests that it fails to take account of the different functions of criminal law. The criminal law has three primary functions.

First, it defines and announces the conduct that is prohibited (or required) by the criminal law. Such 'rules of conduct', as they have been called, provide *ex ante* direction to the members of the community as to the conduct that must be avoided (or that must be performed) upon pain of criminal sanction. This may be termed the *rule articulation* function of the doctrine.

When a violation of the rules of conduct occurs, the criminal law takes on a different role. It determines whether the violation merits criminal liability. This second function, setting the minimum conditions for *liability*, marks the shift from prohibition to adjudication.[1] It typically assesses *ex post* whether the violation is sufficiently blameworthy 'to warrant the condemnation of conviction'.[2]

Finally, where liability is to be imposed, criminal law doctrine assesses the relative seriousness of the offence, usually as a function of the relative blameworthiness of the offender. This sets, in a general sense, the amount of punishment to be imposed. While the first step in the adjudication process, the liability function, requires a simple yes or no decision as to whether the minimum conditions for liability are satisfied, this second step of the adjudication process, the *grading* function, requires judgements of degree. It must take account of such things as the relative harmfulness of the violation and the level of culpability of the actor.

This Part argues that these three primary functions of criminal law —rule articulation, liability assignment, and grading—are a useful way in which to analyse and organize criminal law doctrine. The first chapter in the Part describes and segregates current doctrines according to the function that each performs. The next three chapters consider each of the three functions respectively and illustrate how the failure to take account of a doctrine's function causes errors and distortions in the formulation the doctrine.

---

[1] For a general discussion of the distinction between rules of conduct and principles of adjudication, see Paul H. Robinson, 'Rules of Conduct and Principles of Adjudication' (1990) 35 *University of Chicago LR* 729; Paul H. Robinson, 'A Functional Analysis of Criminal Law' (1994) 88 *Northwestern ULR* 857.

[2] This is a Model Penal Code phrase: see e.g. Model Penal Code, § 2.12(2).

6

A Functional Analysis of Criminal Law

Modern criminal codes commonly acknowledge that criminal law serves each of the three functions described above but fail to see that a given code provision may serve one function but not another; the entire undifferentiated code is seen as serving these functions together. The Model Penal Code, for example, describes '[t]he general purposes of the provisions governing the definition of offenses' as:

[1] to forbid and prevent conduct that unjustifiably and inexcusably inflicts or threatens substantial harm to individual or public interests;

[2] to give fair warning of the nature of the conduct declared to constitute an offense;

[3] to safeguard conduct that is without fault from condemnation as criminal;

[4] to subject to public control persons whose conduct indicates that they are disposed to commit crimes;

[5] to differentiate on reasonable grounds between serious and minor offenses.[1]

The first two purposes embody the rule articulation function, the second two the liability assignment function, and the last the grading function. This Chapter dissects current criminal law doctrine in terms of these three functions, and demonstrates that one can identify specific doctrines as serving specific functions.

The functional differences among doctrines have not been obvious in the past, in part because the current organizing structure of criminal law uses distinctions that obscure the law's different functions. The central organizing distinctions in criminal law doctrine have traditionally been those between offences and defences and between 'actus reus' and 'mens rea' requirements. Yet, as Chapter 3 demonstrates, each of these categories, as well as the subcategories into which they commonly are divided, contains doctrines that perform each of the three functions of rule articulation, liability assignment, and grading.

---

[1] Model Penal Code, § 1.02(1) (The order of the subsections is altered from the original).

A. The Standard Conceptualization

One might initially estimate that the 'actus reus' requirements define the prohibited conduct, the rule articulation function, and that the 'mens rea' requirements, with the help of the general defences, define the minimum requirements of liability for a violation, the liability function. A closer examination, however, suggests that the functional structure of criminal law is somewhat different from this.

1. 'Actus Reus' Requirements

The conduct and circumstance elements of offence definitions do contribute to the definition of the prohibited conduct, the rule articulation function, but result elements do not. Unlike conduct and circumstance elements, result elements are not necessary to define the prohibited conduct. It is an actor's conduct, and not its results, that the criminal law prohibits; it is only the actor's conduct that the law can influence. The law may prohibit a particular result but what is intended is to direct actors not to engage in conduct that would bring about (or risk bringing about) that result. An actual resulting harm may make the violation more serious, as some argue, but the fortuity of whether the result actually occurs does not alter the nature of the conduct that constitutes the violation. The conduct remains objectionable notwithstanding the happenstance that the result does not occur.[2] Result elements, then, serve only to aggravate an actor's liability, the grading function.

The role of the causation requirement—defining the relation between an actor's conduct and a result that gives rise to an actor's accountability for the result—similarly serves the grading function and not the rule articulation function. Like the requirement of a result, the causation rules determine when an actor's liability is aggravated because the actor is accountable for a harmful result. Because result elements and causation requirements are not necessary to define the conduct prohibited by the criminal law, it is not surprising that liability does not necessarily depend upon them. If a prohibited result does not occur or if a required causal connection is not established, the actor commonly is liable for a lesser offence, such as an attempt.[3]

Many of the omission and possession rules, allowing liability for an omission to perform a legal duty or for possession of contraband even in the

---

[2] In some instances, however, as when less serious harms are only risked, the societal harm of the conduct may be too small to justify criminal condemnation. Conduct creating a low risk of a less serious harm may fall below the line of minimum seriousness required for adequate blameworthiness, unless the harm actually occurs.

[3] This is always true for intentional offences in jurisdictions that have general attempt statutes, as nearly two-thirds of the states have. See the general attempt statutes cited at Paul H. Robinson, *Criminal Law Defenses* (St Paul, Minnesota, 1984), i, § 81(b), nn. 16, 17 & § 83(f), n. 60 (hereinafter *Criminal Law Defenses*). See also Draft English Code, ¶¶ 49, 50.

absence of an affirmative act, contribute to the criminal law's definition of the conduct that is prohibited or required. Without the special duty requirements or the special prohibition for the possession of contraband, the law would not provide a complete description of what is acceptable and unacceptable conduct. Thus, this aspect of the actus reus serves the rule articulation function.

On the other hand, other aspects of these actus reus rules do not serve the rule articulation function. The voluntariness aspect of the act requirement, the physical capacity to perform requirement of the omission doctrine, and the requirement in the possession liability rules that the actor know of his possession for a period sufficient to terminate the possession, do not define prohibited conduct but rather define minimum conditions for holding an actor condemnable for a violation by commission, omission, or possession, respectively. The rules of conduct continue to prohibit possession of certain drugs, even if the actor who had possession of such a drug is not held liable because he did not know of such possession for a period sufficient to terminate it. Filing an income tax return remains a duty, although the actor at hand is not punished for her failure because it was physically impossible for her to file. In other words, the actus reus requirements of voluntariness, capacity, and knowledge of possession serve a liability function, in the same way that many mens rea requirements do. Under the mens rea requirements, taking another person's property without permission remains a violation of the rules of conduct although the actor at hand is not held liable for such a taking because he was unaware of a risk that the property belonged to another person.

2. 'MENS REA' REQUIREMENTS

We may think of all 'mens rea' or 'culpability' requirements as serving analogous functions, the liability function of establishing the minimum culpability required for liability for a violation. Purposely, knowingly, recklessly, and negligently are defined as alternative levels of culpability. According to the Code, liability for an offence ordinarily may not be imposed unless one of these culpability levels is proven as to each objective element of an offence.[4] But as with 'actus reus' requirements, by treating all 'mens rea' requirements as a group, the doctrine obscures the different functions that different requirements perform. Many culpability requirements

---

[4] '[A] person is not guilty of an offence unless he acted purposely, knowingly, recklessly, or negligently, as the law may require, with respect to each material element of the offence': Model Penal Code, § 2.02(1). See also Draft English Code, ¶ 20. Thus, if the objective elements of an offence require that an actor take property of another without the owner's consent, the culpability elements of an offence might require, for example, that the actor purposely take what he knows is property while being reckless as to it belonging to someone else and reckless as to the owner's lack of consent. For a discussion of the sometimes complex and confusing process of determining the culpability requirements of an offence, see Paul H. Robinson and Jane A. Grall, 'Element Analysis in Defining Criminal Liability: The Model Penal Code and Beyond' (1983) 35 *Stanford LR* 681 at 705–19 (hereinafter 'Element Analysis').

do serve the liability function, but others do not. Let us examine more closely the nature of culpability requirements.

First, note that the four levels of culpability do not apply in a symmetrical way to the three kinds of objective elements. When we talk of culpability as to the existence of a *circumstance* element, we refer to the actor's culpability as to the then *present* circumstances. Any of the four culpability levels can apply. As to the circumstance that an actor's sexual partner is less than 16 years old, for example, the actor may desire his partner to be under 16, he may be practically certain (know) that the partner is under 16, he may be aware of a substantial risk that the partner is under 16, or he may not be aware, but should be, of a substantial risk that his partner is under 16. (Apparently the Model Penal Code drafters see no practical significance in the difference between an actor desiring that a circumstance exists and knowing so. The Code defines 'purposely' as to a circumstance as requiring only that the actor 'believes or hopes' that the circumstance exists.[5]) These culpability requirements may be called instances of 'present circumstance culpability', to remind us that they refer only to culpability as to then present facts.

When we talk of culpability as to a *result*, in contrast, we necessarily are talking of an actor's culpability as to a then *future* event. Culpability as to an actor's conduct causing a result, which the concurrence requirement demands exist at the time of the conduct, necessarily must be culpability as to causing a result that does not at that moment exist. Again, any level of culpability can apply. As to an actor's culpability in causing another's death, for example, the actor may desire to cause the death, he may be practically certain (know) that his conduct will cause the death, he may be aware of a substantial risk that his conduct will cause the death, or he may not be aware, but should be, of a substantial risk that his conduct will cause the death. These kinds of culpability may be called instances of 'future result culpability'.

When we talk of culpability as to a *conduct* element, the full range of culpability levels does not apply. An actor can only be 'purposeful' as to his or her *own* conduct. Absent a serious disability, an actor engages in conduct only if he desires to do so, if such is his 'conscious object'. An actor either wishes to engage in certain conduct or he does not. Except for persons with control dysfunctions, it makes no sense to speak of an actor who knows or is aware of a risk that he is engaging in or will engage in certain conduct but does not desire to. The Code recognizes this in part when it fails to define 'recklessly' and 'negligently' with respect to a conduct element.[6]

---

[5] Model Penal Code, § 2.02(2)(a)(ii). Similarly, the Draft English Code defines 'intentionally' as to a circumstance as either hoping or knowing that it exists: Draft English Code, ¶ 18(b).

[6] See Model Penal Code, § 2.02(2)(c)&(d). The Code does define 'knowingly' as to conduct, however; an actor is 'knowing' as to conduct when the actor 'is aware that his conduct is of that nature'. Model Penal Code, § 2.02(2)(b)(ii). What does the Code mean by being aware of the 'nature' of one's conduct? Presumably, it means that the actor must be aware

Recall, only 'purposely' is meaningful with regard to one's performing conduct: we may wish to call this kind of culpability 'conduct intention'.

Another important difference that characterizes culpability as to one's own conduct is that it can concern either *present or future* conduct. For all commission offences, a 'present conduct intention' is required. This requires little more than showing that the actor did in fact intend to perform the bodily movements that he performed. An actor does not satisfy this culpability requirement if he does not intend to push the victim, but rather does so accidentally as he catches his balance from his own fall. A requirement of present conduct intention is essentially redundant with the voluntariness requirement discussed above.

The requirement of a 'future conduct intention', on the other hand, has a critical independent role to play. It shows that the actor is planning to do more than what he has already done. Most prominently, attempt liability requires that the actor must intend, must have the 'purpose', to engage in the conduct constituting the offence.[7] Such a future conduct intention also is present in substantive offences that are or that contain codified inchoate offences. Burglary, for example, requires that an actor enter a building 'with purpose to commit a crime therein'.[8] Note that the requirement of a present conduct intention applies to a corresponding objective element of offence definition, the conduct element, which the actor also must satisfy, just as the requirements of a present circumstance culpability and a future result culpability typically apply to a corresponding objective element. A requirement of a *future* conduct intention, in contrast, by definition has no corresponding objective element but rather exists on its own; the actor need not be shown to have performed the conduct.

In some instances the law requires that the actor have culpability as to *another person's* conduct. For example, the general inchoate offences of conspiracy and solicitation, as well as complicity liability, require that the actor agree with or solicit or aid another with some level of culpability

of the circumstances and results of the conduct. But, if this is what is intended, the drafters have created a troublesome overlap between culpability as to conduct and culpability as to a circumstance and a result, which the Code defines separately and differently. In any given circumstance or result element, how are we to know whether the definition of culpability as to a circumstance or as to a result is to apply, or whether the circumstance or result is to be subsumed into the 'nature of the conduct' and the definition of culpability as to conduct is to apply. The Code has no provision that gives a means of distinguishing 'conduct', 'circumstance', and 'result' elements. One may also wonder, if this broad interpretation of 'conduct' is adopted—'conduct' includes the circumstances and results of conduct—why the Code does not allow for culpability lower than knowing: one can be reckless or negligent as to the result or circumstances of one's conduct. The better view is to treat the circumstances or results of one's conduct as circumstance or result elements, each with a distinct culpability requirement (and to disregard the Code's definition of 'knowingly' as to conduct). See generally Robinson and Grall, 'Element Analysis', n. 4 above, at 719–25. The Draft English Code does not define any level of culpability ('fault') as to a conduct element. See Draft English Code, ¶ 18. That approach is consistent with that proposed here.

[7] Model Penal Code, § 5.01(1)(c); Draft English Code, ¶ 49(1)&(2).
[8] Model Penal Code, § 221.1(1). Similarly, see Draft English Code, ¶ 147(1)(a).

as to the other person engaging in conduct constituting an offence.[9] While one normally can be only 'purposeful' as to one's own conduct, one can have any level of culpability as to causing or assisting another's conduct. One may hope and desire that another will engage in certain offence conduct; one may not desire it but may know (be 'aware that it is practically certain'[10]) that the other will engage in the conduct; one may be aware only of a substantial risk that the other will engage in the conduct; or one may not be aware, but should be, of a substantial risk that the person will engage in the conduct. Such culpability may concern another's present or future conduct. When it concerns another's present conduct, it is simply an example of a present circumstance. When it concerns another's future conduct, more often the case, as in solicitation, conspiracy, and complicity, it is a form of a future result. This form of culpability requires a showing that, when the actor solicited, conspired with, or aided another, the actor had a given level of culpability as to causing or assisting the resulting offence conduct by the other person. Culpability as to another's conduct thus does not appear to present a culpability requirement different from 'present circumstance culpability' and 'future result culpability'.

Here, then, are four distinct kinds of culpability requirements—present circumstance culpability, future result culpability, present conduct intention, and future conduct intention—that are grouped together under current doctrine's standard purposeful-knowing-reckless-negligent scheme. The reformulated distinctions described above are significant because they capture the different functions of mens rea requirements that current doctrine does not.

Only the requirements of a present circumstance culpability and a present conduct intention serve the liability function that we typically ascribe to culpability requirements. They set the minimum requirements for imposing criminal liability for a violation. We might call these 'base culpability' requirements. Indeed, as noted above, even a present conduct intention has little practical effect in serving the liability function. It is rarely in dispute and, where it is, it is redundant with the voluntariness requirement. Thus, present circumstance culpability requirements are nearly the exclusive kind of culpability requirement that establish minimum liability conditions.

Just as result elements are never a minimum requirement for liability, their corresponding future result culpability requirements are never part of the minimum requirements of liability. (As we shall see in a moment, however, this may not be true where the future result culpability exists by itself in attempt liability, where no actual result is required.) Thus, future result culpability typically serves as part of the grading function. This is also the case for many future conduct intentions, such as the future conduct intention in burglary that turns the misdemeanour of trespass into the felony of burglary.

---

[9] See e.g. Model Penal Code, §§ 2.06(3)(a), 5.02(1), 5.03(1).
[10] Model Penal Code, § 2.02(2)(b).

Both future result culpability and future conduct intentions also serve a grading function when they are used to distinguish among different grades of violations with identical objective elements. The culpability requirements for homicide—murder (purposeful or knowing killing), manslaughter (reckless killing), and negligent homicide—are not designed 'to safeguard conduct that is without fault from condemnation as criminal'. Rather, they define the conditions for distinguishing between grades of unlawful homicide. Assault with intent to commit rape is another example.[11] The 'intent to commit rape' is used as a basis for increasing the grade of the offence over that of an assault without the intention. Burglary, noted above, is a similar example. These culpability requirements serve 'to differentiate on reasonable grounds between serious and minor offences', to use the Model Penal Code phrase.[12] Future result culpability and future conduct intention, serving the grading function, might be termed instances of 'aggravation culpability', to distinguish them from the base culpability requirements serving the liability function.

Base and aggravation culpability may be the most common functions of culpability requirements, but in a few instances, chiefly in the definition of inchoate conduct, culpability requirements serve a rule articulation function in defining the rules of conduct. That is, they are necessary to describe to the public the conduct that the criminal law prohibits. In the general attempt offence, for example, the conduct and circumstance elements of the substantive offence definition only begin a statement of the criminal law's prohibition. A definition of what conduct is prohibited by the attempt offence requires something more. The requirement, common in modern codes, that the conduct constitute a 'substantial step toward commission of an offence',[13] is inadequate in itself. As a purely objective matter, some conduct may constitute a 'substantial step toward commission of an offence' but in fact may be entirely innocent and acceptable conduct and is not prohibited. Such conduct becomes unacceptable and a societal harm only when accompanied by an intention to violate the substantive rules of conduct.

Lighting one's pipe is not a violation of the rules of conduct, unless it is a step in a plan to ignite a neighbour's haystack. Giving a young girl a ride is not a violation of the rules of conduct, unless it is done with the intention of sexually assaulting her. Thus, to describe the minimum requirements of prohibited conduct, the definition of a criminal attempt must include a state of mind requirement—the intention to engage in conduct that constitutes a rule violation.[14] (In contrast, the law can prohibit

---

[11] Cal Penal Code, § 220 (West 1988).   [12] Model Penal Code, § 1.02(1)(e).
[13] Model Penal Code, § 5.01(1)(c). The same is true of the Draft English Code, clause 49(1) requirement that a person 'does an act that is more than merely preparatory'.
[14] The same analysis may be made for conspiracy and solicitation. Otherwise acceptable and innocent conduct may become a violation of the prohibition against conspiracy or solicitation if accompanied by an intention to conspire with or to solicit another to commit a substantive violation of the rules of conduct. On the other hand, conspiracy and solicitation

homicide without having to refer to the actor's mental state.) Here, the culpability requirements play a role similar to the conduct and circumstance elements of offence definitions.[15] Typically, such a rule articulation function for culpability requirements appears in 'secondary prohibitions', such as the prohibitions against complicity and inchoate offences, and involves an intention to violate a 'primary prohibition'.[16]

Consider the kinds of culpability requirements that serve this rule articulation function. In the most typical attempt offence of incomplete conduct toward a substantive offence, a future conduct intention serves the rule articulation function. The examples above are of this sort: the actor's intention to engage in future conduct, the conduct necessary to burn the haystack or sexually to assault the hitchhiker, makes his otherwise acceptable conduct unacceptable.

may be distinguishable from attempt. One could argue that agreements with or solicitations of another to violate the rules of conduct should be prohibited, even if such is not done with the intention of causing a violation of the rules. Any agreement (even unilateral) to commit an offence and any solicitation of another to commit an offence may be seen as harmful conduct. The harmfulness of the conduct might not necessarily depend upon the actor's subjective state of mind. Therefore, the rules of conduct may appropriately prohibit all agreements and solicitations to commit an offence, no matter whether intentional or inadvertent. That is, the rules may require one to avoid conduct that even accidentally gives the appearance of such an agreement or solicitation. Recall Henry II's rhetorical question, 'Won't someone rid me of this troublesome priest?', which was mistaken as a directive to kill Thomas à Becket. While lack of intent may suggest a lack of blameworthiness, we nonetheless may wish to announce that even inadvertent agreements and solicitations should be avoided in the future. There is no analogously harmful 'unintended attempt', it might be argued.

[15] An offence containing a criminalization mental element commonly contains culpability mental elements as well. In attempted assault, for example, the intention to engage in the conduct constituting the assault is a criminalization mental element; it is necessary for a description of the prohibited conduct. The same offence contains a culpability mental state requiring at least recklessness as to the victim being a person. Under Model Penal Code section 211.1, for example, the assault must be to another human being. Model Penal Code § 2.02 (1) requires proof of culpability 'with respect to each material element of the offence'. That is, the definition of the prohibited conduct is complete even without this requirement; actors are warned not to attempt to assault persons even though this actor will not be punished for his assault because he was faultless or only negligent as to the victim being a person (e.g. he attempted to abort what he believed to be an inviable foetus or he set a hunting trap for what he thought was a dog stealing his chickens).

[16] The conduct and circumstances elements of specific offence definitions define the 'primary prohibitions' of the criminal law. But the criminal law prohibits not only conduct that violates primary prohibitions, but also conduct toward that end. These 'secondary prohibitions' proscribe assisting, attempting, soliciting, and conspiring to commit prohibited conduct. The secondary prohibitions thus enlarge the primary prohibitions: just as one may not violate a primary prohibition, neither may one assist or attempt or solicit or conspire to commit such violation. Secondary prohibitions typically are of two sorts: (1) doctrines expanding the primary prohibition by imputing to the actor the conduct of another, as in complicity, and (2) doctrines expanding the primary prohibition by prohibiting conduct short of the substantive harm or evil, as in the inchoate offences of attempt, conspiracy, solicitation, and possession. Secondary prohibitions sometimes are contained in general code provisions that incorporate by reference the offence definition containing the primary prohibition, as with general inchoate offences and complicity provisions. Secondary prohibitions also sometimes are contained in specific offences, such as special codified attempt provisions (i.e. assault with intent to rape, burglary, and possession of burglar's tools).

In other, perhaps more unusual, attempt cases, the actor has completed the conduct necessary for commission of the offence (but some other required objective element is missing). The actor pulls the trigger to a gun, which would kill another except that the gun is inoperative. The cases and literature call this a case of 'factual impossibility'. It was punished (as an attempt) at common law and is punished in all American jurisdictions.[17] It is not the actor's intention to engage in future conduct that makes the actor's conduct criminal, but rather his future result culpability, his culpability as to causing another's death.

In still other cases, an actor's otherwise acceptable conduct is criminalized by his present circumstance culpability. The actor buys sugar believing that it is an illegal drug. It is not his intention to perform some future conduct that makes his conduct unacceptable, nor his culpability as to causing a prohibited result (in the future). The conduct itself is entirely acceptable but is made criminal by virtue of the actor's belief that the powder is an illegal drug. Such a case was not punished at common law and is not punished in a minority of jurisdictions today. It is punished under the Model Penal Code and the majority of American codes.[18] The American literature refers to this as a case of 'legal impossibility'. In the English literature, that phrase often is reserved for cases of mistake as to whether specific conduct is an offence (such as taking pictures of a military installation or importing foreign currency); the sugar-believed-to-be-drugs case is labelled as another form of 'factual impossibility'. The common law distinction is useful in the following discussion, so let me follow the American terminology, which more easily signals it: factual impossibility v. legal impossibility (with the English 'legal imposibility' cases as a third category that might be called impossibility due to mistake as to the existence of the offence).

To summarize, the incomplete conduct ('substantial step') dealt with under subsection (1)(c) of the Model Penal Code's attempt provision[19] requires a future conduct intention. The completed conduct but missing result (factual impossibility) dealt with under subsection (1)(b) of the Code's provision requires a future result culpability. The completed conduct but missing circumstance (legal impossibility) dealt with under subsection (1)(a) requires a present circumstance culpability. Note that the functional distinctions identify and explain differences between the culpability requirements of the attempt categories used in modern codes. This is true even though the Code's provisions give no hint that identifiably different

---

[17] See e.g. Model Penal Code, § 5.01(1)(a); Ira Robbins, 'Attempting the Impossible: The Emerging Consensus' (1986) 23 *Harvard Journal on Legislation* 377 at 419–22; Robinson, *Criminal Law Defenses*, i, n. 3 above, at § 85; see also Draft English Code, ¶ 50(1). This form of attempt liability even more heavily relies upon an actor's subjective state of mind to justify liability, for the possibility of a successful violation exists only in the actor's mind.

[18] See Robinson, *Criminal Law Defenses*, i, n. 3 above, at § 85(c).

[19] Model Penal Code, § 5.01.

culpability requirements are called for. The functional distinctions also are useful in making the common law's notoriously difficult factual–legal impossibility distinction noticeably more workable. They also can better focus the debate over whether liability should be imposed in cases of legal impossibility, as it is imposed in cases of factual impossibility. In determining whether the two kinds of cases are meaningfully different, one can ask whether present circumstance culpability is for some reason less appropriate as grounds for criminalization than future result culpability.

While traditional analysis does not distinguish among culpability requirements other than to distinguish among the levels of culpability—purposely, knowingly, recklessly, and negligently—a functional analysis suggests different relevant groupings of 'mens rea' requirements—present conduct intention, present circumstance culpability, future result culpability, and future conduct intention. As the following three chapters will more fully illustrate, these functional distinctions can be useful in both applying and analysing current doctrine.

The functions that different kinds of culpability requirements perform are summarized in the table below:

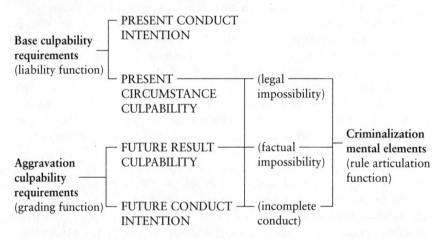

The presence of 'base culpability' suggests that an actor's conduct constituting a violation of the rules of conduct is blameworthy. Present circumstance culpability requirements do most of this work. 'Aggravation culpability' serves to aggravate an actor's liability over the minimum. Future result culpability and future conduct intention requirements perform most of this function.[20] Finally, on occasion, 'criminalization mental elements' are necessary

---

[20] Empirical evidence suggests that people perceive some sorts of culpability requirements as being more significant to grading than others. In a recent study, subjects were given a number of scenarios describing similar instances of property destruction where the actor's culpable state of mind is different in each scenario. In one set of scenarios, his culpability as to causing the damage (a future result intention) is varied among the set. In another set of scenarios, his culpability as to the property being property of another (a present circumstance culpability) is varied among the set. (In each instance, his culpability level as to all other ele-

to define the conduct to be prohibited by the criminal law. In incomplete conduct cases, future conduct intention performs this function. In completed conduct cases, the function is performed either by future result culpability ('factually impossible' attempts) or, in those jurisdictions that permit it, by present circumstance culpability ('legally impossible' attempts).

3. DEFENCES

One might initially be tempted to see defences as serving the liability function; the absence of any defence is a minimum condition for liability for a violation of the rules of conduct. That is, the presence of a defence bars liability for what otherwise would be a blameworthy violation. But, as with 'actus reus' and 'mens rea' requirements, not all defences serve the same function. Many do serve the liability function, but some serve a rule articulation function and a few even serve a grading function. Current doctrine's conceptualization of defences as relating to either irresponsibility, justification, and other, does not track the functional differences. Irresponsibility defences serve a liability function, but so do many 'other' defences and some aspects of modern codes' justification defences. Justification defences serve primarily a rule articulation function, but the common subjective formulation of justification defences, as discussed in Chapter 5, section C,[21] gives them a liability function as well. 'Other' defences include a mix of defences that include all functions.

The commonly used term 'defences' includes many very different sorts of doctrines and obscures important distinctions among them. As discussed in Chapter 5, a more useful conceptualization distinguishes absent element defences, offence modification defences, (objective) justifications, excuses, and non-exculpatory defences.[22] Let me structure the following discussion around these distinctions, for they correspond somewhat better to the differences in defence functions.

Absent element defences, which are simply instances of negating a required offence element, were discussed above in the context of 'actus reus' and 'mens rea'. For example, mistake that negates a base culpability requirement (required culpability as to a present circumstance or intention as to present conduct) serves a liability function. Mistake that negates an

ments is held constant.) Subjects varied the degree of liability that they assigned to the actor according to his level of culpability as to causing the damage. His liability did not vary so much when his culpability as to ownership of the property varied. The subjects apparently perceived the actor's level of culpability as to causing the damage as being much more important in determining the proper level of liability than the actor's level of culpability as to ownership: see Paul H. Robinson and John M. Darley, *Justice, Liability and Blame: Community Views and the Criminal Law* (Oxford, 1995), at 84–96. This suggests that subjects in fact perceive the future result culpability as performing a grading function, while the present circumstance culpability does not. Without further research, it is unclear whether this pattern holds for other present circumstance culpability and future result culpability requirements.

[21] This issue will be taken up again later in this Part. See Ch. 7, sect. C.

[22] See Paul H. Robinson, 'Criminal Law Defenses: A Systematic Analysis' (1982) 82 *Columbia LR* 199 (hereinafter 'Systematic Analysis'); 1&2 Robinson, *Criminal Law Defenses*, n. 3 above.

aggravation culpability requirement (required culpability as to a future result or future conduct) serves a grading function.

Many offence modification defences, which appear outside and independent of offence definitions, serve the rule articulation function. These doctrines, such as the consent defence, further modify or refine the conduct rules. While the rules prohibit conduct that risks causing bodily harm, an exception to the prohibition is admitted where the victim consents to a risk of minor injury or where the risk arises from participation in a lawful sporting event.[23] But other offence modifications perform a liability function. They serve to assure adequate blameworthiness for liability. The *de minimis* defence, for example, bars liability if the actor's conduct caused the harm or evil prohibited by the offence 'only to an extent too trivial to warrant the condemnation of conviction'.[24] Other defences, such as renunciation, similarly refine the normal blameworthiness requirements for inchoate offences.[25]

Justification defences (defined objectively) perform exclusively a rule articulation function. The law recognizes that in some instances a greater harm can be avoided or a greater good can be achieved by allowing a person to violate the law's prohibition. Burning another person's property would normally be a violation, but is tolerated (even encouraged) if the burning creates a firebreak to save a town. Striking another person without consent normally is a violation, but not if necessary to overcome resistance to a lawful arrest. To give a full account of what the law requires of persons, it must define the instances in which an actor is permitted, even encouraged, to do what would otherwise be deplored. In contrast, excuse defences—such as insanity, immaturity, involuntary intoxication, and duress—serve exclusively a liability function. They define the instances in which an actor is held blameless for a violation of the rules of conduct. Non-exculpatory defences serve none of the traditional functions of the criminal law, and are therefore disfavoured and narrowly limited.[26]

B. Rule Articulation, Liability Assignment, and Grading

Having pulled apart current law to show how different doctrines serve different functions, let me reassemble it along the lines of the three basic functions. The doctrines that serve the rule articulation, liability, and grading functions are summarized in the following chart:

---

[23] See e.g. Model Penal Code, § 2.11.   [24] Model Penal Code, § 2.12(2).

[25] Complete and voluntary renunciation, as defined in modern codes, see e.g. Model Penal Code, § 5.01(4), undercuts an actor's blameworthiness, it may be argued, by suggesting that the actor's earlier apparent intention to commit the offence was not in fact sufficiently resolute to warrant condemnation.

[26] For a general discussion, see Robinson, 'Systematic Analysis' n. 22 above, at 229–32.

Rule Articulation Function	Liability Function	Grading Function
Violation Doctrines	**Culpability Doctrines**	
Primary Violations:	Base culpability requirements: primarily present circumstance culpability	Result elements of offence definitions
Conduct and circumstance elements of offense definitions		Causation requirements
Legal duty requirements for omission liability; possession of contraband prohibition in possession offences	Offence modification defences relating to criminalization mental elements, such as renunciation defence, or to base culpability requirements	Aggravation culpability requirements: typically limited to future result culpability and future conduct intention
Offence modification defences relating to conduct or circumstance offence elements, such as consent	Doctrines imputing culpability requirements, such as doctrines of voluntary intoxication and substituted mental elements	Doctrines imputing aggravated culpability, such as felony murder
Secondary Violations:		Miscellaneous offence mitigations and aggravations
Conduct toward a violation, such as attempt	De minimis defence, setting minimum harm or evil requirements	
Assisting another in a violation	**Excuse Doctrines**	
Criminalization mental elements	Voluntariness requirement, in commission offences	
Justification Doctrines	Physical capacity requirement, in omission offenses	
Justification defences	Requirement of knowledge of possession for a sufficient time to terminate the same, in possession	
	Excuse defences	

Traditionally thought of as:

 = actus reus ░░░ = mens rea ▓▓▓ = defences

In determining which doctrines serve which function, the previous discussion has grouped the doctrines as if a doctrine served exclusively one function or another. In fact, the interrelation of the doctrines is more complex than this. A complete description of the minimum requirements for liability requires not only reference to the doctrines serving the liability function but also to the doctrines serving the rule articulation function. In other words, one prerequisite of liability is violation of the rules of conduct, as described by the doctrines serving the rule articulation function. Similarly, the criminal law's grading function cannot be performed by reference to the doctrines of grading alone. The doctrines of liability define the minimum grade in each instance. The doctrinal functions—ordered as rule articulation, liability, and grading—may best be thought of as having a cumulative relation: the doctrines serving a function include those serving previous functions. Their interrelation might be depicted as:

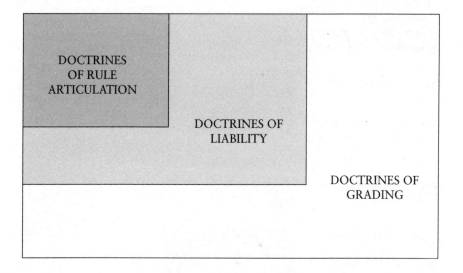

Comparison of this conceptualization to the current law conceptualization diagramed in Chapter 1 yields the following:

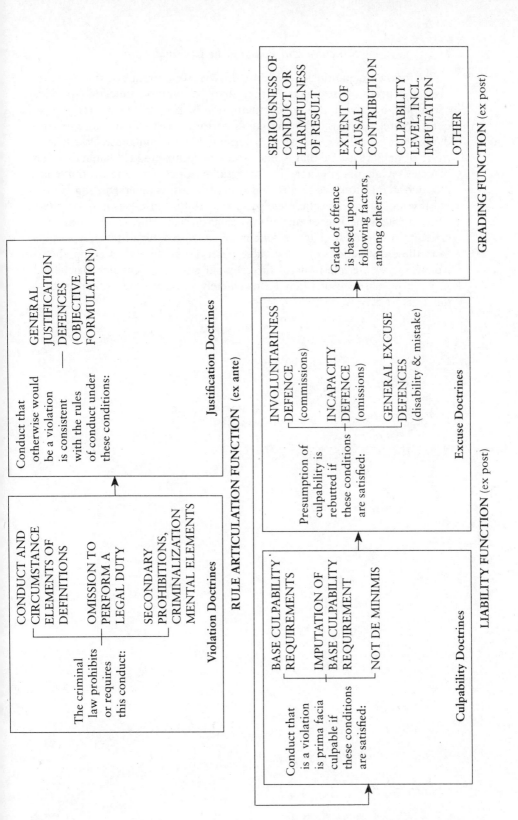

CONDUCT AND
CIRCUMSTANCE
ELEMENTS OF
DEFINITIONS

OMISSION TO
PERFORM A
LEGAL DUTY

SECONDARY
PROHIBITIONS,
CRIMINALIZATION
MENTAL ELEMENTS

The criminal
law prohibits
or requires
this conduct:

Violation Doctrines

Conduct that
otherwise would
be a violation
is consistent
with the rules
of conduct under
these conditions:

GENERAL
JUSTIFICATION
DEFENCES
(OBJECTIVE
FORMULATION)

Justification Doctrines

RULE ARTICULATION FUNCTION (ex ante)

BASE CULPABILITY
REQUIREMENTS

IMPUTATION OF
BASE CULPABILITY
REQUIREMENT

NOT DE MINIMIS

Conduct that
is a violation
is prima facia
culpable if
these conditions
are satisfied:

Culpability Doctrines

INVOLUNTARINESS
DEFENCE
(commissions)

INCAPACITY
DEFENCE
(omissions)

GENERAL EXCUSE
DEFENCES
(disability & mistake)

Presumption of
culpability is
rebutted if
these conditions
are satisfied:

Excuse Doctrines

LIABILITY FUNCTION (ex post)

SERIOUSNESS OF
CONDUCT OR
HARMFULNESS
OF RESULT

EXTENT OF
CAUSAL
CONTRIBUTION

CULPABILITY
LEVEL, INCL.
IMPUTATION

OTHER

Grade of offence
is based upon
following factors,
among others:

GRADING FUNCTION (ex post)

The following questions arise: does this view of current doctrine—grouping the aspects of the doctrine that share a common function—provide useful insights? Does this conceptualization help us to answer the central questions regarding the criminal law's performance? Do the rules of conduct suffice to tell persons what the criminal law commands? Do the doctrines of liability assure that blameworthy violators are held liable and that blameless violators are not? Do the grading doctrines capture our common moral intuitions as to how much punishment is deserved for a blameworthy violation? The three chapters that follow offer insights on these issues through the lens of the rule articulation-liability-grading prism. I do not suggest that these chapters contain an exhaustive list of possible insights from these distinctions nor that these observations provide a comprehensive answer to the questions of the criminal law's performance articulated above. The observations that follow merely illustrate the usefulness of a functional analysis.

7

The Rules of Conduct

What does the criminal law command? It is not too much to ask of a society that it tell its people in a form they can understand what the criminal law expects of them. Indeed, our condemnation and punishment of criminals, as distinguished from civil violators, rests upon an assumption that a criminal violation entails some consciousness of wrongdoing or at least a gross deviation from a clearly defined standard of lawful conduct. How can this assumption be sustained if the commands of the law are unclear? How can we condemn and punish violations of the rules of lawful conduct if the rules are not and cannot reasonably be known by the general public? One also may wonder how effective the criminal law can be in deterring criminal conduct if the law's prohibitions are unclear. The criminal law has a great interest in effectively communicating the rules of conduct. This is, in part, expressed by the law's commitment to the 'legality principle' or 'rule of law'.

A. OBSCURING RULES OF CONDUCT WITH AN OVERLAY OF LIABILITY AND GRADING RULES

Do current criminal codes tell citizens the commands of the criminal law? What would it take to construct a rough approximation of the rules of conduct from a modern criminal code? One could begin by reading the offence definitions but then most of the culpability requirements would have to be removed. Of course, some culpability requirements must be retained, those that serve the rule articulation function, such as the future conduct intention in attempt, as Chapter 6 discusses. And all result elements must be excluded. Result offences, without the results, are only risk-creation offences, many of which already exist in the code. Manslaughter without death is reckless endangerment. In other words, some entire offences, such as manslaughter, exist not to serve a rule articulation purpose but only to serve a grading purpose. These 'grading offences' also must be excluded in an approximation of the rules of conduct. Also excluded are all of the doctrines of aggravation, mitigation, and grading, noted in Chapter 6. Some defences also must be excluded, notably excuses and non-exculpatory defences, while others are kept, such as justification defences.

(Although, as we shall see, only some provisions or parts of provisions relating to justification bear on the rules of conduct.) Another way of visualizing the difference between the rules of conduct and current criminal codes is to compare the chart of current conceptualization, at the beginning of Chapter 1, to the first column of the functional analysis summary, at the beginning of Chapter 6.

One may wonder whether it is possible for anyone other than a criminal law scholar to derive even a rough approximation of the criminal law's rules of conduct from a modern criminal code. The task is all the more difficult with the less systematic older codes that codify frequently arcane common law doctrine. Certainly, a statement of the rules of conduct will look substantially different from a code's collection of specific offence definitions. The undifferentiated commixture of rules of conduct, liability, and grading in a single code introduces significant complexity that obscures the rules of conduct. It seems unrealistic to expect the average person to read, understand, and govern his or her conduct by the rules of conduct embedded in any current criminal code.

In reality, the average person is left to ascertain the law's commands from his or her own moral intuitions about what ought to be prohibited, by word of mouth, or from press reports of criminal case dispositions. But each of these methods of communicating rules of conduct has serious shortcomings, many of which again are created or exacerbated by present law's commixture of doctrines serving different functions.

Press reports of criminal case dispositions are necessarily *ad hoc* and frequently of questionable accuracy. Some criminal law teachers and lawyers would suggest that the press gets the liability rules wrong more often than it gets them right (sometimes for good reasons discussed below). Word of mouth can be worse; like the child's 'telephone' game, every telling can introduce a slight variation in the story. And the original source of word-of-mouth information frequently is a press report. More on press accounts and word-of-mouth in the next section.

A community's shared intuitive notions provide some guidance for the most serious offences. Members of every culture probably understand that killing another is wrong. But even here, most cultures recognize exceptions, and the nature of these exceptions may not be quite so clear. (Can you kill a thief if that is the only way you can stop his persistent theft of the garden vegetables that you need to feed your family?) But especially in a multi-cultural society such as ours, which is predicted to grow even more diverse in the future, it is dangerous to rely too heavily upon shared intuitive understandings as the source of society's conduct rules. While one might expect some shared notions of culpability and blame, which necessarily are matters of intuitive judgement, it is less clear that a citizen can reasonably be expected to intuit her tax obligation or the contours of criminally fraudulent conduct. Shared notions of desert may govern the liability and grading functions, but utilitarian concerns for protecting societal interests may heavily influence the definition of prohibitions and duties. Further, the existence of an intuitive understanding of conduct rules no doubt depends in some part on confirmation and reinforcement of such rules by existing moral authority, which in many societies is the criminal law as much or more than any other institution.

B. Confusing Conduct Rules and Liability Judgements: Ambiguous Acquittals

The difficulties inherent in an informal and *ad hoc* dissemination process are made all the more severe by the tendency of current doctrine to obscure the meaning of publicly-reported dispositions. Reports of criminal case dispositions, in the press or by word of mouth or by combination, are doomed to be confused or inaccurate because our public adjudication system frequently fails to give adequate information to determine the meaning of a disposition for the rules of conduct. A verdict of 'not guilty' may mean either (1) that the actor's conduct in the case *did not* violate the rules of conduct, or (2) that the actor's conduct *did* violate the rules of conduct but he does not have the minimum blameworthiness required to be held criminally liable for the violation. Thus, any acquittal may be taken either to approve or to disapprove the actor's conduct.

The acquittal of the officers who beat Rodney King illustrates the point. Many people found the acquittal outrageous because it seemed to condone the use of excessive and unnecessary force. Recall the quotes from laypersons critical of the acquittal, set out in Chapter 5, section C.6.2.[1] But the issues at trial went beyond the propriety of the conduct; the trial also focused on the blameworthiness of the officers, including an examination of the danger that the officers felt, the confusion and uncertainty of the situation from the officers' perspective, the emotion generated by the preceding high-speed chase, and the training that the officers had for dealing with such a situation. Recall Chapter 5's quotations from people equally confident in their support of the acquittals.[2]

The conflict in perspectives is created in part because the simple verdict of 'not guilty' fails to tell the whole story in a most important respect. The jurors voted for it presumably because they did not think the *officers* were sufficiently blameworthy to merit criminal conviction. Many persons hearing the verdict took it as approval of the officers' *conduct*. That is, the 'not guilty' verdict was taken by some as condoning the conduct, when it might have been reached by the jury upon finding inadequate

---

[1] See Ch. 5, text accompanying notes 139–42.
[2] See Ch. 5, text accompanying notes 136–8.

blameworthiness, a subjective assessment, for what might well have been objectively excessive conduct.

What is needed here is a verdict system that distinguishes 'no violation' acquittals from 'blameless violation' acquittals. If one were to follow the form of the 'not guilty by reason of insanity' verdict, one might ask a jury to return a verdict of 'no violation' (or just 'not guilty') where the rules of conduct have not been violated, and a verdict of 'not guilty by reason of mistake [or excuse]'[3] where the rules of conduct have been violated but where the violation is not blameworthy. (Chapter 11, section E, discusses the issue further and Appendix B contains a suggested verdict system in Article 41.)

If the Rodney King jury had returned the latter verdict, it might have better assured other citizens that the conduct they saw on tape was disapproved, not condoned. It might also have made it clearer to police officers that they are not authorized to engage in such conduct under similar circumstances in the future. But, as the next section illustrates, the success of such a verdict system depends upon the doctrine in fact distinguishing between the rule articulation issue and the liability issue. In the Rodney King case, that means that the doctrine must put distinct questions to the jury: (1) was the conduct a violation? (2) if so, was the violation blameworthy? As we shall see, the doctrine governing the use of force in law enforcement, and indeed all justification defences, mixes these questions.

Instead of clarifying and reinforcing the rules of acceptable conduct in people's minds, the current verdict system often undercuts and confuses an understanding of the rules. The tendency of current dispositions to confuse rather than educate may explain why we are not rushing off to insist on wider dissemination of such dispositions or to insist on more careful reporting of them. The natural play in press and word-of-mouth accounts may well have a corrective effect, adding insights about what the disposition means for the rules of conduct, insights that the verdict itself fails to provide.

C. Mixing Rule Articulation and Liability Functions by Defining 'Justified' Conduct Subjectively: The Failure to Define the Justified Conduct Rules

The rules of conduct are obscured not only by the overlay of liability and grading doctrines, as section A of this Chapter discusses, but also by mixing functions in the formulation of a single doctrinal provision. An example with broad effect is the tendency of current codes, following the lead of the Model Penal Code, to obscure the rule articulation doctrines

---

[3] The jury might be asked to give the particular grounds of excuse—'not guilty by reason of duress' or 'not guilty by reason of mistake as to a justification'—but there seems little benefit as it requires that the jurors come to agreement on the ground of exculpation.

of justification by combining them inseparably with doctrines of liability. (The reader will see that the issue here is the same issue discussed in Chapter 5, section C.3, regarding the dispute over whether the theory of justification defences should look to the nature of the *deed* or the nature of the actor's *reasons* for the deed.)

Was the use of force shown on the ghastly videotape of Rodney King being beaten, justifiable? The justification provision for use of force in law enforcement in most jurisdictions is defined subjectively: '[T]he use of force upon or toward the person of another *is justifiable when* the actor is making or assisting in making an arrest and *the actor believes* that such force is immediately necessary to effect a lawful arrest'.[4] This same form is used for most justification defences. Self defence commonly is defined to provide: '[T]he use of force upon or toward the person of another *is justifiable when the actor believes* that such force is immediately necessary for the purpose of protecting himself against the use of unlawful force by such other person on the present occasion'.[5] Thus, according to the Code, King's beating is justifiable as long as the officers 'believed' at that moment that it was necessary for the arrest, no matter if their belief was wrong.

It is this claim that the conduct was 'justified' that outraged many in the acquittal of the officers. For, as the previous section illustrated, many people reasonably take a finding of 'justification' to mean that the conduct was proper and is condoned. In fact, the finding may reflect the opposite conclusion, that the conduct is disapproved. It is 'justified' only in the sense that, when viewed from the actor's unique and possibly mistaken perspective, the actor is not blameworthy. This crucial ambiguity ensures confusion over the meaning of an acquittal for the rules of conduct to occur in most justification cases.

The Model Penal Code drafters are not ignorant of the distinction between acceptable and unacceptable conduct. In a somewhat obscure provision (the definition of 'unlawful force'), the Code refers to 'privileged' conduct, which cannot lawfully be resisted (it is not 'unlawful force' and therefore does not trigger a right to use defensive force).[6] Unprivileged conduct can lawfully be resisted. But the Code includes both privileged and unprivileged conduct within 'justifiable' conduct. An actor's conduct is 'justifiable' if it is within the rules of conduct ('privileged') or if it violates the rules of conduct under the actual facts (unprivileged) but the actor mistakenly believes that it is justified.[7] Because of this formulation

[4] Model Penal Code, § 3.07(1).
[5] Model Penal Code, § 3.04(1). See, similarly, Draft English Code, ¶ 44(1).
[6] Model Penal Code, § 3.11(1) (definition of 'unlawful force' as used in justification defences). The comparable Draft English Code provision, in cl. 44(3), is an improvement in some respects over the Model Penal Code approach. Recall the discussion in Ch. 5, at text accompanying section C.5, n. 122.
[7] In the unprivileged justification case, the actor may receive a complete defence, despite his mistake, if his mistake is reasonable; if his mistake is honest but unreasonable, many jurisdictions provide a mitigation in liability: see e.g. Model Penal Code, § 3.09(2).

of justification defences, a jury is never asked to determine whether the conduct is objectively proper. The jury need only determine whether the actor's conduct was *either* in fact proper, or improper but he believed that it was proper. (Note that the members of the jury need not even agree among themselves as to which of these two alternatives is true. Thus, even the members of the jury, then, may not be able to clarify an ambiguous acquittal.) The ultimate effect of this is that, even if a more refined verdict system were in place, the Code's subjective formulation of justification defences leaves it unclear whether a jury should select a no-violation or a blameless-violation verdict.

To be clear, an excuse, or mitigation, for mistaken (unprivileged) justification is entirely appropriate, even necessary, as a means of imposing liability and punishment that matches the actor's blameworthiness. The difficulty with subjectively defined justifications is not that they provide such a defence but that they fail to distinguish this excuse from liability from a defence arising from objectively justified ('privileged') conduct. The failure can mislead people into thinking that conduct in violation of the rules of conduct is acceptable. Such subjective formulations of justification defences would better be replaced with objective formulations, which accurately state the rule of conduct, and with separate provisions that give an excuse or mitigation for a mistake as to a justification.[8] A defence under the objective justification provision gives a no-violation acquittal; a defence under the mistaken justification excuse gives a blameless-violation acquittal.

D. Mixing Conduct Rules of Risk-Creation with Liability Judgements of Risk-taking: The Failure to Define Criminal Risks

Another instance in which current doctrine combines and thereby confuses a rule articulation issue with a liability issue occurs in defining what constitutes a criminal risk. Because danger may be created in an infinite number of ways and in an infinite number of situations, the prohibition must use risk as the defining concept; no specific set of acts and circumstances adequately defines the prohibited conduct.

Admittedly, the task of describing the risks that the criminal law prohibits is a formidable one. It is unwise to say simply: 'No person shall engage in conduct that may cause injury to another person or damage to another's property'. Some risks, even risks of personal injury to other persons, are tolerated by the criminal law. Chapter 6 notes at least three

---

[8] For a rare example of a code that segregates the issues of justification and mistake as to a justification, by defining justifications objectively and providing a separate excuse provision, see ND Cent. Code, §§ 12.1–05–03, –04, –07, –08, –12.

doctrines that tolerate risks. A victim's consent to a non-serious risk of injury is a defence. Creating a risk that avoids a greater risk typically gives rise to a justification defence. A prosecution for creating a trivial risk is subject to dismissal under the *de minimis* infraction defence. But consensual, justified, and trivial risks described by these doctrines represent only a minority of the tolerated-risk situations. In nearly every instance of potential harm, the criminal law prohibits and punishes only the creation of risks of a certain probability and severity of harm under certain circumstances. If you decide to build a factory, drive to the theatre, or open your umbrella, you necessarily create risks to others that did not previously exist. Part of the criminal law's rule articulation function is to tell people beforehand which risks—what probability of how serious a harm under what circumstances—must be avoided. Yet, as we shall see, the doctrine fails to give even a clear general formula by which one can determine which risks are criminal.

The persons put at risk by your factory-building, driving, or umbrella-opening have not consented to such risks, in the way that the consent defence of the criminal code would require.[9] Nor is the creation of such risks justified, in the way that the justification defences of the criminal code require.[10] The *de minimis* defence gives only a most general standard for determining whether a violation is *de minimis*: 'too trivial to warrant the condemnation of conviction';[11] it provides little help in distinguishing criminal from non-criminal risks.[12] As we shall see, however, the reasons the law tolerates some risks is similar in some respects to why the law recognizes the consent, justification, and *de minimis* defences.

To determine whether creation of a risk is proper or improper, whether its creation is a violation of the rules of conduct, we need to know, among other things, the probability of the harm and the seriousness of the harm risked. Negligible risk of even serious harm is tolerated as the price we all pay to be part of a modern, industrialized society. We have all, in a sense, consented to such risks by choosing to remain in society knowing that such risks exist and are tolerated. Substantial risk of minor harm is tolerated for similar reasons. It is only significant risk of significant harm that is criminalized, using a sliding scale between the two factors: the lower

---

[9] Consent is a defence if it 'negatives an element of the offense or precludes the infliction of the harm or evil sought to be prevented by the law defining the offense': Model Penal Code, § 2.11(1).

[10] The lesser evils defence, the only justification that may be applicable, requires that the offence avoid a greater harm or evil. It does not authorize violations in order to create a *benefit*, such as financial profit from a factory or the entertainment from attending the theatre. Nor is the harm of your getting wet likely to be sufficient to justify conduct that is otherwise criminal. As the text discusses, however, the lesser evil defence's normative valuation of the actor's conduct has similarities to the assessment made in the definition of a criminal risk. [11] Model Penal Code, § 2.12(2).

[12] For example, it fails to give the most basic, and most obvious, guidance of directing attention to the extent of the harm risked and the probability of the harm occurring.

the probability, the greater the potential injury must be to reach the point of criminalization.

In addition to the extent of the risk, the societal benefits of the risk also are relevant to whether it is tolerated. In an analysis analogous to justi-fication defences, we tolerate a greater risk (probability of harm) if the effect of the risk is sufficiently desirable. The risks created by demolish-ing an old building may be justified but not if only in order to entertain the members of an explosives club. Whether any risk is justified by its purpose is a function of the relative values that society gives to the conflict-ing interests. Thus, each assessment of risk-creation requires an actor not only to make a complex judgement of probability and potential harm but also to balance competing community interests. An actor may find some guidance in whether such a risk in such circumstances has been tolerated in the past.[13]

Modern codes are not insensitive to the need to define the risks that are prohibited by the criminal law. The Model Penal Code, for example, includes in its definition of culpable risk-taking ('recklessness' and 'negli-gence') the following:

> The risk must be *of such a nature and degree that, considering the nature and purpose of the actor's conduct* and the circumstances know to him, [its disregard/ the actor's failure to perceive it] involves a gross deviation from *the standard of [conduct/care] that a [law-abiding/reasonable] person* would observe in the actor's situation.[14]

The nature and degree of the risk and the purpose for which it is under-taken are all taken into consideration. Further, these factors must be assessed in light of the community's standard of conduct.

But while the quoted provision accurately identifies the major factors that define criminal risk, it serves primarily to obscure the definition. To start, the provision quoted above is not a definition of what constitutes *crim-inal risk-creation*. Rather, it is a definition of *culpable risk-taking*. The dis-tinction is important. The definition above does not define what risks are criminal; it does not define the real-world risk-creation that is prohibited. Instead, it defines when an actor is culpable for taking a risk; it defines

---

[13] But assumed knowledge of past 'accepted' practice is a weak reed on which to hang the notice called for by the legality principle. Further, to define an aspect of the rules of con-duct by referring to 'the standard of conduct [of] the [law-abiding/reasonable] person' is slightly circular. No doubt the drafters assume that some shared understanding of 'accepted' risks exists within the community. They may be right about this, but the law's reliance upon such an intuitive standard certainly ought to make us feel uncomfortable about whether this aspect of the rules of conduct adequately performs the notice function that the legality prin-ciple demands. On the other hand, no obvious alternative mechanism has as yet presented itself. The definition of criminal risk in a given instance is a complex matter that cannot (yet) be reduced to a more precise form. An actor's obligation under the rules of conduct is to try to discern 'the standard of conduct [of] the [law-abiding/reasonable] person' and to avoid creating risks that, in light of this standard and nature, degree, and purpose of the risk, are criminal.   [14] Model Penal Code, § 2.02(2)(c)&(d) (emphasis added).

the mental risk-taking as to the existence of a circumstance or as to caus-ing a result that makes the conduct blameworthy. The former issue—real world risk-creation—presents a rules of conduct issue: what is the kind and degree of risk of harm that an actor is prohibited from creating?[15] The latter issue—mental risk-taking—presents a liability issue: when is an actor to be held blameworthy for 'taking a risk' that his conduct violates the rules of conduct? The distinction is between creating a risk of caus-ing a harm and taking a risk of violating a rule.[16] The Code defines what risk-taking is culpable but does not define what constitutes a criminal risk.

As a doctrine of liability, the provision does well. It is properly sensit-ive to the subtle difficulties in assessing whether the actor's risk-taking is culpable. The decision-makers must take account of 'the circumstances known to [the actor]' and place the law-abiding/reasonable person 'in the actor's situation'. That latter requirement in particular permits courts great latitude to individualize the objective standard in judging the actor's culp-ability.[17] Finally, the provision permits liability only if the actor's conduct is a 'gross deviation' from the standard of conduct of the law-abiding/reasonable person. The 'gross deviation' standard is designed to give actors some, albeit vague, margin of error in adhering to the 'standard of con-duct of the [law-abiding/reasonable] person'. Together, these requirements are meant to assure, as the doctrines of liability are obliged to do, that an actor is held criminally liable for an offence only if he reasonably could be expected to have avoided the violation. But by formulating the definitions to perform the liability function, the code fails in its rule articulation function.

By mixing the two functions, the Code invites a similar confusion in its readers. The following passage by a thoughtful and respected scholar is typical of descriptions found throughout the literature:

[15] There is no comparable risk-creation for violations not involving a prohibited result. Where the prohibition is defined only in terms of conduct in certain circumstances, the cir-cumstance either exists or it does not. One does not *create* a risk of a circumstance; one can only *take* a risk that a circumstance exists. That is, one can act in disregard (or ignorance) of such a risk of the existence of the circumstance. As the text notes, determining whether an actor has engaged in such mental risk-taking is part of the liability function.

[16] See Paul H. Robinson, 'Rules of Conduct and Principles of Adjudication' (1990) 57 *University of Chicago LR* 729 at 745–9 (hereinafter 'Rules of Conduct').

[17] The commentary makes clear that 'in the actor's situation' may be interpreted as broadly as the court chooses. It may include not only the objective circumstances of the actor's 'situ-ation' but also characteristics of the actor.

> 'The standard for ultimate judgement invites consideration of the "care that a reas-onable person would observe in the actor's situation". There is an inevitable ambigu-ity in "situation". If the actor were blind or if he had just suffered a blow or experienced a heart attack, these would certainly be facts to be considered in a judgement involving criminal liability, as they would be under traditional law. But the heredity, intelligence or temperament of the actor would not be held material in judging negligence, and could not be without depriving the criterion of all its objectivity. The Code is not intended to displace discriminations of this kind, but rather to leave the issue to the courts.'

Model Penal Code, § 2.02, comment 4 at 242 (1985). In this respect, the drafters stray somewhat from the spirit of the legality principle.

Criminal liability is frequently predicated on negligence, which is *conduct that creates an unreasonable risk of harm* to an interest protected by the criminal law (negligence as to result), *or an unreasonable though sincere belief* that one's conduct is not conduct which, under another description, is proscribed by the criminal law (negligence as to conduct). Negligent homicide is an example of a crime based on negligence as to result—i.e. *the creation of an unreasonable risk of death* that in fact eventuates in a death. Bigamy is an example of a crime that can be based on negligence as to conduct, as (for example) in those cases where one *unreasonably* believes in the validity of a prior divorce. The Model Penal Code's definition of criminal negligence is representative: [quotation of Model Penal Code section 2.02(2)(d)].[18]

Note the interchange of risk-creation and risk-taking. Both are seen as a form of the single concept of 'negligence', rather than as applications of the two very distinct functions of rule articulation and liability assessment. If 'negligence' is meant to refer to the liability function of assessing whether a violation is sufficiently culpable, then analogous culpability requirements exist for both circumstance elements and *result elements*, bigamy and *negligent homicide*. Just as the prosecution must show that the bigamist's belief in the validity of the prior divorce was unreasonable, so too must it establish that the killer's failure to perceive the criminal risk of causing death was unreasonable. The difference between risk-creation and risk-taking is not related to the difference between result elements and circumstance elements, as the quoted passage suggests, but rather is the difference between the rule articulation function—defining the risks prohibited by the criminal law—and the liability function—defining the culpability that must accompany a violation before liability may be imposed.

Even if courts are able to dissect the provision above, to pull from it the factors and analysis necessary to assess whether a risk is prohibited—the nature, degree, and purpose of the risk, and the community's balance of these as manifested in the standard of conduct of the law-abiding/reasonable person—the Code fails in its function of defining the risks that are criminal. The quoted provision is contained in the definition of 'recklessly' and 'negligently'. Thus, the dissection exercise is available only where the offences criminalizing risk-creation use the terms 'recklessly' or 'negligently'. This is sometimes the case, as in homicide.[19] But more frequently the Code defines risk-creation offences as prohibiting a 'substantial risk' or just a 'risk' or a 'danger' of a particular harm, using different phrases in

---

[18] Lawrence Alexander, 'Reconsidering the Relationship Among Voluntary Acts, Strict Liability, and Negligence in Criminal Law', in E. Paul, F. Miller, Jr., and J. Paul (eds.), *Crime, Culpability, and Remedy* (Oxford, 1990), 88–9 (emphasis added).

[19] A person is guilty of manslaughter 'if he *recklessly causes* the death of another human being': Model Penal Code, §§ 210.1(1) & 210.3(1)(a). 'A person is guilty of criminal mischief if he . . . *recklessly causes* another to suffer pecuniary loss': Model Penal Code, § 220.3(1)(c).

different contexts.[20] The effect of this is to exclude from the analysis of whether the actor has created a criminal risk, the consideration of most of the factors that the Code drafters themselves seem to agree are relevant: the nature, degree, and purpose of the risk, and the community's balance of these as manifested in the standard of conduct of the law-abiding/ reasonable person. 'Risk' might be taken to mean any risk; 'substantial risk' might be taken to focus only on the degree of the risk (or, possibly, its nature). Nothing in the language suggests the need to assess the purpose of the risk-creation or the balance of competing interests.

The effect of the Code's failure to provide guidance in defining criminal risks might seem to be minimized by the tendency of the Code to prohibit the most egregious risk-creation through offences that require actual results, such as homicide offences. That is, if an actual result is required, it might be argued, we avoid the problem of defining the mere risk of the harm that is criminal. But as most thoughtful readers have already discerned, requiring that the actual result has occurred does not avoid the need to determine whether the risk was criminal.[21] By defining reckless homicide (manslaughter) to require a death, for example, one does not avoid the need to determine whether the actor's conduct in causing that death created a risk that was criminal. An actor might have caused the death through the creation of a risk that itself is non-criminal. To punish such an actor for manslaughter is to fail to distinguish him from the actor who causes a death by creating a risk that is itself criminal. This problem is the subject of Chapter 9, section A.

The need for clear guidelines in assessing the criminality of the risk is made all the more important by the human tendency to exaggerate the degree of a risk when it comes to fruition. The empirical literature reports the common phenomenon of persons significantly overestimating the extent of a risk if the risked result occurs.[22] This phenomenon may lead to

---

[20] For example, the Code prohibits creation of a 'substantial risk' of causing death (in section 211.1(2)(a), aggravated assault; 'serious bodily harm' is defined in section 210.0(3)), creation of a 'danger' of death or a 'substantial risk' of death (in section 211.2, reckless endangerment), creation of a 'substantial risk' of loss of entrusted property (in section 224.13), and creation of a 'danger' of damage or destruction of a building (in section 220.1(2)(b), reckless burning or exploding). The Code prohibits the 'risk' of causing terror or serious public inconvenience (in section 211.3, terroristic threats). Also prohibited are a 'risk' of causing a 'substantial risk' of death, through restraint (in section 212.2(a), felonious restraint) and a 'risk' of causing a catastrophe (in section 220.2(2), risking catastrophe).

[21] The use of result offences to punish criminal risk-creation not only does not avoid the need to define criminal risk but also creates several other special problems of its own. For example, the resulting array of overlapping offences may define the prohibited risk differently. In some instances of overlap between result and risk-creation offences, the conduct creating a risk is prohibited and punished only if the harm comes about, but whether the harm will occur is a fact that the actor cannot know at the time he engages in the conduct: see Robinson, 'Rules of Conduct', n. 16 above, at 748–9.

[22] Baruch Fischoff, 'Hindsight Does Not Equal Foresight: The Effect of Outcome Knowledge on Judgment Under Uncertainty' (1975) 1 *Journal of Experimental Psychology* 288 at 298.

an assessment of liability for creating a criminal risk when in reality the risk created was not criminal. A death can occur even where the risk created is sufficiently low as to be non-criminal. Yet, without a definition of criminal risk, how can this determination be made?[23]

A better approach is to give independent definitions of criminal risk and of culpable risk-taking. Risk-creation offences, then, are properly defined to prohibit creation of a 'criminal risk' of the specific harm, incorporating by reference the general formula. This replaces the current practice of defining these offences by using either undefined terms such as 'risk' or 'substantial risk' or by using culpability terms that drop the requirement that the prohibited risk actually be created.

Using the language of the Model Penal Code, one can construct the definition of criminal risk given below:

> An actor creates a 'criminal risk' of a result or 'criminally risks' a result when he creates a substantial and unjustified risk that the result will occur. A risk is substantial and unjustified if, given its nature, degree, and circumstances, its creation is a gross deviation from the standard of conduct of a law-abiding person.

One can construct culpability definitions, again using Model Penal Code language, as follows (remember that the culpable risk-taking terms must be defined with respect to both result and circumstance elements):

> A person acts 'recklessly' with respect to an element of an offence when he consciously disregards a risk that the circumstance exists or that his conduct will cause the result, as the case may be. [Same second sentence as in Code.]
>
> A person acts 'negligently' with respect to an element of an offence when he should be aware of a risk that the circumstance exists or that his conduct will cause the result, as the case may be. [Same second sentence as in Code.[24]]

The only real change to the Code's current culpability definitions is deletion of the phrase 'substantial and unjustified' modifying the term 'risk' in the first sentence of each definition. The substantiality and justifiability of the risk are matters of concern in defining criminal risk-creation, but they add nothing to the definition of culpable risk-taking that is not already covered by the culpability definitions' call, in the second sentence, to judge the blameworthiness of the actor's disregard or unawareness of the risk:

> The risk must be of such a nature and degree that, considering the nature and purpose of the actor's conduct and the circumstances known to him, [its disregard/ the actor's failure to perceive it] involves a gross deviation from the standard of

---

[23] Nor is it enough, as discussed above, that the definition of culpable risk-taking tells us whether the actor's risk-taking was culpable. Liability for manslaughter is appropriate only if the actor was culpable and the risk created in fact is prohibited. At very least, the doctrine should distinguish reckless homicide convictions where the risk created is criminal from those where it is not. The current doctrine's failure to do this is examined more closely in Ch. 9, sect. A.   [24] See quotation in text at next note.

[conduct/care] that a [law-abiding/reasonable] person would observe in the actor's situation.[25]

Presumably, juries will more easily find 'a gross deviation' where the risk is more 'substantial' or more 'unjustified'.

To illustrate the use of these terms, manslaughter can be defined as follows: 'An actor commits manslaughter if, with recklessness as to causing the death of another human being, he creates a criminal risk of such death and death results.' Of course, one can avoid such stilted definitions by having a general principle that liability for a substantive offence of risk-creation (as opposed to an inchoate offence) requires proof that the criminal risk in fact was created. With such a principle, which courts could supply even in the absence of a statutory provision, and a definition of a criminal risk, one can define manslaughter as simply 'recklessly causing the death of another human being'.

To conclude, my claim here is not that the Model Penal Code drafters are insensitive to factors that are important to the definition of criminal risk-creation or to the definition of culpable risk-taking. That is, there seems nothing better that one can do in giving guidance on these issues than to give general formulae. My claim here is that, by failing to see that the issues of risk-creation and risk-taking are distinct, the general formula that the Code gives is less likely to be effective in performing either task. (The discussion here focuses on the difficulties that such mixture of function creates for the rule articulation function, in failing to provide a definition of criminal risk. The difficulties that this mixture creates for the grading function, in using culpability terms to define prohibited risks, are examined in Chapter 9, section A.)

E. Conclusion

Does the criminal law tell people what the law commands of them? For a society that complains of the breakdown of shared understandings of acceptable behaviour, we do considerably less than we could to make the rules of acceptable conduct accessible to the average person.

The rules of conduct are clearer, it is suggested, if they are segregated into a separate code designed to be read by the average person rather than attorneys and judges. We can improve the educational effect of criminal adjudications by removing the ambiguity of acquittals and dismissals. This requires that two alternative, and contradictory, grounds for acquittal be distinguished: no liability because no violation of the rules of conduct, and no liability, despite a violation of the rules of conduct, because the violation is not blameworthy. Ambiguities of this sort inherent in the

---

[25] Model Penal Code, § 2.02(2)(c) & (d).

formulation of doctrines also can and should be remedied. This means, for example, defining justification defences objectively, and providing a separate excuse defence or mitigation for a mistaken justification. It also means defining criminal risks objectively so that people can better judge the risks that are prohibited. The blameless creation of a prohibited risk can be exempt from liability under separately-defined culpability requirements. Is it not possible, and desirable, to have a simpler, clearer statement of the rules of conduct? Might it not be useful to produce a set of rules the basics of which school children could begin to discuss in their 'citizenship classes' and that could form the basis for discussion of a citizen's obligations in classes continuing through high school or beyond?

8

The Doctrines of Liability

The liability function of criminal law doctrine, recall from Chapter 6, is performed by two sets of doctrines. The doctrines stating the rules of conduct make up the first part of the liability inquiry; liability cannot be imposed in the absence of a violation of the rules. The additional doctrines that contribute to the liability function, the 'doctrines of liability', include such doctrines as those that establish the minimum offence culpability requirements, those imputing culpability requirements, and the excuse defences.[1]

Because of the special condemnatory nature of criminal law, most doctrines of liability are designed to gauge whether an actor's violation of the rules of conduct was performed with sufficient blameworthiness to merit the condemnation of criminal conviction. If an actor's violation is blameless, the actor ought to be free from liability even though he may well have brought about the prohibited harm or evil. If an actor's violation is blameworthy, he ought to be liable.

Does current doctrine impose liability on blameworthy violations and avoid liability for blameless violations? The legal literature contains a number of criticisms of current doctrine for perceived failures. Two well-known examples are the lack of a general defence for a reasonable mistake as to the lawfulness of one's conduct and continued use of the felony-murder rule. A functional analysis suggests some less obvious failures, failures both in setting culpability requirements and in formulating excuse defences. This Chapter gives an example of each.

A. Elevating Base and Aggravation Culpability Requirements to the Status of Criminalization Mental States: Improperly Limiting Attempt Liability

Chapter 6 describes several distinguishable kinds of culpability requirements: future conduct intention, present circumstance culpability, and future result culpability.[2] Only the first is used as a criminalization mental state

---

[1] For a more complete list, see the chart in Ch. 6, sect. B.
[2] The present conduct intention is somewhat superfluous.

in cases of incomplete conduct toward an offence. The failure to see that the future conduct intention in attempt plays a different function from the other culpability requirements in an incomplete attempt has confused many courts and code drafters into treating all attempt culpability requirements as if they perform the rule articulation function. It is true that this 'purpose' or 'intention' requirement is an appropriate additional requirement —beyond that required by the substantive offence—but it does not follow that this same elevated level of culpability should be applied to all other culpability requirements of attempts, which may serve other functions.

Consider a prosecution for attempted murder. Must it be the actor's conscious object (purpose) to cause the death, or is it sufficient, as it is for murder liability, that the actor know that his conduct is practically certain to cause the death? It is true that the actor's purpose to complete the conduct that would cause the death must be clear. Without this intention, the justification for criminalizing the otherwise innocent conduct disappears. But why should the minimum culpability requirements of the object offence—such as the culpability as to causing the death, a future result culpability—be elevated to purpose? Similarly, in a prosecution for attempted statutory rape,[3] must the actor have as his purpose that his partner is under-age or is it enough that he is aware that his partner might be under-age (recklessness as to under-age), as is sufficient for liability for the completed offence? Clearly, his intention to go through with the intercourse, his future conduct intention, must be shown. In its absence there is no justification for criminalization. But why is recklessness as to age, a present circumstance culpability, no longer adequate in establishing the minimum culpability for liability?

The clumsiness of the common law's mental-elements scheme may explain why the common law could not make the distinction between a criminalization mental state and a culpability mental state. Attempt was said to be a 'specific intent offence'.[4] It thus required more in the way of proof of culpable state of mind than a 'general intent offence', where it was thought that the actor's intention could be inferred from his conduct. But the 'general intent offence'–'specific intent offence' scheme, which did not distinguish between mental states as to different elements of the offence, made it impossible to require purpose as to completing the offence conduct but to require mental states of less than purpose as to the elements of the substantive offence. Thus, once it was agreed that attempt had a purpose requirement, which it surely had (the purpose to engage in the conduct constituting the substantive offence), it followed that this same purpose requirement applied to all offence elements.

[3] See e.g. *State* v. *Davis* (1967) 108 NH 158, 229 A (2d) 842 (conviction for attempted rape of a 'woman child under the age of 16 years', NH Rev. Stat. Ann., § 585:16, affirmed).
[4] See e.g. *People* v. *Trinkle* (1977) 68 Ill. (2d) 198 at 204, 369 NE (2d) 888 at 892; *R.* v. *Whybrow* (1951) 35 Cr. App. R 141.

The Model Penal Code replaces the common law 'offence analysis' notion that each offence has a single culpability requirement with 'element analysis'.[5] Section 2.02(1) expressly requires a showing of culpability 'with respect to *each material element of the offence*'. Yet it appears to hold to the common law rule that attempt liability requires the actor to be purposeful as to a result element even if the substantive offence attempted requires less. The commentary explains: 'The general principle is . . . that the actor must affirmatively desire to engage in the conduct or *to cause the result that will constitute the principal offence*'.[6]

But why should this be the rule? Assume an actor places a bomb in a military services draft board knowing it will kill the persons therein. He does not want to kill such persons, his object is only to destroy the building, but he knows that when he pushes the detonator the people are practically certain to be killed. If he is caught by police after the explosion causes deaths, he is liable for murder. If he is caught just before he presses the detonator, he is not liable for attempted murder. He is not liable even though the prosecution can prove beyond a reasonable doubt that it was his purpose to engage in the conduct constituting the offence, pushing the detonator, and can prove that he has the culpability required for murder, knowledge that his conduct is practically certain to cause the death of people. He may be liable for other offences but escapes liability for attempted murder because it is not his *conscious object* to cause death.

The same principle elevates culpability as to a circumstance element to the same 'purpose' required as to future conduct, just as it elevates culpability as to a result element. Under this approach, a person caught in bed on the verge of committing statutory rape is free from attempt liability even if he is aware that his partner may be under-age and it clearly is his purpose to engage in intercourse. To be liable for the attempt, it must

---

[5] See generally Paul H. Robinson, 'Element Analysis in Defining Criminal Liability: The Model Penal Code and Beyond' (1983) 35 *Stanford LR* 681; R. A. Duff, *Criminal Attempts* (1997), [250].

[6] Model Penal Code, § 5.01 comment 301 (1985) (emphasis added). Although modern codes have shifted to 'element analysis', in which different culpability requirements may apply to different elements of the same offence, many modern courts and codes have followed the common law rule that attempt requires purpose as to the elements of the object offence. In *People v. Trinkle*, for example, after being refused further service, the resentful defendant fired a shot into a tavern, wounding a patron within: (1977) 68 Ill. (2d) 198, 369 NE (2d) 888. The court affirmed a reversal of the defendant's conviction for attempted murder because, while murder required only 'knowing' (or sometimes less) as to causing death, attempted murder required a specific intention, or purpose, to kill. The court reached this result despite the presence of an attempt statute that explicitly provided that attempted murder required only that the actor '*knows* [his] act creates a strong probability of death or great bodily harm': 68 Ill. (2d) at 201, 369 NE (2d) at 890. The court's conclusion was said to be required by the common law rule that 'attempt is a specific intent offence' and attempt liability requires not only that the actor intend to engage in the conduct constituting the substantive offence but that the actor intend the prohibited result and the required circumstances of the substantive offence.

be his 'purpose' that his partner is under-age.[7] One may wonder whether
the law is wise to limit attempt liability in this way.[8] (While nothing on the
face of the Model Penal Code's incomplete conduct provision suggests a different rule regarding elevation of culpability as to a result than as to a circumstance, the Code's commentary can be read to suggest that culpability
as to a circumstance element need not be elevated.[9] The Draft English Code
expressly provides for no elevation of culpability as to a circumstance.[10])

----

[7] Unlike the definitions as to conduct or results, 'purpose' is defined with regard to a
circumstance ot require either a desire or an awareness of circumstances: see Model Penal
Code, § 2.02(2)(a)(ii) ('he *believes* or hopes'). Thus, 'purpose' as to a circumstance requires
no more than does 'knowing' as to a circumstance. The same is true of the Draft English
Code, clause 18(b)&(i) definition of 'intentionally'.

[8] There is some authority for a contrary view. In *State* v. *Galan*, for example, the defendant was charged with attempted trafficking in stolen property. The substantive offence
required only recklessness as to the property being stolen but the defendant claimed that
the indictment was defective because 'an attempt . . . requires a specific intent which is in-
compatible with a reckless state of mind'. (Ariz. Ct. App. 1982) 134 Ariz. 590 at 590, 658
P (2d) 243 at 244. The attempt statute was similar to the Model Penal Code provision,
except for the substitution of the term 'intentional' for 'purposeful', a common grammatical alteration. The court concluded:

> 'A common sense reading of the provision leads to the conclusion that the words in-
> tentionally engages in conduct refers, in this case, to the actions that make up trafficking
> like buying property . . . and that the words *acting with the kind of culpability other-*
> *wise required for the commission of an offence* requires only that the acts be accom-
> panied by a reckless state of mind as to the circumstances attending the status of the
> property. A contrary conclusion would mean that the words *acting with the kind of*
> *culpability otherwise required for the commission of an offence* are superfluous.'

134 Ariz. at 591–2, 658 P (2d) at 244–5 (emphasis in original). (Deleted from the passage
quoted are dicta that suggest that 'intentionally engages in conduct' might also require proof
that the actor intended to resell the property. This might well be required by the substantive offence of trafficking but it is hard to see how such a requirement be drawn from the
'engages in conduct' language.)
      Some jurisdictions take a similar approach with respect to the culpability required as to
a result. They require only that level of culpability as to causing a result that is required
by the substantive offence; there is no elevation of culpability as a result required for attempt. Indeed, some jurisdictions drop the Model Penal Code's 'purpose' or belief language,
leaving only the requirement that the actor be 'acting with the kind of culpability otherwise required for commission of the offence': Model Penal Code, § 5.01(1). As the Utah
Supreme Court concluded, in *State* v. *Maestas*:

> '[R]egardless of any requirements which the common law may impose concerning
> [specific intent in] "attempt" crimes, Utah law requires only "the kind of culpability
> otherwise required for the commission of the [completed] offence". Thus, there can be
> no difference between the intent required as an element of the crime of attempted first
> degree murder and that required for first degree murder itself.'

(Utah 1982) 652 P (2d) 903 at 904.

[9] See Model Penal Code, § 5.01(1) comment 27 (Tent. Draft No10, 1960). (This unofficial
revision in the commentary has not been noticed by many jurisdictions that use the Code's
attempt provision.) But in support of elevation of culpability as to circumstance elements,
see the commentary quoted in the text at note 6 above (requiring a positive desire '*to en-*
gage in the conduct or to cause the result *that will constitute the principal offence*'). And
recall the Code's broad meaning of 'conduct' to include the attendant circumstances of the
conduct, e.g. 'having intercourse with a person under 16'.

[10] See Draft English Code, ¶ 49(2). This was a late change of mind by the Law Commission. See vol. 2, ¶¶ 13.44–45.

The better approach considers the criminalization mental state, such as the actor's intent to engage in the conduct constituting the offence (future conduct intent), as distinct from the culpability mental states required by the substantive offence, such as the culpability as to causing a result in homicide (future result culpability) or the culpability as to the partner's age in statutory rape (present circumstance culpability). The actor's future conduct intention is central to the definition of what constitutes a criminal attempt; the actor must have as his *purpose* to engage in the conduct that constitutes the offence. There is no apparent reason, however, why the culpability requirements of the substantive offence, which serve the liability function, must be elevated to purposeful. It seems more appropriate to consider the culpability requirements that adequately serve the liability and grading functions for the substantive offence as adequate to serve those functions for attempt liability. If negligence as to a sexual partner's age is sufficient to establish culpability for statutory rape, why not for attempted statutory rape? If knowing as to causing a death is adequate for murder, why not for attempted murder?

One dramatic effect of the elevation-to-purposeful approach is that it bars liability altogether for conduct designed to create a prohibited risk of harm, specifically where the actor's attempt to create the risk is foiled. Consider the actor who is caught just as he is about to discharge toxic chemicals near a school soccer field, knowing that the chemicals may cause the death of one or more of the school children. He cannot be liable for reckless homicide because no one is actually killed. He cannot be liable for endangerment because he had not yet created a risk of death or serious bodily injury (and did not believe that he had yet created such a risk).[11] One would think, however, that where we are lucky enough to catch him before he creates the risk, he should be liable for attempted endangerment. Similarly, where an actor is caught just before he buries toxic waste near the town reservoir, knowing that, once completed, his conduct will create a risk of catastrophe, he ought to be liable for an attempt to commit the offence of risking catastrophe.[12] But under the elevation-to-purposeful approach, neither actor can be held liable.[13] While the actors' awareness that the planned conduct creates the prohibited risk is sufficient for full offence liability if the risk is created, only purposeful is adequate for liability where only attempt is charged. That the actor's objective is to avoid the costly disposal fees, not to endanger people, protects them from attempt liability.

The drafters defend the Code's position by arguing that liability for attempts to create a prohibited risk would spread liability too far.[14] But it is

---

[11] See Model Penal Code, § 211.2.   [12] See Model Penal Code, § 220.2(2).

[13] Presumably, some regulatory offence governing the handling of toxic chemicals will impose some liability, but this hardly recognises the seriousness of the violation.

[14] The approach of the Model Code is not to treat such behaviour as an attempt. Instead the Code creates a separate crime, a misdemeanor, for recklessly placing another person

hard to see why the actual creation of the risk ought to be determinative of liability. The successful and unsuccessful attempters have the same subjective culpability (and probably the same dangerousness). Indeed, it is precisely this argument that the Code drafters use to support their view that the absence of resulting harm generally ought not reduce the grade of an offence; attempts generally are graded the same as the completed offence.[15] Yet, here, under their definition of attempt, the actor's failure successfully to create the intended risk does even more than reduce the grade of the violation, it exempts the actor from liability altogether.[16] The Draft English Code takes an in-between position on this issue, requiring intention as to all elements except as to a circumstance element, which is not elevated.[17]

The discussion so far has focused on the most common case of incomplete conduct toward an offence. Is the analysis different for those cases where attempt liability is imposed because the actor's conduct is complete but the offence is factually or legally impossible? Where the actor's conduct is complete, no future conduct intention need be shown. We have the actor's conduct as evidence of his intention to engage in the conduct constituting the offence. Thus, even the analogy to the future conduct intention in incomplete conduct cases does not explain a wish to elevate the required culpability above that required as to the circumstance and result elements of the substantive offence.

Reconsider the draft board terrorist who plans to bomb the draft board knowing that it will kill the security guard but not wanting the guard to be killed. If his bomb kills the guard, he is liable for murder; knowing as to causing death is sufficient. As noted above, if he is caught just before he triggers the bomb, he is not liable for attempted murder because his knowing culpability is insufficient; attempt liability here requires that he be purposeful as to the killing. Consider the case where he triggers the bomb but the explosive does not function because it has become wet. His conduct toward the offence is complete—we know for certain that he was willing to carry the offence through to completion—but the result did not come about. Ought the actor escape liability for attempted murder because of the factual impossibility of completion?

in danger of death or serious bodily injury. The Institute's judgement was that the scope of the criminal law would be unduly extended if one could be liable for an attempt whenever he recklessly or negligently created a risk of any result whose actual occurrence would lead to criminal responsibility. While it was believed that the reckless creation of risk of death or serious bodily harm was grave enough for general coverage, even for this behavior misdemeanor penalties seemed more apt than the severer sanctions attached to felony attempts.

Model Penal Code, § 5.01 comment 303–4 (1985) (footnotes omitted).

[15] Model Penal Code, § 5.05(1).

[16] Also note that such attempt liability is limited to those few instances in which the code creates a substantive offence that punishes an actor for causing or risking a specified result. Result elements typically appear only in homicide, personal injury, and property damage offences.   [17] See Draft English Code, ¶ 49(2).

All would agree that he ought not escape attempt liability. Even the Code agrees with this result. It creates an exception to the elevate-to-purpose requirement for cases in which the actor has completed his conduct but the result does not occur. Model Penal Code section 5.01(1)(b) provides that an actor is guilty of attempt if, 'when causing a particular *result* is an element of the crime, [he] does or omits to do anything with the purpose of causing or *with the belief* that it will cause such result without further conduct on his part'.[18] Such a reduction in the minimum culpability as to result from purpose to knowing is justified, in the drafters' view, because where the actor's conduct is complete, the manifestation of the actor's dangerousness is just as great—or very nearly as great—as in the case of purpose conduct. In both instances a deliberate choice is made to bring about the consequence forbidden by the criminal law, and the actor has done all within his power to cause this result to occur.[19]

Some courts have reached the same conclusion, and have argued that the common law's specific intent requirement might even be satisfied by such a belief that the result will occur.[20]

But the exception does not save the Code's provision from the criticisms voiced above. It does avoid elevation in the narrow case of substantive offences, like murder, where knowledge as to causing a result is required and the conduct is complete. It does not, however, avoid the questionable results that occur where the actor's conduct is incomplete. The draft board bomber who is caught just before he detonates the bomb still escapes liability for attempted murder. The knowing culpability required for murder is still elevated to purpose for attempted murder.

Nor does the Code's exception avoid elevation and improper results where the substantive offence requires less than knowing as to causing a result. Consider the case of the toxic dumper who completes his conduct in dumping the chemicals but finds that suspicious investigators have substituted a similar-looking non-toxic chemical. If the actor knows that his conduct creates a risk of death, then he may be liable for attempted endangerment under the Code's special rule (only knowing is required as to a result for completed conduct attempts). But assume that the actor is only reckless as to causing death. This is sufficient for the offence of reckless endangerment, but the Code does not permit liability for attempted

---

[18] Model Penal Code, § 5.01(1)(b) (emphasis added). The Code's commentary notes: 'Thus when the charge is attempted murder or assault with intent to kill, it is error to permit conviction on a finding of reckless disregard for human life or intent to inflict grievous bodily harm': Model Penal Code, § 5.01 comment 306–7 (1985).

[19] Model Penal Code, § 5.01 comment 305 (1985).

[20] See e.g. *State* v. *Krovarz* (1985) 697 P (2d) 378. The *Krovarz* court upheld a conviction where a psychologically unstable defendant attempted robbery with a putty knife. The court quoted language from the Model Penal Code section 5.01(1)(b) commentary and concluded: '[w]e agree with [the Model Penal Code] reasoning; a knowing attempt to attain a proscribed result is a sufficient culpable mental state to justify imposition by the legislature of attempt liability': *ibid*. 382.

reckless endangerment. This is so even though the actor has the culpability required for the substantive offence and has completed the conduct required for the offence. He cannot be held liable because the Code elevates the culpability requirement for attempt over that required by the substantive offence.

It is true that there can be no such thing as an 'accidental attempt', in the sense that to 'attempt' an offence one must intend to complete the conduct that would constitute that offence. One must have a future conduct intent. There is, however, such a thing as an attempt to cause an 'accident', in the sense of an attempt to engage in conduct that creates the opportunity for an 'accident', that is, conduct that creates a risk. As long as the law is careful to require that it is the actor's conscious object to engage in the *conduct constituting the offence*, there seems little reason that attempts to create risks and attempts that create risks ought not be punished.

The better course here is to see that the special intention requirement quite appropriately required in cases of incomplete conduct attempts is distinct from the other culpability requirements in such cases and has no application where the conduct is complete. No greater culpability than that required by the substantive offence ought to be required for attempt liability.[21]

B. Obscuring the Voluntariness Requirement's Shared Liability Function with Excuses: Distorting the Involuntary Act Defence

The voluntariness requirement typically is classed as part of the actus reus of each offence, as Chapter 3 notes.[22] Recall from Chapter 6 that most

---

[21] This position is not insensitive to the problems inherent in imposing liability where the actor has not gone far toward committing the offence. The culpability requirements become harder for the prosecution to meet as the actor does less toward commission of the offence. As a practical matter, a future conduct intention is harder to prove than a present conduct intention. Where the actor's offence conduct is incomplete, the prosecution has a significant burden in proving the actor's future conduct intention. Where the offence conduct is complete, the prosecution's task is easier. In completed-conduct attempts, the required criminalization mental state is transformed from a burdensome future conduct intention to an almost pro forma present conduct intention. No special elevation of the object offence's culpability requirements is needed to reach this sliding scale between the extent of conduct and the importance of proving culpability.

[22] Voluntariness might be thought to be more akin to mens rea than to actus reus elments. Culpability elements at least concern the issue of accountability for harm caused; objective elements more clearly define the nature of the harm or evil. But this characterization is problematic as well. Under it, for example, an actor's involuntariness might be denied a defence to a strict liability offence on the ground that proof of culpability is not required. See e.g. Roger Clark, 'Accident—Or What Became of Kilbride v. Lake?', in Roger Clark (ed.), *Essays on Criminal Law in New Zealand* (Wellington, 1971), 65 (discussing denial of involuntariness defence in strict liability case and arguing inappropriateness of such denial). But while public policy may support the imposition of strict liability for an offence, it does

aspects of the actus reus serve a rule articulation or grading function, describing the harm or evil of the offence and its seriousness. I want to elaborate here on my claim in Chapter 3, section C.3. that the voluntary act requirement, or 'involuntary act defence', is analogous to the criminal law's system of excuses. Like the excuses, it serves the liability function.

Admittedly the cases dealt with under the voluntary act requirement are different from other excuses in that they are at the extreme of the lack-of-volition spectrum. Such involuntariness represents the most non-volitional form of conduct and is thus the most convincing ground for excuse, but it is not functionally different from other traditional excusing conditions such as insanity, immaturity, duress, and involuntary intoxication.

Like the general excuse defences, the involuntariness defence is not unique to the particular offence at hand. Involuntariness does not mean the absence of the harm or evil of the offence, as does absence of other objective elements. When an actor assaults another during a seizure, our conclusion is not that the assault is not harmful and regrettable (indeed, civil liability may be permitted) but rather that the assault is undesirable but condemnation is not appropriate in light of the involuntariness of the conduct. Nor is involuntariness consistent with a normal actor with normal capacities. It suggests either abnormal conduct or an abnormal actor, as do the conditions of excuse defences. The other elements of an offence, in contrast, are consistent with an actor of normal capacities.[23]

The failure of current doctrine to see the functional similarity of the voluntary act requirement and the general excuse defences has resulted in distortion in the formulation of the former. Because it is not conceptualized as an excuse, the voluntary act requirement has escaped significant limitations that routinely are placed on excuse defences. The two most important are the requirement of a specific cause of the lack of control (the requirement of a specific 'disability') and the requirement that the disability cause a certain degree of control dysfunction.

As to the first requirement—a specific disability requirement—the traditional excuses, such as insanity, duress, and involuntary intoxication, require proof that the actor's lack or impairment of control comes from a

---

not follow that it supports the imposition of liability on involuntary actors, who are blameless under general principles of excuse. General excuses remain available to offences of strict liability. And involuntariness, like the general excuses, ought similarly be available, without regard to the culpability requirements of the particular offence definition. The doctrine can make this point clear by characterizing involuntariness as a general excuse rather than an offence element.

[23] One can maintain the conceptual similarity between involuntariness and other excuses by treating all excuses as negative elements of each offence. Indeed, the Model Penal Code seems to move toward this approach when it defines 'elements of an offence' to include the absence of all general defences, including excuses: Model Penal Code § 1.13(9)(c). However, such an approach hides the important conceptual distinctions between elements of an offence definition and general defences: see Paul H. Robinson, 'Criminal Law Defenses: A Systematic Analysis' (1982) 82 *Columbia LR* 199 at 243-91 (hereinafter 'Systematic Analysis').

specific identifiable cause, mental illness, physical coercion, or intoxication, respectively. An involuntary act defence, in contrast, is permitted without regard to the cause of the involuntariness. Anything that causes an actor to perform a criminal act that 'is not a product of [his or her] effort or determination' will qualify for the defence. The absence of a specific disability requirement may be justified on the ground that the lack of control in many involuntary act cases is so complete and dramatic that no other requirement is needed to assure blameworthiness. It is irrelevant whether the muscular movement comes from a *grand mal* seizure or from a reflex action. Such total lack of volition is an obvious and convincing ground for exculpation. No additional requirement is necessary.

But the absence of a disability requirement has the collateral effect of broadening the defence to cases beyond instances of complete lack of volition. That is, the freedom from a specific disability requirement gives the involuntariness defence a special role in the system of excuses, as the catch-all excuse, to be used where the actor's control is impaired by a disability other than one of those recognized in the traditional excuse defences.[24] Hypnotism, for example, is not a recognized form of mental illness or defect or unlawful force or intoxication or any of the other disabilities or sources of disability recognized by traditional excuse defences. If an actor is to be excused for his conduct under hypnosis, it must be done under the involuntary act defence, for there no specific disability is required.

This catch-all use of the involuntariness defence allows its use in cases where the actor's control is admittedly impaired but decidedly less impaired than the complete or near complete lack of control of a *grand mal* seizure or a reflex action, and this can be problematic. Available evidence suggests that hypnotism, for example, can cause significant impairment of control under certain circumstances for certain persons, but not total loss or even near total loss of volition.[25] Somnambulism ('sleepwalking')

---

[24] In *Bradley* v. *State* (1925) 102 Tex. Crim. 41, 277 SW 147, for example, the defendant was startled from sleep and in a somnambulistic state began randomly shooting in to a dark room, killing his companion; court held that defendant lacked 'conscious volition' and therefore could not be held liable. For other examples of this extended use of the involuntariness defence to cases of impairment, see *Regina* v. *Charlson* [1955] 1 All ER 859 (defence of automatism permitted for defendant who suffered from a cerebral tumor which gave rise to outbursts of impulsive violence; defendant acquitted); *People* v. *Newton* (1970) 8 Cal. App. (3d) 359, 87 Cal. Rptr. 394 (allowing complete defence to charge of criminal homicide for physical injury causing subsequent action without awareness); *Fulcher* v. *State* (Wyo. 1981) 633 P (2d) 142 (blow to head producing 'traumatic automatism', a condition affecting ability to control conduct and to perceive environment, is a defence).

[25] Conduct under hypnosis typically is not robotic, as is popularly thought, yet nonetheless can be odd and out of character: see e.g. Glanville Williams, *Criminal Law: The General Part* (2nd edn., London, 1961), 768–9 (arguing that it is wrong to assume that the hypnotized actor is under complete control of the hypnotist and that the hypnotized actor's ego ideal exercises continuous control over relations) (hereinafter *General Part*); Ernest R. Hilgard, *Hypnotic Susceptibility* (New York, 1965), 6 (stating that the change in state under hypnosis is always relative, rather than absolute; thus the hypnotized subject has the ability to initiate action, such as delivering a speech); P. Schilder, *The Nature of Hypnosis* (2nd

similarly has an effect in impairing an actor's control but not one that renders his conduct involuntary in the absolute or near absolute sense.[26] This extension of the involuntariness defence from cases of loss to cases of mere impairment of control is not limited to clever defence counsel or sympathetic courts. The Model Penal Code recognizes acts during both hypnotism and somnambulism as conclusively *involuntary* acts despite the lack of evidence that such disabilities cause such loss of control.[27]

This expansion of the involuntariness defence from cases of loss to cases of mere impairment of control is not itself objectionable. The degree of impairment in such cases may not be severe but nonetheless may be sufficient to merit an excuse. And such impairment may result from disabling conditions as empirically confirmable as the traditional excuse disabilities of involuntary intoxication, insanity, and duress. Thus, this expansion of the defence may be useful because it generates a proper result in cases of blamelessness that otherwise would be denied a defence.[28]

However good the motivation, the characterization of volitionally impaired conduct as involuntary conduct is problematic. Under traditional excuse principles, an excuse for impaired control short of involuntariness requires an inquiry into whether the degree of impairment is enough to render the actor blameless. This requires an examination of the actor's situation and a comparison of the actor's conduct to that of the reasonable person in the same situation. The duress defence, for example, requires not only that, 'the actor engaged in the conduct charged to constitute the offence because he was coerced to do so', but also requires that, 'a person of reasonable firmness in the actor's situation would have been unable to resist [the coercion]'.[29] The excuses of insanity and involuntary intoxication similarly require the jury to assess the *degree* of impairment of volition in the case at hand and to determine whether it is sufficient to support an excuse. The jury must find that, 'the actor at the time of his conduct lacks *substantial* capacity . . . to conform his conduct to the requirements of law'. The standard of 'substantial' capacity is intended by the drafters to be intentionally 'open-ended' in order to induce the jury

---

edn., New York, 1973), 104 (asserting that the hypnotized subject is not a passive tool in the hypnotist's hands and that the subject retains his will and personal attitudes). For a more detailed discussion, see Paul H. Robinson, *Criminal Law* (Boston, 1997), § 9.2.

[26] Paul H. Robinson, *Criminal Law Defenses* (St Paul, Minnesota, 1984), ii, § 172(c) (hereinafter *Criminal Law Defenses*).

[27] Model Penal Code, § 2.01(2)(b)&(c). The Draft English Code, clause 33(1)(a)(ii), requires that the actor be deprived of effective control of the act, referring to 'sleep' as one of the conditions in which this occurs.

[28] A hypnotic state can serve the purposes that a disability typically serves. The presence of a hypnotic state can be scientifically confirmed by a change in brain wave patterns. And, typically, the hypnosis is caused by another person. This last characteristic makes the abnormality particularly effective in the blame-shifting function. Like the coercer in duress, the hypnotist presents an easy recipient for the blame.

[29] Model Penal Code, § 2.09(1). See, similarly, Draft English Code, ¶ 42(3)(b).

to use their own intuitive sense of justice to determine whether the degree of impairment is enough to merit an excuse.[30]

To presume irrebuttably exculpating involuntariness in the absence of this inquiry into the extent of the impairment, as the Model Penal Code does, is to risk giving excuses that are not deserved. In cases of hypnotism and somnambulism, or in any other cases where disabilities impairing control are treated as instances of lack of control, an actor may fail to meet the standard of impairment that a jury would require for excuse yet nonetheless may gain an excuse if it is brought within the involuntary act defence. Indeed, whenever the voluntary act requirement is the claimed basis for a defence, it creates the potential for improper exculpation if the actor's self-control is only impaired, not lost.

One can avoid these difficulties by recognizing the voluntariness issue as serving the same liability function as the excuse defences and imposing analogous requirements. If volition is not lost but impaired, the doctrine ought to demand the same inquiry into degree as do the excuse defences. This can be done by adopting a new excuse of *impaired consciousness*,[31] for use in cases short of involuntariness, where the disability causing the impairment is other than one of the disabilities recognised as a traditional excuse.[32]

The central point here is that, where an actor seeks excuse on a claim that he lacked adequate ability to control his conduct, the jury should inquire into the actual extent of the impairment to determine whether it is enough to render him blameless for his violation. The failure to include this basic requirement of excuse defences in the formulation of the voluntary act requirement is consistent with a failure to see that these two aspects of criminal law doctrine in fact perform the same function and properly should have analogous requirements. This failure also creates problems in the realm of procedure. Treatment of the voluntary act requirement as a universal actus reus element, rather than as an excuse defence, also complicates the allocation of the burdens of proving the issue. Most jurisdictions allocate the burden of offence elements to the state but

---

[30] Model Penal Code, § 4.01 comment 172 (1985).

[31] Such an excuse has been proposed by Glanville Williams for slightly different reasons. See Williams, *General Part*, n. 25 above, at 482–90.

[32] The defence provision might look something like the following:

'*Impaired Consciousness.* An actor is excused for his conduct constituting an offence if,
  (1) as a result of any physiologically confirmable disease or defect not specifically recognised or rejected as a basis for exculpation by another excuse,
  (2) the actor

    (a) does not perceive the physical nature or foresee the physical consequences of his conduct or does not know his conduct is wrong or criminal [lacks substantial capacity to appreciate the criminality/wrongfulness of his conduct], or
    (b) is not sufficiently able to control his conduct so as to be justly held accountable for it [lacks substantial capacity to conform his conduct to the requirements of law].'

may have the defendant carry the burden for defences. Thus, while voluntariness is functionally similar to the excuse defences, the state is likely to be given the burden of proving voluntariness.[33] Indeed, one may read existing Supreme Court cases as requiring this allocation if voluntariness is conceived as of as an offence element.[34]

C. CONCLUSION

Does the criminal law impose liability on blameworthy violators and only blameworthy violators, its liability function? Confusion over the function of different aspects of the doctrine results in formulations that fail in this regard. Current doctrine fails to impose deserved liability on some attempt violations, for example, because it requires elevation of all culpability requirements of the object offence to purposeful in the mistaken view that the very demanding future conduct intention required for criminalization of incomplete attempts must be applied to all other culpability elements, including those that serve only liability or grading functions. Similarly, current doctrine's involuntariness defence fails to require a showing of sufficient impairment of control to exculpate because it fails to see that both the voluntariness requirement of the 'actus reus' and the general excuse defences perform analogous liability functions and ought to have analogous minimum requirements.

[33] The conditions supporting any of the general excuses are statistically rare; the actor has engaged in admittedly wrongful conduct, and the facts supporting the defence are uniquely within the knowledge of the defendant. Because of this, a jurisdiction may wish to give the defendant the burdens of proof on general excuses. In contrast, offence elements are in issue in every case, and proof of the actus reus elements traditionally is required to establish that the actor has caused a societal harm, a burden traditionally and appropriately placed on the state. Allocation of the burdens of proof for excuses to the defendant is common. See Robinson, *Criminal Law Defenses*, ii, n. 26 above, at § 73(a), n. 7. See generally Robinson, 'Systematic Analysis', n. 23 above, at 243–64. The failure to distinguish involuntariness from the offence elements makes it more difficult to see the propriety of allocating the burden to prove involuntariness to the defendant. Regarding the burden of persuasion, compare *People* v. *Furlong* (1907) 187 NY 198, 79 NE 978 (placing the burden of persuasion on the defendant) and *State* v. *Caddell* (1975) 287 NC 266, 215 SE (2d) 348 (court determined that defence of unconsciousness (or automatism) is affirmative defence; therefore burden rests with defendant) to *People* v. *Hardy* (1948) 33 Cal. 2d 52 at 64–5, 198 P (2d) 865 at 872 (placing the burden of persuasion on the prosecution).

[34] Supreme Court decisions permit the burdens of production and persuasion to be shifted to the defendant for excuses but demand that they be allocated to the state for all offence elements: *Patterson* v. *New York* (1977) 432 US 197. To treat voluntariness as an offence element, then, is to foreclose the possibility of placing on the defendant either the burden of persuasion or the burden of production for involuntariness, no matter how strong a jurisdiction may judge the policy arguments in support of such allocation. This is particularly troubling given the use of the involuntariness defence as a catch-all, where the degree of impairment of control may be similar or even less than the degree of impairment of the traditional excuses, for which the burden of proof may be constitutionally shifted to the defendant. The common occurrence of conflicting expert opinions on matters of involuntariness, especially of the catch-all type, as is common for many, if not most, general excuse defences, makes a beyond-a-reasonable-doubt standard difficult to meet.

The first error—the culpability requirements for attempt—occurs because the doctrine fails to see that two doctrines, different mental elements in attempt, are functionally different. The second error—too broad an involuntariness defence—illustrates the reverse sort of error, where the doctrine fails to see that two doctrines are functionally similar; the involuntariness defence serves the same function as the general excuse defences.

9
The Doctrines of Grading

Once it is determined that an actor has violated the rules of conduct and once the doctrines of liability determine that such violation was sufficiently blameworthy to deserve the condemnation of criminal conviction, the doctrines of grading operate to determine the general range of punishment to be imposed, as described in Chapter 6.

Just as the doctrines of liability look primarily to whether the actor's violation was accompanied by the minimum blameworthiness for criminal conviction, the doctrines of grading also typically focus on blameworthiness, in this instance the *degree* of the actor's blameworthiness, taking account of such things as the seriousness of the violation and the actor's level of culpable state of mind. If the criminal law claims moral authority for itself, the amount of punishment imposed must match the degree of an actor's blameworthiness, no more and no less. There is less agreement in the context of grading doctrines than in the context of liability doctrines, however, that desert ought to be the governing criterion. It is not uncommon for desert considerations to be pushed aside in grading, as in sentencing generally, in order to advance policies thought better to reduce crime. The use of extended terms of imprisonment for offenders predicted to commit future crimes, for example, is an increasingly common practice.[1]

The doctrines of grading, recall from Chapter 6, include doctrines that either aggravate or mitigate the grade of a violation. Common are doctrines that provide a higher grade for an offence with a result element than the same offence conduct without the result, as in manslaughter versus endangerment. Aggravation of grade also occurs, for example, where an actor's culpability level is higher than the minimum required for liability, as in murder versus manslaughter versus negligent homicide.

This Chapter illustrates some of current doctrine's failures properly to grade violations, failures that a functional analysis reveals. One kind of failure comes through the misformulation of a doctrine through a failure to see its grading function. The subjective definition of criminal risks, for example, gives liability treatment (focusing on an actor's belief that a risk

---

[1] I disagree with such use of non-desert criteria in the formulation of the doctrines of grading, for reasons given in Paul H. Robinson and John M. Darley, 'The Utility of Desert' (1997) 91 *Northwestern ULR* 453.

is created) to a grading issue (which ought to take account of whether the prohibited risk actually is created, not just the actor's belief in the same). More on this in section A.

A more common failure is the tendency of current doctrine to overlook the relevance to grading of many factors previously taken into account in the rules of conduct or in liability assignment. This happens with such doctrines as those concerning causation, complicity, and excuse. On other occasions, the doctrine recognizes that a factor is relevant to grading but is unsystematic or incomplete in varying grade with changes in the factor. This is the situation with the seriousness of the offence, harm or evil and the actor's level of culpability.

A. Mixing Liability and Grading by Using Culpability Terms to Define Prohibited Risks: Aggravation of Grade for Risk-Creation in the Absence of a Criminal Risk

Chapter 7, section D, describes the Model Penal Code's failure to define the risks that are criminal. Instead, the Code frequently defines risk-creation offences by using the culpability terms of 'recklessness' and 'negligence'. Manslaughter is 'recklessly causing a death'; negligent homicide is 'negligently causing a death'. Because culpability terms are necessarily subjective or individualized, the criminalization of these offences is correspondingly subjective or individualized. This is problematic because, under this formulation, the Code punishes a case where a criminal risk actually is created the same as one where it is not created, where the actor only mistakenly believes that it is created. Most jurisdictions take the view that the actual occurrence of the offence, harm, or evil increases the grade of liability. Thus, the actual creation of a criminal risk is graded more seriously than where the actor does not actually create the criminal risk, all other things being equal.

Consider the case of the actor who speeds at 75 miles per hour to avoid being late for an appointment and, in the process, kills a child who runs into the road. Assume there is no question that he believes that he is taking a substantial and unjustified risk as to causing such a death, that given the circumstances known to him, his conduct is a gross deviation from the standard of care, etc., as the definition of recklessness requires, and that his conduct causes the death. Under the Code, he is liable for manslaughter. Assume, however, that in fact his speedometer is broken. He is travelling at only 55 miles per hour, the posted speed limit. His conduct admittedly creates a risk but no greater risk than that of any other lawful driver on that road, a risk that is not, as an objective matter, a violation of the rules of conduct. Is liability for manslaughter still appropriate?

Criminalizing subjective risk-taking as to a result (the belief that one's conduct creates a prohibited risk) is not itself improper, for it is no different from punishing criminal attempts. Modern criminal law commonly bases liability upon an actor's externalization of her culpable state of mind. A difficulty arises here, however, because instances of criminalization of subjective risk-taking are not labelled or identified as instances of inchoate liability and are punished as full substantive offences, as if the prohibited risk had actually been created. Under the Code, an actor is liable for manslaughter if he causes a death and, at the time of his conduct, he has the required culpability as to the death (recklessness). The Code allows conviction for the full offence even if no criminal risk in fact is created.

If the actual harm or evil should aggravate liability—for example, the actual creation of a prohibited risk—then liability for manslaughter is problematic. The actor's conduct is analogous to an impossible attempt. From his mistaken perspective, he satisfies the requirements of an offence by creating a criminal risk to pedestrians, but in fact he is wrong in his belief. If he is held criminally liable based upon his mistaken belief, by analogy to an impossible attempt, then only attempt liability is appropriate, not full liability for the substantive offence.

In defence of the Model Penal Code drafters, it should be noted that they can argue that it is appropriate to punish an actor's subjective risk-taking the same as where the actor, with the same culpability, actually does create a prohibited risk. For example, while the Code is somewhat inconsistent in its implementation, it generally punishes attempts the same as the completed offence.[2] That is, the Code has the extent of the harm or evil attempted affect the offence grade but not its actual occurrence. The Code is not theoretically inconsistent, then, when it subjectivizes the definition of criminal risk.[3] Believing one is creating a prohibited risk and actually creating the risk are graded the same.

But if a jurisdiction disagrees with the Code's view that actual harm and actual risk are irrelevant, as a majority do, the code drafters in the jurisdiction must reverse the Code's provisions to reinstate the significance of the occurrence of the harm or evil. It is easy enough to see that the Model Penal Code's provision grading attempt the same as the completed offence, for example, must be dropped. And this typically is done.[4] But it

---

[2] See Model Penal Code, § 5.05(1).

[3] Of course, the subjectivization of criminal risk is inconsistent with those aspects of the code that do give significance to resulting harm, such as the grading difference between first degree felonies and attempted first degree felonies, Model Penal Code § 5.05(1), and between offences that differ only in the respect of a resulting harm, such as that between manslaughter and reckless endangerment, Model Penal Code §§ 210.3(1)(a), 211.2. See generally Paul H. Robinson, 'The Role of Harm and Evil in Criminal Law: A Study in Legislative Deception?' (1994) 5 *Journal of Contemporary Legal Issues* 299 (hereinafter 'Harm and Evil').

[4] See *ibid.*, n. 18.

is less obvious that the Code's treatment of criminal risk must be altered to eliminate its subjectivization of criminal risk. No jurisdiction that rejects the Code's disregard for resulting harm and evil also desubjectivizes the Code's definition of criminal risk, as they should.

The problem is not unique to manslaughter. Whenever the Code uses an actor's culpability as the basis for liability, without requiring proof that the actor's conduct violates the rules of conduct, it creates a potential for full substantive liability for an actor who only believes, mistakenly, that his conduct is prohibited. The peculiarities go unnoticed because the rule articulation, liability, and grading doctrines are not distinguished. If one drafts rules of conduct, a purely subjective definition of criminal risk becomes obviously out of place. It does not stand out in the current codes because the subjectivization is entirely appropriate in service of the code's liability function.

B. Incomplete and Unsystematic Use of Central Grading Factors

The most prominent distinction between the rule articulation and liability functions, on the one hand, and grading determinations, on the other, is between the yes–no nature of the former as compared to the gradient nature of the latter. Both rule articulation and liability determinations set minimum requirements. The grading determination must set each violator at the appropriate place on a spectrum of punishment. Yet, the doctrine frequently reverts to cut-off judgements with regard to issues that in reality are issues of grading, and this occurs in part because the doctrine fails to see grading as distinct from rule articulation and liability. Many of the issues of rule articulation and liability have an effect in assessing grade and, in that capacity, they require formulations that call for continuous rather than cut-off judgements.

It may seem that the doctrine fails to make degree judgements with regard to some of the most important determinants of grade, such as the seriousness of the offence harm or evil or the actor's level of culpability. That is, each offence typically requires proof of a given minimum culpability level and minimum harm or evil. But, when looked at as a whole, rather than one offence at a time, the doctrine can be seen as doing somewhat better. Many offences exist only to establish a higher grade of liability over a 'lesser included offence'. For example, the doctrine takes account of the degree of the seriousness of a threatened harm by creating different offences to punish different harms. Thus, intentionally causing a death is murder, a first degree felony; intentionally causing serious bodily harm is aggravated assault, a second degree felony; intentionally causing bodily injury with a risk of death (use of a deadly weapon) is a third degree felony; intentionally creating a risk of death or serious bodily injury is endangerment, a misdemeanour.[5]

On the other hand, degrees of seriousness in some forms of harm are ignored by modern codes. Destroying a twenty-storey apartment building with an explosive and slightly scorching the side of an abandoned house trailer are the same grade offence.[6] The actor who causes permanent brain damage by repeatedly beating a robbery victim with a hammer is liable for the same grade offence as one who swings at the victim with the hammer but misses then flees.[7] If the only role of result elements is grading, and the code shows its appreciation of this fact by altering grade according to some harms, as in personal injury, one may wonder why the code does not more systematically alter grade according to the seriousness of the offence harm or evil.[8]

The doctrine also uses culpability levels to grade offences, usually varying grade with the level of future result culpability. This is done in homicide, for example, where an intentional killing is murder, a first degree felony, a reckless killing is manslaughter, a second degree felony, and a negligent killing is negligent homicide, a third degree felony.[9] Similarly, knowingly causing a catastrophe is a second degree felony, while recklessly doing so is a third degree felony.[10]

But, again, varying the grade of a violation with the level of the actor's culpability as to the harm or evil is the exception rather than the rule. Few offences other than homicide have their grade altered according to the actor's culpability level. This failure is particularly peculiar in the context of culpability as to result when one considers that culpability as to result elements, like result elements themselves, serve *only* a grading function, thus one would expect the grading issue to be paramount in the drafters' minds. Yet, under most modern codes, an actor's culpability level

---

[5] Model Penal Code, §§ 210.2(2), 211.1(2)(a) & (b), 211.2. Similar distinctions are found in the Draft English Code. Compare ¶¶ 54(1), 70(1), 72, 75(a), showing variations in punishment of life, 3 years, and 6 months (see Sched. 1). The Code does not have an endangerment offence.

[6] Model Penal Code, § 220.1(1)(a) & (4) (definitions of arson and 'occupied structure'). Similarly, see Draft English Code, ¶ 180.

[7] Model Penal Code, § 222.1(1). The Draft English Code does seem to distinguish these two cases. On the other hand, it provides the same maximum punishment for intentionally causing another's death and intentionally causing serious personal harm but not death: see Sched. 1 for ¶¶ 54(1) and 70.

[8] One might argue that the failure to recognize these differences in grading reflects a belief that actual resulting harm is irrelevant to the degree of liability; it is only the actor's subjective culpability that is relevant. But if that is the case, why does the Code include result elements at all? Why not define offences in purely subjective terms? If subjective culpability is to be so centrally determinant of grade, one would expect the Code to generally take account of culpability level in grading. But, as the text notes, this is rarely done. See generally Robinson, 'Harm & Evil', n. 3 above, at 312–22.

[9] Model Penal Code, §§ 210.2(2), 210.3(2), 210.4(2). Similarly, compare Draft English Code ¶¶ 70 and 71 (life for intentionally causing serious personal harm; 5 years for recklessly causing). [10] Model Penal Code, § 220.2.

as to causing a harmful result is frequently treated as irrelevant to the grade of his offence.[11] The actor who starts a fire knowing that it will destroy another's building and the actor who is only reckless in doing so are liable for the same grade offence.[12] The actor who purposely creates a risk of catastrophe and the actor who recklessly does so are liable for the same grade offence.[13] The actor who purposely creates a risk of death and the actor who recklessly does so are liable for the same grade offence.[14] If culpability level is relevant to grading, why should not a code's grading scheme systematically reflect it?

C. Dichotomous v. Continuous Judgements: Using Rule-articulation and Liability-assignment Forms in Grading

While modern codes are incomplete in taking account of the seriousness of the harm and the culpability level in grading a violation, they commonly fail to see the grading significance of some issues altogether. Causation, for example, is treated by modern codes as a simple yes–no issue. It is presented as a fixed point cut-off: either the actor is causally accountable for the result or she is not. This places the actor on one of only two points on the continuum of punishment, at the same point as where no result has occurred (the punishment point for an unsuccessful attempt, for example) or at the point of full causal accountability for the full result. This dichotomous rather than continuous nature of the current formulation of causation does not stand out as unusual under current codes because such discrete forms are common, even typical, of the rule articulation and liability functions. But when we see causation as having a grading function, one may more naturally ask whether, like other grading issues, it too ought to be formulated to generate results along the continuum of punishment.

A recent empirical survey gave subjects a series of murder scenarios that varied from one another only in the actors' degree of causal connection with the death. The causal connection varied in both how necessary it was for the death to occur and in the remoteness of the result from the actors' conduct. The subjects assigned liability in the scenarios in a pattern that suggested that they were sensitive to the same factors that current doctrine recognizes as relevant to determining causation—the requirements of a necessary ('but for') cause and that the result not be 'too remote or accidental'—but saw the issue of causation as one of degree rather than as dichotomous. The subjects did not require some minimum closeness in the causal connection then to impose full liability. Instead, the degree of liability assigned by the subjects ranged across a wide spectrum. Where the causal connection was weakest, by traditional necessary cause and remoteness criteria, the point of punishment was close to that for an unsuccessful attempt at murder. As the causal connection grew stronger, as death more directly and more immediately followed the actor's conduct, the subjects' imposition of liability increased.[15] This pattern is, of course, characteristic of grading factors.

Some writers have noted the analogy between causation and complicity.[16] An accomplice's aid to a perpetrator is a form of causal contribution to the offence. It should be no surprise, then, to find the same pattern of shared intuitions on causation, noted above, evident with regard to an actor's degree of assistance to a perpetrator. Current doctrine treats complicity as it does causation, as a dichotomous issue. In other words, it treats it in a fashion consistent with a rule articulation and minimum-liability function. But in an empirical survey similar to that discussed above, the subjects saw the nature and extent of complicity as an issue highly relevant to the grade of the violation. When given a series of scenarios similar in all respects except for the degree of the accomplice's causal contribution to the principal's offence—necessary v. sufficient, extent of contribution compared to the perpetrator and others—the subjects assigned different degrees of liability according to their perception of the degree of the accomplice's contribution.[17] This means, for example, that the subjects never assigned the same degree of liability to an accomplice helping unload a drug shipment as to the organizer of the operation, as current doctrine does.

Note that the issue of grading according to degree of assistance to a perpetrator goes beyond the grading issue in causation in an important way. Causation is a grading issue from start to finish. Assisting a perpetrator, in contrast, is in its base requirement a rule articulation issue. Some minimum degree of complicity is required for liability. What this illustrates is that many factors relevant to rule articulation, or to the minimum requirements of liability, may well be relevant to grading as well. What are identified in Chapter 6 as the 'doctrines of grading' are those doctrines that serve only a grading function. Recall the cumulative serial relation among the doctrines that serve the three functions, discussed in Chapter 6.

To illustrate the point further, consider the current doctrine's treatment of excuse defences as part of the liability function. They assure that criminal liability will not be imposed unless the actor could reasonably have

[15] Paul H. Robinson and John M. Darley, *Justice, Liability, and Blame: Community Views and the Criminal Law* (Oxford, 1995), 181–9 (hereinafter *Justice Liability and Blame*).

[16] See e.g. Sanford H. Kadish, 'Complicity, Cause and Blame: A Study in the Interpretation of Doctrine' (1985) 73 *UCLA LR* 323; George P. Fletcher, *Rethinking Criminal Law* (Boston, 1978), 582.

[17] Robinson and Darley, *Justice Liability and Blame*, n. 15 above, at 33–42.

been expected to have avoided the violation. The failure to gain a duress defence, for example, means that, while some coercion may have been present, it was not sufficient coercion to render the actor blameless for the violation. Does it follow, however, that the actor who fails to get a duress defence is as blameworthy as the actor who commits the same offence with no coercion whatever? While the degree of mitigation may not be dramatic, it seems likely that most people would distinguish the two cases. When subjects in a research study were given a series of scenarios that differed in the amount of coercion exerted on the offender, subjects gave a complete defence in the extreme case but also varied the degree of liability in less severe cases according to the degree of coercion they perceived.[18] If codes were to reflect this view, they would allow reductions in grade for excusing conditions short of a complete defence.

D. Grading v. Sentencing: The Arguments Against Judicial Sentencing as a Substitute for Grading

One might agree that the ideal code takes account of many more factors but still argue that a code can only do so much. To take account of even the most significant factors in grading requires a document even more complex than current codes. The complexity of the punishment judgement requires, the argument continues, that the task be left primarily to the discretion of sentencing judges.

Three kinds of arguments stand against this claim that codes must generally defer to judicial sentencing discretion: we need not defer, we ought not defer, and increasingly we do not defer.

Codes need not defer to judicial sentencing discretion. It is within our current ability to draft codes that take account of the most significant grading distinctions. This is the point demonstrated in Part IV. It admittedly would be difficult to make codes more sophisticated in their grading assessments in their current mix-function form. But Part IV demonstrates that there is much that can be done to gain greater sophistication with greater simplicity through structural changes such as separate codes for separate functions. Such a system is illustrated in Appendix B, articles 30 and 31.

There is great efficiency in using general principles, for example, to adjust an offence grade up or down according to culpability level, extent of the harm, causal contribution, degree of an actor's responsibility for his conduct, or some other relevant factor. Thus, a code can take account of a wide range of factors in setting the grade of a violation without requiring that the factors be redefined and restated in every offence

---

[18] *Ibid.* 147–55.

definition.[19] So, for example, recklessness as to causing property damage might be a Class D misdemeanor, while purposely causing the same damage might be a Class C misdemeanor. (Such a system is likely to have many more offence grades than the seven or eight typical of current codes, however.)

Part IV provides many other illustrations of improved drafting approaches. Let me leave the discussion until then but here make just two general points. First, the grading task requires less than the task of sentencing generally. Only the amount of punishment issue need be addressed in grading, the method of sanction issue (prison v. house arrest v. probation v. fine, etc.) may be left to the discretion of sentencing judges without injuring the legality and related interests discussed below, as long as the sanctioning method or methods selected impose the amount of punishment called for.[20]

Secondly, the need for simplicity in application is greatest where a document is intended for wide public dissemination and quick application, as with rules of conduct. If the grading rules are segregated from the functionally-mixed provisions of current codes, they can be considerably more complex than they might otherwise be. With training and education we can expect criminal adjudicators to apply more complex and more sophisticated provisions than the untrained and uninstructed citizen. The adjudication process allows an opportunity for thoughtful and thorough application of grading rules that the real-world application of conduct rules would not always permit.

Assuming that it is possible to draft a workable yet more sophisticated code grading system, why should we bother? A second set of arguments makes the case for why a code ought not to defer to the discretion of sentencing judges. The arguments essentially track the reasons for our long-held support for the legality principle. We ought to articulate as much as we can about the factors that affect the amount of punishment to be imposed because such articulated rules increase the uniformity of punishment among similar cases sentenced by different judges. Such articulated rules give notice of what conduct is deemed more serious and what less serious, and this in turn makes the deterrent threat for more serious offences clearer. Such rules also can more systematically assure that each additional harm or evil will trigger additional punishment. Where a more-harm-more-punishment principle is adhered to, an articulated grading system can better announce the principle and thereby better deter additional harms. Finally, an articulated grading system more effectively preserves for the legislature judgements about the relative seriousness of various societal

---

[19] See generally Paul H. Robinson, 'A Sentencing System for the 21st Century' (1987) 66 *Texas LR* 1 at 34–8 (hereinafter '21st Century').

[20] See Paul H. Robinson, 'Desert, Crime Control, Disparity, and Units of Punishment', in A. Duff *et al.* (eds.), *Penal Theory and Practice* (Manchester, 1994), 93–105.

harms, a judgement appropriately made by the legislative branch in a democratic system. No doubt there is a limit to how precise a grading system can be. The thrust of these arguments is simply to suggest that we ought to adopt a system that embodies as much of the grading judgement as our current understanding allows us to articulate.

The need for more comprehensive codification of grading factors also is suggested by the tendency of some people, including sentencing judges and commissioners, to conclude that if the criminal code takes account of a factor it can no longer be relevant to grading. Consider the treatment of excusing conditions short of a complete defence by the United States Sentencing Commission. As a Commissioner, I proposed that the federal sentencing guidelines contain a general principle of adjustment to account for excusing conditions that fall short of providing a complete defence.[21] The strongly held view of most of my colleagues was that the defendant had raised and lost on such issues at trial and ought not be able to raise them again. That is, they saw the code's present treatment of the issue, as a dichotomous liability issue, as meaning that the factor could not properly be considered as well on the issue of grading. This is not an unreasonable conclusion to draw. It suggests, however, that where a code does not make clear that a factor is relevant to grading, judges and sentencing commissioners may mistakenly assume that it is not relevant, especially if the code recognizes and uses the factor in its liability function.[22]

Finally, a third set of arguments in support of an articulation of grading factors and principles is found in the reality that this is in essence what many states and the federal system are doing as they develop more articulated 'sentencing' systems. The movement has been characterized as one of *sentencing* reform, but in truth the vast majority of the reforms have been to do precisely what the *grading* provisions of a criminal code do, set some general limits on the sentencing discretion of judges for a given kind of offence and offence circumstances. We have kept this false grading–sentencing distinction because constitutional rulings on proof of *offence* elements limit the nature of possible reforms if those reforms are seen as touching the criminal code, where offence elements are set out. But it is not always easy to distinguish legislative grading from legislatively authorized binding limits on judicial sentencing, other than by the difference in their location in and out of the code. This is not an argument for petrifying sentencing systems as constitutional rulings have done to much

---

[21] See Robinson, '21st Century', n. 19 above, at 34–8.

[22] I think it wrong to draw this implication from the code's failure to use a factor in grading. A better interpretation of the code's treatment is that some factors are more important in grading than others and that some are more easily reduced to defensible categories than others. Note that the Commission was persuaded that degree of complicity should be adopted as a grading/sentencing factor even though it is a factor recognized by the code and used only in a minimum-requirements role: see United States Sentencing Commission, Guidelines Manual (Nov 1990), §§ 3B1.1 & 3B1.2.

of criminal codes but rather an argument for allowing legislatures more freedom in structuring new ways to assess criminal punishment, perhaps by deconstitutionalizing some aspects of the proof requirements for criminal offences.

E. CONCLUSION

Does the criminal law properly distinguish among different grades of violations? Confusion in the function of doctrines may account for an under-utilization or failure to take account of factors that have a significant effect on grade, at least as significant as factors that the doctrine does take account of. In some cases, the failure is obscured because the functional confusion is hidden within a misconceived doctrinal formulation. This is the case, for example, where culpability terms, designed for a liability function, are used to define prohibited risk, a rule articulation function. The resulting effect is to distort the grading function by aggravating a violation for actually creating a criminal risk when in fact the risk existed only in the actor's mind.

Under-utilization of grading factors is more apparent where the doctrine fails to take account in grading of significant differences in such things as the extent of resulting harm and differences in culpability level. Relevant grading factors are ignored altogether in some instances, as with such factors as differences in an actor's degree of causal accountability for a result, differences in causal contribution to a violation by another, and differences in the degree of dysfunction and impairment short of complete excuse. It is possible that these weaknesses in current grading schemes result in part from a failure to make an independent assessment of the doctrine's performance of this function.

Part IV
Using Structure to Advance Function

Part III explains the various functions that a criminal code performs. The code announces the law's commands to those whose conduct it seeks to influence. It also defines the rules to be used in deciding whether a breach of the law's commands will result in criminal liability and, if so, the grade or degree of that liability. In serving the first function, the code addresses all members of the public. In performing the second and third functions, it addresses lawyers, judges, jurors, and others who play a role in the adjudication process.

In part because of the different audiences, the different code functions call for different kinds of documents. To communicate effectively to the public, the code must be easy to read and understand. It must give a clear statement, in objective terms if possible, of the conduct that the law prohibits and under what conditions it is prohibited. Readability, accessibility, simplicity, and clarity are the central virtues if the code is effectively to articulate and announce the criminal law's rules of conduct.

The adjudicators, on the other hand, can tolerate greater complexity. Clarity and simplicity are always a virtue, but the judgements required of adjudicators necessarily limit how simple the adjudication rules can be. While the public can be told rather easily and clearly that 'you may not cause bodily injury or death to another person',[1] when a prohibited injury or death does occur, the adjudicators need rules to determine whether the injurer ought to escape liability because he or she had no culpability, was insane, mistakenly but reasonably believed that the force used was necessary for self-defence, or for any number of other reasons. If liability is appropriate, the adjudication rules must determine the degree of liability that is appropriate, taking account of the level of the actor's culpability, the extent of the injury, and a variety of other mitigating and aggravating circumstances. Many, if not most, of these liability and grading factors must use complex and sometimes subjective criteria.

The use in current practice of a single code to perform all three functions means that none of the functions is performed as well as it could

---

[1] App. A, § 3 (Injury to a Person).

be.[2] Could one draft two codes—a code to articulate the rules of conduct, written for lay persons, and a code to govern the adjudication process, written for criminal justice professionals? If one were to pull out of a current criminal code only those provisions that a lay person must know in order to remain law-abiding, what would such a document contain and what would it look like? If one were to organize a code to capture the decisional process for criminal adjudication, what would such a document contain and what would it look like? Chapters 10 and 11 attempt to answer these questions. Their tentative conclusion is that distinct codes of conduct and of adjudication can be drafted that will allow the criminal law to perform both functions more efficiently and successfully.

Separate codes for separate functions can be created by examining the function performed by each rule of criminal law. Most rules need be included only in the code of conduct or the code of adjudication, not both. For example, to communicate effectively to the members of the public the rules needed to conform their conduct to the requirements of law, it is not necessary to communicate the subtleties of the insanity defence, the detailed definitions of culpable states of mind, or the operation of the entrapment doctrine. That is, a code of conduct and a code of adjudication can be created by segregating the doctrines of criminal law into one or the other code according to the function that each doctrine performs. (There is no suggestion by this segregation that the code drafted for adjudicators be kept secret from the public, as we shall see below.[3])

This Part shows how a code of conduct and a code of adjudication should be drafted, and how, taken together, the two codes will better perform each of the three functions of criminal codes. Chapter 10 discusses strategies for drafting an effective code of conduct, Chapter 11 for drafting a code of adjudication. Both discussions use examples from the complete models for a draft code of conduct in Appendix A and a draft code of adjudication in Appendix B. These codes are not refined, ready-to-enact models, but rather are meant simply as illustrations of the drafting principles developed in the two chapters.[4]

---

[2] See generally Paul H. Robinson, 'A Functional Analysis of Criminal Law' (1994) 88 *Northwestern ULR* 857; Paul H. Robinson, 'Rules of Conduct and Principles of Adjudication' (1990) 57 *University of Chicago LR* 729.

[3] See Ch. 11, sect. F.

[4] Most of the material in this Part is taken from Paul H. Robinson, Peter D. Greene, and Natasha R. Goldstein, 'Making Criminal Codes Functional: A Code of Conduct and a Code of Adjudication' (1996) 86 *Journal of Criminal Law & Criminology* 304.

10

Drafting a Code of Conduct

How can one create a clear statement for the public of the rules of conduct, one that is easy to read, understand, and apply in daily life, even in the situations of anxiety and confusion in which the potential for criminal conduct sometimes arises? Here are five drafting principles toward that end.

A. Eliminate Liability and Grading Language

The feature of current criminal codes that most hurts its communication to the public, unnecessarily so, is its inclusion of much more than the rules of conduct. The conduct rules are hidden among the much longer and more complex rules governing the adjudication of liability and grading. Even if the conduct rules could be understood, they cannot be found. At under 2,300 words, including headings, the draft code of conduct in Appendix A is one-fifteenth the length of the Model Penal Code, although it covers essentially the same material.[1]

Consider an example, perhaps an extreme one. The Model Penal Code's definition of assault is set out in the margin.[2] In essence, the Code's section 211.1 criminalizes causing bodily injury to another. Eliminating the

---

[1] The relevant provisions of the Model Penal Code—Part I (excluding Articles 6 and 7) and Part II—are approximately 35,000 words in length: see Model Penal Code (Official Draft 1985). The comparable parts of the Draft English Code total less than 33,000 words.

[2] Model Penal Code, section 211.1 (Assault) provides:

'(1) Simple Assault. A person is guilty of assault if he:

   (a) attempts to cause or purposely, knowingly, or recklessly causes bodily injury to another;

or

   (b) negligently causes bodily injury to another with a deadly weapon; or
   (c) attempts by physical menace to put another in fear of imminent serious bodily injury.

Simple assault is a misdemeanor unless committed in a fight or scuffle entered into by mutual consent, in which case it is a petty misdemeanor.

(2) Aggravated Assault. A person is guilty of aggravated assault if he:

   (a) attempts to cause serious bodily injury to another, or causes such injury purposely, knowingly or recklessly under circumstances manifesting extreme indifference to the value of human life; or

liability and grading language from the provision leaves a fairly readable
and understandable rule (the number at the beginning of the excerpt is
the section number of the provision in the Appendix):

3. INJURY TO A PERSON
   You may not cause bodily injury or death to another person.

Gone are all culpability requirements, as well as other language defining
grades of assault. Indeed, this simple rule of conduct is not only a substitute for the Code's definitions of simple and aggravated assault in section 211.1, but also for the definitions of criminal homicide in section
210.1, murder in section 210.2, manslaughter in section 210.3, negligent
homicide in section 210.4, and reckless endangerment in section 211.2.[3]
Together these offence definitions take up some 490 words in the Model
Penal Code, 475 more than the fifteen words of the draft code of conduct provision quoted above.

   Similarly, the Model Penal Code's provisions relating to complicity,
solicitation, and conspiracy, in Code sections 2.06, 5.02, 5.03, 5.04, and
5.05, contain 1,600 words. The rule of conduct they contain is reducible
to this:

50. ACTING WITH ANOTHER TOWARD COMMISSION OF A CRIME (COMPLICITY,
CONSPIRACY, AND SOLICITATION)
   You may not agree with, ask, assist, or encourage another to commit a crime.

Gone are all culpability requirements, doctrines of mitigation and aggravation, and special defences, for none of these are needed to tell people what
this aspect of the law commands of them.

   Also gone from the code of conduct are all excuse defences and non-
exculpatory defences. Only justification defences are kept, and then only
their objective requirements. To remain law-abiding, people need to know
the rules that allow them to use otherwise unlawful force. It is not necessary, however, that they also know, for example, the conditions that will
give a duress excuse or the kind of mistake that will mitigate their level
of liability.[4]

> (b) attempts to cause or purposely or knowingly causes bodily injury to another
> with a deadly weapon.
>
> Aggravated assault under paragraph (a) is a felony of the second degree; aggravated
> assault under paragraph (b) is a felony of the third degree.'

[3] The substitute for reckless endangerment also requires reference to App. A, sect. 51
(Creating a Prohibited Risk).

[4] People may well find some information in the adjudication code useful. For example,
the relative seriousness of offences as reflected in their grading may be useful in judging the
justification of conduct. The point here is simply that conveying the basic rules of conduct
is an important function that can be improved by keeping the statement of rules as simple
and straightforward as possible. The code of adjudication should remain available to lay
persons, as the criminal code is now, so that such information as the relative grades of
offences will remain available: see Ch. 11, sect. F.

B. Consolidate Overlapping Offences

Eliminating grading language from offence definitions has a second beneficial effect. Many offences in current codes prohibit conduct identical to that prohibited by other offences; the offences are defined separately only for grading purposes. For example, an offender frequently is held liable for the same conduct under different offences depending upon whether a prohibited harm actually results. Thus, reckless endangerment[5] and reckless homicide[6] prohibit the same conduct (or at least should prohibit the same conduct[7]), with the latter applicable where the risk created results in death and the former applicable where it does not. Where the conduct results in injury but not death, a third offence applies, assault; the assault offence for which the offender is liable may vary with the extent of the injury caused.[8] In other words, grading distinctions are made both by creating subsections within an offence and by creating separate offences, and all of these distinctions can be eliminated in drafting a code of conduct that has as its purpose only a description of the law's commands.

Consolidation is possible for every set of offences that differ from one another only in that one prohibits causing a result and another prohibits engaging in conduct that risks the same result. Model Penal Code section 220.2(1) defines the offence of causing a catastrophe; section 220.2(2) defines the separate offence of risking a catastrophe. The only difference is one of grading: recklessly causing a catastrophe is a third degree felony, while only risking it, with the same culpable state of mind, is a misdemeanour.[9]

A similar proliferation of offences in present codes occurs where multiple offences punish the same conduct but at different liability levels because of different levels of culpability. For example, the Model Penal Code distinguishes among three homicide offences—murder, manslaughter, and negligent homicide—according to the actor's level of culpability as to causing the result—purposeful or knowing, reckless, and negligent, respectively.[10]

Another source of proliferation is illustrated in the theft offences, where each of several different offences criminalizes a particular form of taking, using, or transferring another's property without consent.[11] Model Penal Code section 223.2(1) criminalizes taking or exercising control over movable property. Section 223.3 prohibits obtaining property by deception. Section 223.4 criminalizes obtaining property by extortion. Section 223.7

---

[5] Model Penal Code, § 211.2 (Recklessly Endangering Another Person).

[6] Model Penal Code, § 210.3 (Manslaughter).

[7] For discussion of the Model Penal Code's failure to provide a general definition of criminal risk that governs both offences, see Paul H. Robinson, 'A Functional Analysis of Criminal Law' (1994) 88 *Northwestern ULR* 857 at 886–7.

[8] Model Penal Code, § 211.1 (Assault).

[9] Model Penal Code, § 220.2(1)–(2) (Causing or Risking Catastrophe).

[10] Model Penal Code, §§ 210.2 (Murder), 210.3 (Manslaughter), 210.4 (Negligent Homicide).

[11] See Model Penal Code, Article 223 (Theft and Related Offences).

covers theft of services, while section 223.8 targets theft by failure to make required disposition of funds received.[12] The rule of conduct for these offences (and for property damage offences) is reducible to this:

24. DAMAGE TO OR THEFT OF PROPERTY

You may not damage, take, use, dispose of, or transfer another's property without the other's consent. Property is anything of value, including services offered for payment and access to recorded information.

Another kind of proliferation is found in offences that combine prohibitions already contained individually in other offences. The offence of robbery,[13] for example, simply prohibits a combination of theft and assault. It may be that such conduct ought to be graded higher than it would be if punished separately as a theft and an assault. If this is so, then such a policy should be reflected in the adjudication code. But creation of a robbery offence adds nothing to the law's statement of prohibited conduct; the theft and assault prohibitions already make it clear that the conduct described in the robbery offence is criminal.

The same is true of burglary, which combines trespass and attempt to commit another substantive offence, such as theft.[14] Similarly, arson combines reckless endangerment and criminal mischief.[15] All of these combination offences can be eliminated by a code of conduct without loss of coverage. Beyond providing a shorter, clearer statement of the rules of conduct, consolidation of offences exposes inadvertent loopholes in offence prohibitions. A set of overly specific, related provisions may criminalize remarkably similar conduct, yet overlook a few significant variations.[16]

C. SIMPLIFY JUSTIFICATION DEFENCES

Current justification defences nicely illustrate the kinds of errors that code drafters commit when they fail to distinguish the functions of a code of

---

[12] The grading of these offences in Model Penal Code, section 223.1(2) (Consolidation of Theft Offences; Grading; Provisions Applicable to Theft Generally) is not tied to the mode of theft defining each offence, which may justify that Code's use of separate offences, but, rather, depends primarily on the value of the item stolen.

[13] Model Penal Code, § 222.1 (Robbery); Draft English Code, ¶ 146.

[14] See Model Penal Code, § 221.1 (Burglary) (committed by an actor who 'enters a building or occupied structure . . . with purpose to commit a crime therein, unless . . . the actor is licensed or privileged to enter').

[15] See Model Penal Code, §§ 220.1 (Arson and Related Offences), 211.2 (Recklessly Endanger-ing Another Person), 220.3 (Criminal Mischief). Similarly, Model Penal Code section 251.3 (Loitering to Solicit Deviate Sexual Relations) combines loitering (§ 250.6) and solicitation (§ 5.02).

[16] For example, the Illinois Criminal Code contains eleven separate prostitution-related offences, criminalizing nearly all forms of prostitution. Yet, while it criminalizes 'touching or fondling of the sex organs . . . for money *or anything of value*', Ill. Rev. Stat., ch. 38, paras. 11–4 (1993) (emphasis added), the Code inexplicably fails to criminalize *sexual intercourse* for 'anything of value', perhaps because the complexity of so many related provisions hid the inadvertent omission. (In its other sexual provisions, the Code defines distinct, parallel offences for unlawful touching and intercourse.)

conduct and a code of adjudication. Current justification defences are frequently detailed and complex; the Model Penal Code's defence of property provision alone goes on for three pages, 1,035 words.[17] (The Draft English Code is significantly briefer. Clause 44 consolidates all defensive force defences and uses fewer than 500 words in doing so.) The portion of the Model Penal Code provision that governs use of force for the recapture of property unlawfully taken, for example, reads as follows:

(1) Subject to the provisions of this Section and of Section 3.09, the use of force upon or toward the person of another is justifiable when the actor believes that such force is immediately necessary: . . .

 (b) to effect an entry or re-entry upon land or to retake tangible movable property, provided that the actor believes that he or the person by whose authority he acts or a person from whom he or such other person derives title was unlawfully dispossessed of such land or movable property and is entitled to possession, and provided, further, that:

  (i) the force is used immediately or on fresh pursuit after such dispossession; or
  (ii) the actor believes that the person against whom he uses force has no claim of right to the possession of the property and, in the case of land, the circumstances, as the actor believes them to be, are of such urgency that it would be an exceptional hardship to postpone the entry or re-entry until a court order is obtained. . . .

(3) Limitations on Justifiable Use of Force . . .

 (c) Resistance of Lawful Re-entry or Recaption. The use of force to prevent an entry or re-entry upon land or the recaption of movable property is not justifiable under this Section, although the actor believes that such re-entry or recaption is unlawful, if:

  (i) the re-entry or recaption is made by or on behalf of a person who was actually dispossessed of the property; and
  (ii) it is otherwise justifiable under paragraph (1)(b) of this Section.[18]

While such complexity may be tolerable in a code of adjudication, it borders on silly to think that a person who comes upon another unlawfully taking his or her property would or could follow these rules, even if he or she had a copy of the rules in hand.

The drafters' failure to understand the natural limitations of a criminal code creates two problems. First, their efforts to alter people's conduct by drafting complex code provisions in one way or another are doomed to fail. For example, the drafters may be right that it is best to have a person resist the temptation to use force to recapture property taken by a person acting under a claim of right, as Model Penal Code section

---

[17] See Model Penal Code, § 3.06.   [18] Model Penal Code, § 3.06 (1)(b), (3)(c).

3.06(3)(c)(i) provides. It may be better to have the parties settle their dispute in court than to allow a clash that could escalate into violence.[19] But can the drafters really believe that by putting such a special rule in the code, among the 1,035 words of the defence of property provision, people being unlawfully dispossessed of property will refrain from resisting because this rule will come to their mind?

I regularly teach the Model Penal Code's defensive force provisions but would be unable to apply the complex rules and exceptions of the Code governing a recapture situation. How can one think that such statutory pronouncements can alter the conduct of the average persons who are not law professors? Whenever criminal code drafters formulate a special rule in the expectation that it will alter people's conduct, they show their ignorance of the code's limited accessibility to the average person.

A more serious effect of the code drafter's ignorance on this point is the unfairness it creates for individual defendants who come within the scope of one of these rules. The actor defending his or her property against an unlawful dispossession, who is unlikely to know anything about the drafters' special rule barring recapture from one acting under a 'claim of right', will be denied a justification defence if he or she violates the rule. Thus, the drafters' erroneous belief that they can change conduct by manipulating complex statutory rules not only fails to change conduct, but also creates unfairness by denying a defence to a person who could not reasonably have been expected to have known to do other than he or she did. To avoid this unfairness, where a code of conduct adopts any rule that cannot be simply stated, the rule ought to correspond to the lay person's intuition of what a just rule for the situation would provide. Section E takes up this issue below.

The draft code of conduct in Appendix A suggests a formulation that reduces the Model Penal Code's 1,035 words to the following thirty-three:

56. DEFENCE OF PROPERTY

You may use reasonable force against a person who is unlawfully threatening property or who has just unlawfully taken property, if such force is immediately necessary to defend or take back the property.

D. USE SIMPLE, ACCESSIBLE LANGUAGE

The previous three drafting principles improve a code's communicative potential by reducing complexity and eliminating unnecessary language. A different kind of improvement is the use of simple and plain language. In other contexts, scholars have noted the benefits of plain language drafting

---

[19] See Model Penal Code, § 3.06 comments 73–4 (1985).

and careful attention to the structure of a code's provisions.[20] Lay comprehension can be improved through careful word choice, sentence structure, and overall organization. Several kinds of reformulations are useful.

First, short, commonly-used words are preferable.[21] Consider Model Penal Code section 240.1, prohibiting the gaining of an advantage by interfering with the exercise of political power:

A person is guilty of bribery, a felony of the third degree, if he offers, confers or agrees to confer upon another, or solicits, accepts or agrees to accept from another:

(1) any pecuniary benefit as *consideration* for the recipient's decision, opinion, recommendation, vote or other exercise of discretion as a public servant, party official or voter.[22]

While the term 'consideration' may have a clear meaning for lawyers, the term does not have the same meaning for the lay person.[23] A code of conduct prohibition might better read something like the following:

45. BRIBERY AND CRIMINAL COMPENSATION
You may not offer or accept any benefit either to influence the future action of or in return for past action by a public official or servant, a party official, or a voter, UNLESS such benefit is a legal fee or salary for such action.

This prohibits the conduct criminalised by the Model Penal Code section (and much more[24]), but replaces the word 'consideration' with the words 'influence' and 'in return for'.

The offence of prostitution provides another example. The Model Penal Code prohibition provides:

A person is guilty of prostitution, a petty misdemeanor, if he or she:

(a) is an *inmate* of a house of prostitution or otherwise engages in sexual activity as a business.[25]

---

[20] See Irving Younger, 'In Praise of Simplicity' (1976) 62 *American Bar Association J* 632 (hereinafter 'Praise of Simplicity'); Richard Wydick, *Plain English for Lawyers* (3rd edn., Durham, North Carolina, 1994) (hereinafter *Plain English*); Michele M. Asprey, *Plain Language for Lawyers* (Sydney, Australia, 1991) (hereinafter *Plain Language*); Mark Adler, *Clarity for Lawyers: The Use of Plain English in Legal Writing* (London, 1990) (hereinafter *Clarity for Lawyers*).
[21] See Wydick, *Plain English*, n. 20 above, at 53–60; Asprey, *Plain Language*, n. 25 above, at 81–97; Adler, *Clarity for Lawyers*, n. 20 above, at 62, 75–81.
[22] Model Penal Code, § 240.1 (Bribery in Official and Political Matters) (emphasis added).
[23] *Webster's Third New International Dictionary* (Springfield, Massachusetts, 1966), 484 defines consideration as 'observation, contemplation; continuous or deliberate thought'. The eighth meaning listed is 'something given as recompense', but this is not the common understanding of the term.
[24] The draft section also includes the prohibitions of Model Penal Code, §§ 240.6 (Compensating Public Servant for Assisting Private Interests in Relation to Matters Before Him), 240.7 (Selling Political Endorsement; Special Influence), 241.6 (Tampering with Witnesses and Informants; Retaliation Against Them), and 224.8 (Commercial Bribery and Breach of Duty to Act Disinterestedly).
[25] Model Penal Code, § 251.2(1)(a) (Prostitution and Related Offences) (emphasis added).

Just as 'consideration' has a meaning for the drafters that is different from its ordinary usage, so too does 'inmate'. In current common usage the term refers to someone incarcerated in a prison rather than to a resident of a house of prostitution. The draft code of conduct replaces this language with the following:

34. PROSTITUTION
You may not engage in, support, or profit from any sexual act that is offered for sale.[26]

This draft provision also covers the prohibitions contained in Model Penal Code sections 251.2(1)(b)–(6) (Prostitution and Related Offences). In this instance, 591 Model Penal Code words are reduced to eighteen.

A second technique to increase comprehension is the use of shorter sentences.[27] The Model Penal Code, in addition to using technical legal language, commonly relies on long, multi-clause sentences. Model Penal Code section 223.5, for example, provides:

A person who comes into control of property of another that he knows to have been lost, mislaid, or delivered under a mistake as to the nature or amount of the property or the identity of the recipient is guilty of theft if, with purpose to deprive the owner thereof, he fails to take reasonable measures to restore the property to a person entitled to have it.[28]

Shorter sentences convey the same information as this sentence of sixty-seven words but increase the likelihood of lay comprehension. The draft code of conduct criminalizes the same conduct as follows:

27. FAILURE TO RETURN LOST OR MISTAKENLY DELIVERED PROPERTY
You may not keep lost or mistakenly delivered property, UNLESS you make a reasonable effort to find its owner and return the property.

A third clarification technique involves the capitalization of connecting words. The quotation above illustrates the use of capitalization to highlight important conditions. The same is useful to highlight connecting words that might easily be missed. Some offences criminalize conduct only if it satisfies several conditions; others may prohibit any one of a list of related actions. The significant difference between such provisions is brought to the attention of the reader by highlighting the connecting words. For example, the draft code of conduct provision defining the justified use of force by a parent, guardian, teacher, or caretaker requires *both* of two conditions:

---

[26] A 'sexual act' is defined in App. A, § 35.
[27] See Wydick, *Plain English*, n. 20 above, at 33–7; Asprey, *Plain Language*, n. 20 above, at 74.
[28] Model Penal Code, § 223.5 (Theft of Property Lost, Mislaid, or Delivered by Mistake).

62. USE OF FORCE BY PARENT, GUARDIAN, TEACHER, OR CARETAKER

If you are a parent, guardian, teacher, or caretaker, you may use reasonable force against a minor or incompetent if:

(a) you are legally responsible for the minor or incompetent's care or supervision, AND

(b) such force is necessary to safeguard the well-being of the minor or incompetent.

In contrast, the duty to act to prevent a catastrophe requires action if *either* of two conditions is met:

26. DUTY TO PREVENT CATASTROPHE

You must make reasonable efforts to prevent or reduce potentially widespread injury or damage from explosion, fire, flood, avalanche, collapse of building, release of other harmful or destructive force or substance, or any other means, if you:

(a) have an official, contractual, or other legal duty to prevent the injury or damage, OR

(b) have contributed to creating the danger.

The capitalization of the connecting words (AND and OR) emphasizes the relation between the two conditions and reduces misunderstanding.[29]

A different kind of reform switches present codes' use of phrases like 'an actor' or 'a person' in describing a prohibition to use of the second person pronoun, 'you'. If the point of the code of conduct is to tell people that each of them has an obligation not to engage in the listed prohibited conduct and that each must perform the listed required conduct, what better way to emphasize the point than through the use of the second person pronoun.[30] The law's prohibitions are not directed at some abstract, nameless, hypothetical person. They are directed at YOU.

Finally, a code of conduct can be made more comprehensive by organizing it in a way that helps readers understand how it works. Notice from the Appendix A table of contents that all offence conduct is collected in Part II, grouped within that Part according to a few basic categories. (The federal criminal code and some state criminal codes, in contrast, intersperse offences with other provisions, organizing all the provisions alphabetically.[31]) Part III of the draft code of conduct expands each of the basic offences by adding general prohibitions against attempting, assisting, or risking any of the offences in Part II. Part IV summarizes the special justifying circumstances in which a person may commit one of the offences

[29] See Wydick, *Plain English*, n. 20 above, at 46–7; Asprey, *Plain Language*, n. 20 above, at 108–9.

[30] See Wydick, *Plain English*, n. 20 above, at 69.

[31] See e.g. 18 USC, chs. 2 (aircraft)–121 (wiretapping) (1988); Del. Code Ann., tit. 22, §§ 2 (abortion)–39 (victims) (1989); Idaho Code, §§ 4 (abandonment)–72 (weights and measures) (1987).

otherwise prohibited, again, grouping the justifications into a few basic categories. This organization not only makes it easy to see the practical connection between similarly grouped provisions, it also allows the reader to better understand the functional differences between each of the types of provisions.

E. Track Community Views Where Possible

One last kind of reform that increases a code of conduct's effectiveness concerns not form but content. Behavioural science research suggests that people better understand rules that mirror their own intuitive judgements about assessing liability. For example, one study of juror comprehension of legal instructions gave true–false questions about legal rules to jurors who had been given legal jury instructions and to jurors who had not.[32] The extent of the superior performance of the instructed jurors, if any, would give an indication of the extent to which the instructions were being understood. The study found that for 63.6% of the questions, jury instructions had no statistically significant effect in increasing juror comprehension of the law.[33] Other studies confirm the poor performance of jury instructions in conveying legal principles to lay persons.[34] The reasons for this include many of the reasons noted above in explaining the weakness of current criminal codes in effectively communicating the rules of conduct.

One interesting and potentially helpful finding of the jury instruction work is that the instructed jurors tended to do better than the uninstructed jurors on issues on which the uninstructed jurors did relatively well,[35] presumably because the legal instructions built upon and articulated the lay jurors' existing intuition of what a just rule would be.[36] Perhaps this occurs

[32] Geoffrey P. Kramer and Doreen M. Koenig, 'Do Jurors Understand Criminal Jury Instructions? Analyzing the Results of the Michigan Juror Comprehension Project' (1990) 23 *University of Michigan Journal of Law Reform*, 401 at 409–10 (hereinafter 'Do Jurors Understand?').

[33] *Ibid.* 425. In another study using similar methodology, instructed jurors had at best a 6% greater success rate than uninstructed jurors in correctly assessing the defendant's liability in a controlled test case: Laurence J. Severance *et al.*, 'Toward Criminal Jury Instructions that Jurors Can Understand' (1984) 75 *Journal of Criminal Law & Criminology* 198 at 205–6.

[34] See generally Paul H. Robinson, 'Are Criminal Codes Irrelevant?' (1995) 68 *Southern California LR*, 159 at 170–2 (summarizing studies on effectiveness of jury instructions).

[35] Kramer and Koenig, 'Do Jurors Understand?', n. 32 above, at 421, 424. One issue was voluntary manslaughter, where 89.3% of instructed jurors correctly answered the questions on the issue as compared to 67.6% of the uninstructed jurors. The second issue was whether second degree criminal sexual conduct always involves injury and penetration, where all instructed jurors correctly answered the questions on the issue as compared to 64.4% of the uninstructed jurors.

[36] *Ibid.* 430. In other words, when a juror's preconceived notions are congruent with instructions, both uninstructed and instructed comprehension levels are quite high. See also Phoebe C. Ellsworth, 'Are Twelve Heads Better Than One?' (1989) 52 *Law & Contemporary Problems* 205 at 220–1.

because the instruction need only identify or remind the juror of the concept; the juror's prior knowledge provides the level of understanding that current instructions by themselves seem unable to provide.[37] In any case, these findings suggest that a similar effect is possible in increasing the comprehension of a code of conduct by having it mirror community views.

Beyond the issue of comprehension, a code of conduct inspires greater compliance if, in the public's view, it describes conduct that the public sees as wrongful. In other words, the code's credibility as an accurate statement of what is wrongful conduct enhances its effectiveness; its lack of credibility can undercut compliance.[38] For example, assume a code still criminalizes consensual sexual intercourse between unmarried persons, so-called 'fornication'. In our present society, that provision will be ignored. But more than that, the inclusion of such a provision may suggest to many people that the code drafters lack reliable judgement about what is indeed wrongful. That lack of credibility is likely to lead some to disregard the code in marginal cases. Presumably all will agree that rape, murder, and mayhem are wrong. But in less obvious cases, such as criminalization of the failure to return lost or stolen property,[39] the authority with which the code speaks, its earned moral credibility, may well influence the rate of compliance.[40]

---

[37] It would be useful to have further study of the change of both comprehension and nullification rates as instructions are more or less divergent from community views. Of course, this kind of research requires, first, research into the community's views on the issues to which the test instructions apply. See generally Paul H. Robinson and John M. Darley, *Justice, Liability and Blame: Community Views and Criminal Law* (Oxford, 1995) (hereinafter *Justice, Liability, and Blame*).

[38] See generally Robinson and Darley, Justice, Liability, and Blame, n. 37 above, at 6–7; Paul H. Robinson, 'A Failure of Moral Conviction?' (Fall 1994) 117 *The Public Interest* 40 at 44–6.

[39] Model Penal Code, § 223.5 (Theft of Property Lost, Mislaid, or Delivered by Mistake). Another example of marginal criminalization is the offence of 'refraining from reporting . . . the . . . suspected commission of any offence' in exchange for any compensation (Model Penal Code, § 242.5, Compounding).

[40] The draft code of conduct in App. A generally does not reflect community views, but rather tracks the prohibitions contained in the Model Penal Code. Reforming the rules of conduct to reflect community views would require empirical research beyond that which is presently available, to determine those views.

11
Drafting a Code of Adjudication

Chapter 10 set out the principles for drafting a code of conduct. This Chapter considers the same questions for drafting a code of adjudication. How can one best draft a code that clearly articulates the subtle distinctions in the complex adjudication decision concerning how much liability ought to be imposed, if any? Here are five drafting principles.

A. Adopt a Code Structure that Matches the Analytical Process

Whether the adjudicator is a prosecutor deciding whether and what to charge, a defence counsel giving advice on a proposed plea agreement, a judge writing jury instructions, or a jury deliberating a verdict, the process of assessing liability has several logical steps. By having a code of adjudication organized around that analytical process, the code can increase the chances that the adjudicator will understand and follow that process.

The analytical process properly follows three questions:

1. Has the defendant violated the rules of conduct?
2. If so, is the violation sufficiently blameworthy that criminal liability ought to attach?
3. If so, how much liability should be imposed?

The code of adjudication in Appendix B is organized around these questions. The process begins by comparing the defendant's conduct to that prohibited by the code of conduct, the same code that has been available to the defendant and all members of the public. Did the defendant's conduct violate the code?

Section 100. Violation of Code of Conduct
A person violates the Code of Conduct, for the purposes of this Code of Adjudication, if the person violates a prohibition or duty in Part II of the Code of Conduct and does not have a justification for such violation under Part IV of that Code.

A few additional provisions may be needed to make this determination with precision, provisions that are not necessary in the code of conduct itself, such as provisions giving more detailed explanations of what constitutes causation, attempt, conspiracy, solicitation, prohibited risk creation, and consent.[1]

Once it is clear that the code of conduct has been violated, the inquiry shifts to whether the violation was blameworthy. Here the relevant inquiries include whether the defendant acted with the required minimum culpable state of mind,[2] whether the defendant is accountable for the offence conduct performed by another,[3] whether the defendant ought to be excused for his culpable conduct because of insanity, immaturity, duress, or some other excusing condition,[4] and whether, despite his blameworthiness, the defendant is entitled to a non-exculpatory defence such as the statute of limitations or diplomatic immunity.[5]

If it is determined that liability is appropriate, the inquiry shifts to grading the violation. Here the adjudication code must take account of such issues as the seriousness of the offence harm or evil,[6] whether the offence harm or evil actually occurred,[7] the offender's level of culpability,[8] the extent of the offender's impaired capacity to avoid the offence, if any,[9] and, if the offender is an accomplice, the extent of the assistance he or she provided.[10] The mechanism used by the draft code of adjudication to take account of this wide range of factors sets a base grade for each violation described in the draft code of conduct, depending upon the seriousness of the offence, harm, or evil,[11] and then adjusts that base grade up or down according to the presence of various aggravating or mitigating factors.[12]

The end result of this process of adjustments to the base grade is a grading classification like that generated by current criminal codes, but one that

---

[1] App. B, §§ 110 (Causation Defined), 111 (Requirements for Violation of Code of Conduct Section 49 (Attempting Commission of a Crime)), 112 (Requirements for Violation of Code of Conduct Section 50 (Acting with Another Toward Commission of a Crime)), 113 (Requirements for Violation of Code of Conduct Section 51 (Creating a Prohibited Risk)), 114 (Consent Defence).   [2] See *ibid.*, § 200 (Minimum Culpability Required).

[3] See *ibid.*, § 212 (Accountability for Conduct of Another).

[4] See *ibid.*, Article 22 (Excuses).

[5] See *ibid.*, Article 23 (Non-exculpatory Defences).

[6] *Ibid.*, § 304 (Base Grade).

[7] *Ibid.*, § 304(49) (reduction in grade where harm, evil or offence has not occurred).

[8] *Ibid.*, § 310 (Adjustment for Greater Culpability).

[9] *Ibid.*, § 313 (Adjustment for Partial Disability).

[10] *Ibid.*, § 311 (Adjustment According to Extent of Participation in Assisting an Offence by Another).

[11] *Ibid.*, § 304 (Base Grade). Though the Model Penal Code served as a general guide for the assignment of base grades, the Code's grading judgements required refinement because the draft adjudication code uses fourteen grading categories (eight grades of felony, five grades of misdemeanor, and one grade of petty misdemeanour) in place of the Model Penal Code's five categories (three grades of felony, one grade of misdemeanour, and one grade of petty misdemeanour). Modern state codes commonly use eight or more categories: see e.g. NY Penal Law § 55.05 (McKinney 1987); Tex. Penal Code Ann., §§ 12.03–.04 (West 1994). The draft code of adjudication uses more categories than usual to allow smaller adjustments to grade.

[12] App. B, Article 31 (Adjustments to Base Grade). This scheme is similar to that used in the United States Sentencing Commission Guidelines and described in Paul H. Robinson, 'A Sentencing System for the 21st Century?' (1987) 66 *Texas LR* 1.

takes account of many more factors with greater sophistication and less complexity. Note that the draft adjudication code in Appendix B takes less than 5,300 words. Even when added to the 2,300 words of the draft conduct code, the two codes together are still approximately one-fifth the length of the comparable provisions of the Model Penal Code.[13] Although it is shorter, the draft adjudication code takes account of relevant factors that the Model Penal Code does not.[14]

B. Include All Articulable Rules Relevant to Adjudication

A code of adjudication is most useful if it includes all rules relevant to the liability decision, and as many rules relevant to the grading decision as feasible. Relying upon common law rules or giving the judiciary authority to create and define liability rules through case law is not an adequate substitute for codification. Comprehensiveness in a code has several important benefits.

First, comprehensiveness helps avoid inappropriate results. It is unrealistic to expect that judges will, in every case, be as effective as a legislature or a criminal code drafting commission in properly formulating doctrines that work together as do the provisions of a comprehensive code. The failure to create or properly to formulate a defence, for example, can result in liability for an actor who deserves to be exculpated. It is unrealistic to expect that a single judge in a single case can more properly formulate a defence than a legislative drafting committee.

Secondly, an uncodified rule is more likely to be applied differently in similar cases than a codified rule. The criteria of the latter are fixed, explicit, and easily available to all officials at each stage in the process. For example, assume a person seriously injures another in the course of a school football match. Can the injured party insist that the injurer be prosecuted for aggravated assault? In a jurisdiction that has no codified consent defence, as many do not,[15] the issue may be left to the discretion of the prosecutor or the judge, to be decided according to whether he or she thinks there should be a consent defence in such a situation. A sports hater, who sees school sports as a dangerous and irresponsible activity, may come to a different conclusion from a fan of the local team.

---

[13] The length of the Model Penal Code's relevant provisions is approximately 35,000 words. See n. 1 in Ch. 10.

[14] The Model Penal Code does not take account of such factors as the extent of participation by an accomplice (see App. B, § 311), a defendant's partial disability (see App. B, § 313), a defendant's selection of victim because of certain victim characteristics (see App. B, § 314). Nor does the Model Penal Code provide a system of special verdict forms (see App. B, Article 41).

[15] See e.g. Cal. Penal Code (Deering 1994); Ga. Code Ann., tit. 16 (1994); NC Gen. Stat., ch. 14 (1994).

The problem is not a hypothetical one. In addition to consent, provisions that are frequently missing from current criminal codes, even recently reformed codes, include such basic rules as those governing the requirements of causation,[16] mistake or ignorance of law or fact,[17] and customary license and *de minimis* infractions.[18] While there are arguments against a comprehensive code, they are outweighed by its advantages.[19]

C. Use General Principles Whenever Possible

A code of adjudication benefits from being shorter and more streamlined, just as Part I showed for a code of conduct.[20] The greatest benefits are achieved through the use of general rules that apply to all offences without having to repeat the rule in each specific offence. A good example is the culpability required for criminal liability. Current codes typically include a statement of culpability requirements in each offence definition, but the functions of culpability requirements suggest that a few general principles can be substituted.

A first principle suggests that criminal liability ought not be imposed in the absence of some minimum level of culpability as to each offence element. This function of culpability requirements is served by a general rule like the following:

Section 200. Minimum Culpability Required
(1) An actor's violation of the Code of Conduct is not criminal unless the actor is at least reckless as to each element of the violation as described in the Code of Conduct . . .

The general rule must be tempered:

. . . except that negligence is the minimum culpability required:
   (a) for a violation of the prohibition against causing the death of another person under Code of Conduct Section 3 (Injury to a Person); and
   (b) as to the age of the victim for a violation of Code of Conduct Section 14(b) or (c) (Criminal Sexual Contact).[21]

A jurisdiction might want additional exceptions; these are the two most common in current codes. The point is, the function of culpability

---

[16] See e.g. Ill. Rev. Stat., ch. 38 (1993); Nev. Rev. Stat. Ann., tit. 15 (1993); NH Rev. Stat. Ann., tit. LXII (1993).

[17] See e.g. RI Gen. Laws, tit. 11 (1993); SC Code Ann., tit. 16 (1992); Wyo. Stat., tit. 6 (1994).

[18] See e.g. Fla. Stat., tit. XLVI (1993); NY Penal Law (Consol. 1992); Wash. Rev. Code Ann., tit. 9–9A (West 1992).

[19] For a good summary of the arguments for and against, see the Draft English Criminal Code, vol. 1, 5–11.

[20] See Ch. 10.   [21] App. B, § 200 (Minimum Culpability Required).

requirements in setting a minimum condition of liability is more clearly and easily served when articulated as a general rule.

For some offences, especially inchoate offences, code drafters may wish to add a more demanding culpability requirement. This too can be provided by special mention within the general provision:

(2) In addition to the culpability requirements of Subsection (1), to be liable for a violation of:

(a) Code of Conduct Section 49 (Attempting Commission of a Crime), the actor must have the purpose to engage in the conduct that would constitute the violation; and

(b) Code of Conduct Section 50 (Acting with Another Toward Commission of a Crime (Complicity, Conspiracy and Solicitation)), the actor must have the purpose to facilitate the conduct constituting the violation.[22]

Culpability requirements perform a second function: increasing the grade of liability where the offender has committed the offence with a higher level of culpability than the required minimum. This is the case in homicide, for example, where the grade of a killing is a function of the actor's culpability as to causing the death. But this function too can be performed by a general principle. In the draft code of adjudication, this is done through the use of a grading table.[23] The base grade for each violation assumes the actor has only the minimum culpability required for liability. If greater liability is present, the grade of the violation is increased by the following general principle of adjustment:

Section 310. ADJUSTMENT FOR GREATER CULPABILITY

(1) The grade of an offence increases:

(a) two grades if the actor is purposeful as to the core elements, or
(b) one grade if the actor is knowing as to the core elements.

(2) Definitions. For the purposes of this Section:

(a) The 'core elements' are those facts that establish the violation in the Code of Conduct and its grade in Section 304 (Base Grade).

(b) 'Purposely', 'knowingly', 'recklessly', and 'negligently' are defined in Section 401 (Definitions).

If special culpability grading distinctions are needed for a particular offence, they need only be noted in the table.[24]

One added benefit of this approach is that it allows differences in culpability levels to be easily taken into account in all cases. While few people disagree with the general principle that greater culpability increases liability, current codes only occasionally alter liability accordingly. The homicide

---

[22] *Ibid.*   [23] *Ibid.*, § 304 (Base Grade).

[24] Note, for example, that reckless and negligent homicide are given special treatment in the grading table. See App. B, § 304(3)(a)–(b).

offences do this, as noted above, as does arson.[25] But most offences do not, including such important offences as statutory rape[26] and theft.[27] For example, negligence as to a sexual partner being under-age may be adequate for liability, but it is clear that greater blameworthiness ought to attach where the actor knows that the partner is under-age. Modern codes typically make no grading distinction between these two cases.[28]

The practice of current codes in ignoring culpability differences may reflect the overwhelming complexity of such a task given the structure of current codes. Recognizing culpability differences through the creation of separate offences or suboffences, the approach of current codes, dramatically multiplies the number of offences in a code. In contrast, with a general adjustment like the one quoted above, no such proliferation of offences is needed.

Other general principles in Appendix B similarly provide more sophisticated grading to take account of other relevant factors without a proliferation of offences. For example, if an actor does not receive a full excuse defence but nevertheless deserves some mitigation because of a substantial impairment of functioning, the following provision guides adjudicators:

Section 313. ADJUSTMENT FOR PARTIAL DISABILITY
The grade of the actor's offence decreases one grade if, at the time of the conduct constituting the offence, the actor suffers a substantial impairment of cognitive or control dysfunction, as defined in a provision in Article 22, but to a degree insufficient to merit a complete excuse.

Rather than creating a mitigation within each excuse defence, this general adjustment provides a set of parallel mitigations, piggybacking on the excuse criteria of each defence in Article 22. Other general adjustments take account of the extent of contribution by an accomplice, a choice of victim that aggravates the seriousness of the offence, and ineffective renunciation by an actor.[29]

D. USE PARALLEL LANGUAGE IN CONCEPTUALLY ANALOGOUS PROVISIONS

The previous subsection discusses the drafting advantages of using general principles when possible, rather than introducing a distinct rule for each factual context. An example is the use of a general principle of adjustment

---

[25] See Model Penal Code, § 220.1 (Arson and Related Offences).
[26] See Model Penal Code, § 213.3(1)(a) (Corruption of Minors and Seduction).
[27] See Model Penal Code, § 223.2 (Theft by Unlawful Taking or Disposition).
[28] See e.g. Model Penal Code, § 213.3(1)(a) (Corruption of Minors and Seduction).
[29] App. B, §§ 311 (Adjustment According to Extent of Participation in Assisting an Offence by Another), 312 (Adjustment for Ineffective Renunciation of Attempt, Conspiracy, or Solicitation), 314 (Adjustment for Selection of Victim).

for culpability level rather than the practice of modern codes of defining special culpability requirements for each offence. Such a tendency to splinter a single conceptual issue into a variety of context-specific rules creates difficulties beyond drafting. Such fracturing also invites inconsistent treatments in the different contexts.

For example, the Model Penal Code bars an intoxication excuse for any offence if the actor was negligent in bringing about the excusing condition, that is, in becoming intoxicated.[30] In the context of duress, in contrast, the actor's negligence only bars the defence for offences of negligence; an actor must be at least reckless as to causing the defence conditions to lose the defence when charged with an offence of recklessness, knowledge, or purpose.[31] In yet another variation, in the context of the lesser evils defence, an actor who is negligent in bringing about the justifying circumstances will lose the defence when charged with an offence of negligence, but recklessness in bringing about the defence conditions bars the defence only for offences of recklessness.[32] In still other instances, however, the Code gives no guidance on how to handle an actor's culpability in causing the defence conditions. This is the case, for example, for a defence for conduct performed under hypnosis.[33] Yet, there is no apparent reason for these different approaches to the problem of culpability in causing the conditions of one's defence. One can only guess that the drafters' penchant for context-specific rules blinded them to the conceptual similarity of the issues.[34]

The draft adjudication code deals with the problem in the following provision:

Section 240. CAUSING THE CONDITIONS OF ONE'S OWN JUSTIFICATION OR EXCUSE DEFENCE

(1) When an actor causes the conditions that give rise to a justification under Part IV of the Code of Conduct or to an excuse under Article 22 of the Code of Adjudication, the actor gains the benefit of the defence despite his or her conduct in causing the defence conditions, but

(2) the actor may be held liable for the violation of the Code of Conduct based upon his or her conduct in causing the defence conditions if, at the time of causing those conditions, the actor has the culpability as to bringing about the violation that is required by Section 200 (Minimum Culpability Required).

(3) As provided by Section 310 (Adjustment for Greater Culpability), the grade of liability for causing the defence conditions under Subsection (2) increases if the actor was knowing or purposeful as to causing the violation.

---

[30] Model Penal Code, § 2.08(4), (5)(b) (Intoxication).

[31] Model Penal Code, § 2.09(2) (Duress).

[32] Model Penal Code, § 3.02(2) (Justification Generally: Choice of Evils).

[33] See Model Penal Code, § 2.01 (Requirement of Voluntary Act; Omission as Basis of Liability; Possession as an Act).

[34] For a general discussion of the inconsistent treatment of causing the conditions of different defences, see Paul H. Robinson, 'Causing the Conditions of One's Own Defense: A Study in the Limits of Theory in Criminal Law Doctrine' (1985) 71 *Virginia LR* 1 at 1–27.

(4) *Defence to Liability for Causing the Conditions of One's Own Defence.* An actor may have a justification or excuse defence to liability under Subsection (2) for his or her conduct in causing the defence conditions.

A similar problem arises from the drafters' failure to see the conceptual similarity among excuses. The insanity and involuntary intoxication excuses use parallel language that makes clear that having the required disability —mental illness or involuntary intoxication—is not in itself enough to merit an excuse. The actor must show, in addition, that the disability caused a substantial impairment of functioning, such that the actor lacked 'substantial capacity either to appreciate the criminality [wrongfulness] of his conduct or to conform his conduct to the requirements of law'.[35] Yet, in the context of other excuses, such as hypnotism and somnambulism, the Code fails to impose such a dysfunction requirement.[36] There is no dispute that hypnosis and somnambulism create a wide variety of degrees of dysfunction, some very debilitating, some not,[37] yet the Code's provisions give a defence without any inquiry into the degree of dysfunction present in a given case. Under the Code's defence formulation, hypnosis or somnambulism provides a complete defence to an actor even if the condition did not cause a lack of 'substantial capacity either to appreciate the criminality [wrongfulness] of his conduct or to conform his conduct to the requirements of law'.[38] The draft adjudication code collects all excuses in Article 22 and uses parallel requirements for each.[39]

[35] Model Penal Code, § 4.01 (Mental Disease or Defect Excluding Responsibility); see *ibid.*, § 2.08(4) (Intoxication).
[36] See Model Penal Code, § 2.01(1), (2)(b)–(c) (Requirement of Voluntary Act; Omission as Basis of Liability; Possession as an Act).
[37] See Paul H. Robinson, 'A Functional Analysis of Criminal Law' (1994) 88 *Northwestern ULR* 857 at 896–901.
[38] For a more detailed discussion of this problem, see *ibid.*, at 896–901; see also Paul H. Robinson, 'Rules of Conduct and Principles of Adjudication' (1990) 57 *University of Chicago LR* 729 at 762–3 (discussing similar problems with Model Penal Code treatment of immaturity defence).
[39] Cases of hypnotism and somnambulism are dealt with under the following excuse defence:

Section 225. Disability Excuse: Impaired Consciousness
(1) An actor's violation of the Code of Conduct is excused if, at the time of the conduct constituting the violation, the actor:
(a) is in a state of impaired consciousness, and
(b) by reason of such impaired consciousness, lacks substantial capacity to:

(i) appreciate the criminality or wrongfulness of his or her conduct, or
(ii) conform his or her conduct to the requirements of law.

(2) 'State of Impaired Consciousness' Defined. For the purposes of Subsection (1)(a), a 'state of impaired consciousness' means a disturbance of consciousness resulting from a physiologically confirmable state or condition not specifically recognised or rejected as a basis for exculpation under any other Section included in this Article.
(3) Presumed Impaired Consciousness. An actor who is unconscious, asleep, or under hypnosis is presumed to be in a state of impaired consciousness as required by Subsection (1)(a).

E. Provide Jury Verdicts That Make Clear Their Meaning

One final proposal addresses the problem of ambiguous jury acquittals and their destructive effect on criminal justice. Let me first remind the reader of the problem, first discussed in Chapter 5, section B, then explain how a properly organized adjudication code can avoid the problem.

A verdict of 'not guilty' under the present system may mean either: (1) that the actor's conduct in the case *did not* violate the rules of conduct, or (2) that the actor's conduct *did* violate the rules of conduct but that he or she is entitled to a culpability defence, excuse, or non-exculpatory defence. Thus, any acquittal may be understood either to approve or to disapprove the actor's conduct, and that ambiguity prevents trial verdicts from educating the public about the commands of the criminal law. Indeed, ambiguous verdicts can affirmatively confuse a rule of conduct that otherwise would have been clear.

Recall the discussion in Chapter 7, section B, using the state court acquittals of the officers who beat Rodney King to illustrate the point. Hearing the verdicts, different people came to different conclusions about what the acquittals were intended to mean: to justify the conduct, or to condemn the conduct but excuse the actors. This conflict in views arises in part because the simple verdict of 'not guilty' fails to tell the whole story in a most important respect. The jurors could have voted not guilty because, while they disapproved of the conduct, they did not think the officers were sufficiently blameworthy to merit criminal conviction. Yet, people could reasonably interpret the verdict as an approval of the officers' conduct, which they reasonably could find an outrageous conclusion.

What is needed is a verdict system that distinguishes 'no violation' acquittals from 'blameless violation' acquittals. With proper organization, a code of adjudication easily can do this. Recall from the first drafting principle for an adjudication code—'Adopt a code structure that matches the analytic process'—that the draft code of adjudication in Appendix B considers separately the questions whether the defendant has violated a rule of conduct and whether that violation is blameworthy. A code that segregates these questions is then in a position to offer alternative verdicts of 'no violation' or 'blameless violation', depending upon the code provision giving rise to the acquittal.

The structure of the draft code of conduct in Appendix A has other similar benefits: it allows jury verdicts to educate the public by distinguishing 'no violation' acquittals from 'justified violation' acquittals. A 'no violation' acquittal confirms that the conduct at issue is not prohibited by the code of conduct and can lawfully be performed by others without any special justification. A 'justified violation' acquittal sends the opposite message about the conduct at issue: it *is* normally prohibited by the code of conduct and cannot lawfully be performed by others unless special justifying circumstances exist.

Assume, for example, that a bus passenger is running through the bus distracting the driver, impairing her view of the road, and endangering the vehicle and its passengers. Despite requests, the passenger refuses to sit down or to leave the bus. The driver then uses force to eject the passenger, causing him to twist his ankle. The driver has violated Section 3 of the draft code of conduct:

3. INJURY TO A PERSON
You may not cause bodily injury or death to another person.

However, because the driver also satisfies the requirements of Section 64, she receives a justification defence:

64. USE OF FORCE BY OPERATOR OF PUBLIC TRANSPORTATION
If you are responsible for the maintenance of safety, control, or order aboard a vehicle, vessel, train, or aircraft, you may use reasonable force if it is necessary to maintain such safety, control, or order.

An acquittal by verdict of 'justified violation' under section 64 reaffirms that bodily injury is not permitted, unless special triggering conditions and force limitations are satisfied (such as the justification provision authorizing a bus driver to respond to the endangerment of her vehicle with the use of non-deadly force[40]).

Finally, the structure of the draft code of adjudication also allows the system to distinguish between conduct that is excused and conduct that remains blameworthy but is not punishable. For example, a blameworthy offender may escape liability because of diplomatic immunity, former prosecution, governmental immunity, incompetence, expiration of the period of limitation for commencement of the prosecution, or entrapment.[41] Because such non-exculpatory defences are collected in one article of the draft code of adjudication, an acquittal based on such a defence can be distinguished from one based on one of the excuse defences, which are collected in a different article of the code.

Making clear whether an acquittal is exculpatory or non-exculpatory is important for the system's credibility. A non-exculpatory acquittal rendered as a simple 'not guilty' may be misperceived by some as a conclusion by the system that the offender is blameless, a conclusion that may lead some to believe that the system has bad judgement on matters of blameworthiness. Poor credibility reduces the system's power to gain compliance.[42] By making clear that such acquittals do not exculpate the offender, but rather

[40] The use of deadly force has additional requirements beyond those in the quoted section 64. See App. A, § 52.   [41] See App. B, Article 23 (Non-exculpatory Defences).
[42] See Paul H. Robinson and John M. Darley, 'The Utility of Desert' (1996) 91 *Northwestern ULR* 453.

result because the offender simply is not punishable, the system protects its credibility. Consider, for example, a person who steals a pack of cigarettes from a convenience store. The conduct is a violation of the code of conduct:

24. Damage to or Theft of Property
   You may not damage, take, use, dispose of, or transfer another's property without the other's consent.

Assume, however, that the actor is the member of the staff of a foreign embassy. Pursuant to the Diplomatic Relations Act of 1978, the person is not subject to prosecution.[43]

Section 232. Diplomatic Immunity
   An actor may not be prosecuted for a violation of the Code of Conduct if he or she has been granted immunity from prosecution pursuant to the procedures of the Diplomatic Relations Act of 1978.

By making clear that the actor's acquittal arises from section 232 of the Code of Adjudication rather than from a failure to violate section 24 of the Code of Conduct, the acquittal reaffirms rather than undercuts the prohibition against theft. It also protects the system's credibility by explaining the reason for the acquittal of what appears to the lay person to be condemnable conduct.

   These kinds of distinctions among acquittal verdicts are possible because of the general organization of the draft codes:

A Draft Code of Conduct
   Part I. . . .
   Part II. Specific Crimes: Prohibited and Required Conduct
   Part III. General Prohibitions
   Part IV. Justified Violations of the Criminal Law

A Draft Code of Adjudication
   Part I. Violation of Code of Conduct
   Part II. Liability Assessment
      Article 20. Minimum Requirements for Liability
      . . .
      Article 22. Excuses
      Article 23. Nonexculpatory Defences
      . . .
   Part III. Grading
   . . .

With this organization, it is possible to provide verdicts that effectively convey their intended meaning. It allows a verdict system like the following:

---

[43] Diplomatic Relations Act of 1978, 22 USC §§ 254a–254e (1988).

Section 410. Verdict Form: No Violation of Prohibitions or Duties

If the trier of fact finds no violation of the prohibitions or duties described in Parts II and III of the Code of Conduct, then the verdict shall be 'No Violation'.

Section 411. Verdict Form: Justified Violation of Prohibition or Duty

If the trier of fact finds that the actor's conduct constitutes a violation of a prohibition or duty under Parts II or III of the Code of Conduct, but finds that the violation is justified under Part IV of the Code of Conduct, then the verdict shall be 'Justified Violation'.

Section 412. Verdict Form: Blameless Violation

If the trier of fact finds that the actor's conduct constitutes an unjustified violation of the Code of Conduct, but:

(1) the minimum requirements for liability contained in Code of Adjudication Article 20 have not been satisfied, or
(2) the actor's conduct is excused under Code of Adjudication Article 22,

then the verdict shall be 'Not Guilty by Reason of Blameless Violation'.

Section 413. Verdict Form: Not Punishable

If the trier of fact finds that the actor is not subject to prosecution, triable, or punishable because of a provision in Code of Adjudication Article 23, then the verdict shall be 'Not Punishable'.

Section 414. Verdict Form: Guilty

If the trier of fact finds that the actor violated the Code of Conduct without justification, satisfies the minimum requirements of liability under Code of Adjudication Article 20, and has no defence under Code of Adjudication Articles 22 or 23, then the verdict shall be 'Guilty'. The verdict shall indicate the grade of the offence as provided by Part III of the Code of Adjudication.

Absent such a verdict system, trial verdicts can undercut and confuse the public's understanding of the rules of conduct instead of clarifying and enforcing those rules. This amounts to a failure by trial verdicts to realize their potential to exemplify and enforce the norms of society.

F. The Case Against 'Acoustic Separation'

At least one writer has suggested there is value in giving the members of the public rules to guide their conduct that are different from the rules given adjudicators to assess liability, and that the latter decision rules ought not to be publicly available.[44] The draft codes here could well be used to construct such a system of 'acoustic separation'. Some readers may think that such is part of the motivation in these proposals, so let me address the issue.

---

[44] See Meir Dan-Cohen, 'Decision Rules and Conduct Rules: On Acoustic Separation in Criminal Law' (1984) 97 *Harvard LR* 625 at 634–46, 667–8.

There are arguments in favour of 'acoustic separation' but on balance they are unpersuasive. A short-term value may result from the law's ability to announce a rule—perhaps denying a defence to help deter crime, for example—but not enforce the rule and thereby avoid the unfairness to the defendant and the cost of imprisonment. But the long-term prospects of such deception are not good. In an open society with an active free press, acoustic separation cannot be maintained. And once the deception is revealed it will only contribute to a cynicism and distrust for the criminal justice system that will make it harder for the system to perform its functions.

A case in point is the once common practice of publicly imposing long prison terms and then systematically releasing offenders long before the end of the terms imposed. The practice provided high deterrent effect at minimum cost. But once the practice was discovered by the general public, the perceived impact of every imposed sentence was reduced accordingly, requiring even higher sentences to maintain the same deterrent effect. Of course, eventually the higher sentences, also unfulfilled, only increased the public's discount rate for judging the severity of the sentences imposed, creating a cycle of exaggeration that often ended in sentences of many hundreds of years being imposed, with little general deterrent effect because of a belief by the public that the offender might still be released in a short time.

Many jurisdictions have shifted to a system of 'real time' sentencing in which offenders must serve most of the sentence imposed, 85 per cent in the federal system.[45] But the legacy of the earlier deception is that many citizens remain sceptical of the sentences. At the same time, having become accustomed to high sentences, many people insist that the new 'real time' sentences are too low to provide the bite needed to deter. The earlier deception may have created the worst of both worlds, longer sentences with less deterrence. Presumably, with time, the system's credibility will return and expectations will adjust.

Our view is that the code of adjudication should be available to anyone who has an interest. Greater public knowledge of its contents will improve the criminal law's credibility (and provide better prepared jurors). The emphasis, however, should be on broad publication of the code of conduct, for this is the document that ought to guide people's daily lives. In the reasonably short and readable form in which it appears in Appendix A, it can be widely reproduced, read, and understood. It can be the basis for secondary school classes on the obligations of citizens and for adult and continuing education through newspapers, magazines, and television. The resulting greater public awareness and understanding will yield greater

---

[45] See e.g. Sentencing Reform Act of 1984, 18 USC § 3624(b) (1987).

compliance with the law's commands and the provision of better notice increases the fairness of the punishment imposed.

The drafting principles suggested in Chapters 10 and 11 are executed in the Draft Code of Conduct and Draft Code of Adjudication contained in the Appendices. It is not suggested that these draft codes are ready for enactment. They are, rather, vehicles to illustrate the principles offered in the text. The drafts reflect the majority view on most policy issues because they seek to focus the discussion on the drafting method rather than the drafts' contents.

*Appendices**

APPENDIX A: A DRAFT CODE OF CONDUCT

* These Appendices are taken, with only slight modification, from Paul H. Robinson, Peter D. Greene, and Natasha R. Goldstein, 'Making Criminal Codes Functional: A Code of Conduct and a Code of Adjudication' (1996) 86 *Journal of Crim. Laws & Criminology* 304.

PART I. SCOPE AND DEFINITIONS

1. Scope of Code
All crimes are defined in this Code. Other prohibitions, defined by other statutes of this state, are not crimes.

2. Definitions
The following terms are defined in the following sections:
'Consent' in section 5.
'Deadly force' in section 53.
'Family member' in section 23.
'Intimate parts' in section 16.
'Property' in section 24.
'Public place' in section 18.
'Sexual act' in section 35.
'Sexual contact' in section 15.
'Unlawful force' in section 54.

PART II. SPECIFIC CRIMES: PROHIBITED AND REQUIRED CONDUCT

OFFENCES AGAINST PERSONS

3. Injury to a Person
You may not cause bodily injury or death to another person.

4. Consent Defence to Minor Injury
You may engage in conduct that causes or risks minor bodily injury IF the victim requests or voluntarily consents to such conduct, as in participation in a sporting event, for example.

5. Consent Defined
'Consent', as used in this Code, means voluntary agreement by a person who understands the nature and consequences of what he or she is agreeing to. Silence is not consent, unless such silence is understood to be consent by prior agreement among the persons involved.

6. Assisting Another's Suicide
You may not assist another's suicide, UNLESS the other:

(a) has a terminal illness,
> AND

(b) voluntarily requests the assistance.

7. Criminal Harassment
You may not repeatedly follow or contact another in a way that causes the other emotional harm or the fear of physical harm.

8. Violation of Privacy
You may not violate another's legitimate expectation of privacy without the other's consent.

9. *Criminal Threat of Committing a Crime*
You may not gain an advantage from another by threatening to commit a crime.

10. *Criminal Threat of Exposure*
You may not gain an advantage from another by threatening to:

(a) accuse anyone of a crime,

OR

(b) accuse anyone of serious misconduct,

OR

(c) expose a secret,

UNLESS you are trying to avoid a danger, right a wrong, or receive restitution for the crime or misconduct.

11. *Criminal Threat of Official Action*
You may not gain an advantage from another by threatening to improperly cause or prevent official action.

12. *Criminal Restraint*
You may not remove, restrain, or confine another without the other's consent.

13. *Welfare of Child*
You may not endanger the physical or emotional well-being of a child.

14. *Criminal Sexual Contact*
You may not have sexual contact with another person:

(a) without that person's consent,

OR

(b) who is under the age of eleven (11),

OR

(c) who is under the age of sixteen (16) if you are four or more years older than that person,

OR

(d) who is in your custodial care,

OR

(e) who is receiving mental health treatment from you.

15. *Sexual Contact Defined*
'Sexual contact', as used in this Code, includes any of the following three types of contact:

(a) contact with another's intimate parts, using a body part, directly or through clothing,

OR

(b) contact with another, using an intimate part,

OR

(c) any form of sexual intercourse, using a body part or object.

16. Intimate Parts Defined

'Intimate parts', as used in this Code, are the buttock, anus, groin, scrotum, penis, vagina, pubic mound, or female breast.

17. Indecent Exposure

You may not expose your intimate parts in a public place, EXCEPT that if you are a female you may expose your breast as needed to breast-feed a child.

18. Public Place Defined

'Public place', as used in this Code, is any area, facility, vehicle, vessel, train, or aircraft to which persons generally have unrestricted access or to which access is restricted to customers and employees.

19. Abortion

You may not terminate a pregnancy after 26 weeks, UNLESS one of the three following conditions applies:

    (a) the failure to terminate would result in substantial and unjustified danger to the life or health of the mother,

            OR

    (b) the foetus would be born with a serious physical or mental defect,

            OR

    (c) the pregnancy is the result of rape or incest.

OFFENCES AGAINST THE FAMILY

20. Bigamy

You may not marry another person if either of you is already married to someone else who is alive.

21. Interference with Custody

You may not interfere with another's legal custody of a child.

22. Duty to Provide Support

You must provide financial support to any present or former spouse or family member or dependent when the support is required by law or by a judgment of a court.

23. Incest

You may not marry or have sexual intercourse or sexual contact with a family member. A family member is a parent by blood or adoption, step-parent, child, step-child, brother, sister, uncle, aunt, nephew, niece, grandparent, or grandchild.

OFFENCES AGAINST PROPERTY

24. Damage to or Theft of Property

You may not damage, take, use, dispose of, or transfer another's property without the other's consent. Property is anything of value, including services offered for payment and access to recorded information.

25. Criminal Trespass

You may not enter or remain in another's building without consent or enter or remain upon another's land if 'no trespassing' signs are posted or if you are told that such entrance is forbidden.

26. Duty to Prevent Catastrophe

You must make reasonable efforts to prevent or reduce potentially widespread injury or damage from explosion, fire, flood, avalanche, collapse of building, release of other harmful or destructive force or substance, or any other means, if you:

    (a) have an official, contractual, or other legal duty to prevent the injury or damage,

        OR

    (b) have contributed to creating the danger.

27. Failure to Return Lost or Mistakenly Delivered Property

You may not keep lost or mistakenly delivered property, UNLESS you make a reasonable effort to find its owner and return the property.

28. Forgery, Bad Cheques, and Fraudulent Practices

You may not injure another person by providing misleading or false information or documents.

OFFENCES AGAINST PUBLIC ORDER OR DECENCY

29. Destruction or Damage of Certain Objects

You may not damage, destroy, or deface any public monument or structure, or any object or place commonly worshiped.

30. Disorderly Conduct

You may not provoke unlawful behavior or a disruption of order in a public place or in a gathering of persons by excessively loud, offensive, or threatening behaviour.

31. Indecent Behavior

You may not commit a lewd and indecent act in a public place that would cause affront or alarm.

32. Creating a Public Alarm or Panic

You may not cause false alarm or panic among a gathering of persons or among persons in a public place.

33. Obstructing a Public Passage

You may not obstruct a public passage.

34. Prostitution

You may not engage in, support, or profit from any sexual act that is offered for sale.

35. Sexual Act Defined

'Sexual act', as used in this Code, includes any of the following acts:

(a) vaginal, anal, or oral intercourse or penetration,
> OR
(b) direct genital stimulation.

36. Obscenity

You may not produce, possess, or exchange written or recorded material that contains a visual record of any of the following:

(a) an actual sexual act involving a person under the age of sixteen (16),
> OR
(b) actual sexual contact between a person of any age and an animal,
> OR
(c) actual mutilation, torture, rape, or death of a human being that is performed for such recording.

37. Criminal Possession

You may not possess:

(a) a weapon without proper authority or license, if such is required by law,
> OR
(b) a controlled substance or drug paraphernalia without proper authority or prescription,
> OR
(c) stolen property.

38. Cruelty to Animals

You may not cause unnecessary suffering, injury, or death to any animal, UNLESS the conduct is specifically authorised by law.

39. Abuse of Corpse

You may not mutilate, destroy, or mistreat a human corpse, UNLESS the conduct is specifically authorised by law.

OFFENCES AGAINST GOVERNMENT ADMINISTRATION

40. Obstruction of Law

You may not obstruct or resist an arrest, obstruct the apprehension or prosecution of a suspected criminal, or obstruct the performance of a public duty.

41. Avoiding Lawful Detention

You may not escape from lawful detention, or fail to return to lawful detention from authorized release.

42. Failure to Appear

You may not fail to appear in court when required to do so.

43. *Abuse of Non-Public Information by Public Official*
If you are a public official, you may not speculate or wager upon, gain an economic benefit from, or cause another to gain an economic benefit from, information not available to the public gained in your capacity as a public official.

44. *Providing False Information*
You may not lie under oath or give false information to a law enforcement officer, firefighter, or other public servant performing his or her public duty.

45. *Bribery and Criminal Compensation*
You may not offer or accept any benefit either to influence the future action of or in return for past action by a public official or servant, a party official, or a voter, UNLESS such benefit is a legal fee or salary for such action.

46. *Governmental Oppression*
If you are a public official, you may not violate another's personal, property, or other civil rights.

47. *Tampering with Records*
You may not tamper with a public document.

48. *Impersonating a Public Official*
You may not impersonate a public official.

PART III. GENERAL PROHIBITIONS

49. *Attempting Commission of a Crime*
You may not attempt to commit a crime.

50. *Acting with Another Toward Commission of a Crime (Complicity, Conspiracy, and Solicitation)*
You may not agree with, ask, assist, or encourage another to commit a crime.

51. *Creating a Prohibited Risk*
You may not act in a way that creates a substantial and unjustified risk of causing a result made criminal by this Code, EXCEPT that conduct creating a risk that would otherwise be a crime is not a crime if it is:

(a) commonly engaged in,

        AND

(b) generally thought by the community at large to be lawful.

PART IV. JUSTIFIED VIOLATIONS OF THE CRIMINAL LAW

USE OF DEADLY DEFENSIVE FORCE

52. *Use of Deadly Defensive Force*
You may use deadly force against another who is threatening you if and only if it is necessary to defend against the other's use or threatened use of unlawful force likely to cause serious bodily injury or death.

53. Deadly Force Defined

'Deadly force', as used in this Code, is force that creates a substantial risk of causing the death of another person. The firing of a firearm is deadly force.

54. Unlawful Force Defined

'Unlawful force', as used in this Code, is force that is criminal and unjustified under this Code.

USE OF NON-DEADLY FORCE BY THE GENERAL PUBLIC

55. Use of Force in Self-defence or Defence of Another

You may use reasonable force against another if it is immediately necessary to defend against the other's use or threatened use of unlawful force.

56. Defence of Property

You may use reasonable force against a person who is unlawfully threatening property or who has just unlawfully taken property, if such force is immediately necessary to defend or take back the property.

57. Use of Force to Prevent Commission of a Crime

You may use reasonable force, including confinement, against another, if it is necessary to prevent the other from acting in a way that is defined as criminal and unjustified by this Code.

58. Use of Force to Assist Law Enforcement

You may use reasonable force against another if it is necessary to assist a law enforcement officer in making an arrest or preventing an escape.

59. Use of Force to Prevent Suicide

You may use reasonable force against another if it is necessary to prevent the other's suicide.

60. Use of Force to Pass a Wrongful Obstructor

You may use reasonable force against another if it is necessary to pass the person who is unlawfully obstructing a public passage.

USE OF FORCE BY SPECIALLY AUTHORIZED PERSONS

61. Use of Force by Law Enforcement Officer

If you are a law enforcement officer, you may use reasonable force against another to make an arrest or prevent an escape. You may use deadly force if and only if:

(a) the force used creates no risk of serious bodily injury to innocent persons,
   AND
(b) it is likely that the other person will cause serious bodily injury if such force is not used.

62. Use of Force by Parent, Guardian, Teacher, or Caretaker

If you are a parent, guardian, teacher, or caretaker, you may use reasonable force against a minor or incompetent if:

(a) you are legally responsible for the minor or incompetent's care or supervision,

AND

(b) such force is necessary to safeguard the well-being of the minor or incompetent.

63. *Use of Force by Penal Officer*

If you are an official of a jail, prison, or other correctional institution, you may use reasonable force against an inmate if it is immediately necessary to maintain control or order within that institution.

64. *Use of Force by Operator of Public Transportation*

If you are responsible for the maintenance of safety, control, or order aboard a vehicle, vessel, train, or aircraft, you may use reasonable force if it is necessary to maintain such safety, control, or order.

65. *Use of Force by Medical Personnel*

If you are a doctor, a person acting under a doctor's supervision, or a paramedic, you may use reasonable force if:

(a) such force is necessary to avoid serious bodily injury or death,

AND

(b) no authorised person is available to consent,

AND

(c) it is likely that the patient would consent if he or she were able to.

General Justifications

66. *Public Duty*

You may act in a way that would otherwise be a crime if your conduct is necessary to perform a public duty, and reasonable in light of the importance of that duty. This Section does not apply if the situation is addressed by a previous section of this Part of the Code.

67. *Lesser Evils*

You may act in a way that would otherwise be a crime if your conduct is necessary to avoid a more serious harm or evil than that caused by your conduct. This Section does not apply if the situation is addressed by a previous section of this Part of the Code.

PART I. VIOLATION OF CODE OF CONDUCT

ARTICLE 10. VIOLATION OF CODE OF CONDUCT

Section 100. Violation of Code of Conduct
A person violates the Code of Conduct, for the purposes of this Code of Adjudication, if the person violates a prohibition or duty in Part II of the Code of Conduct and does not have a justification for such violation under Part IV of that Code.

ARTICLE 11. PROVISIONS RELATING TO ADJUDICATION OF A VIOLATION OF THE CODE OF CONDUCT

Section 110. Causation Defined
An actor is causally accountable for a result if:

(1) his or her conduct is an antecedent but for which the result in question would not have occurred; and

(2) the result is not:

(a) too remote or accidental in its manner of occurrence, or

(b) too dependent upon another's volitional act,

to have a just bearing on the actor's liability or on the gravity of his or her violation.

Section 111. Requirements for Violation of Code of Conduct Section 49 (Attempting Commission of a Crime)

(1) An actor violates Code of Conduct Section 49 (Attempting Commission of a Crime) if he or she engages in conduct that constitutes a substantial step toward the commission of a violation which is strongly corroborative of the actor's culpability.

(2) The following are examples of what constitutes a substantial step:

(a) lying in wait, searching for, or following the contemplated victim of the violation;

(b) enticing or seeking to entice the contemplated victim of the violation to go to the place contemplated for its commission;

(c) reconnoitring the place contemplated for the commission of the violation;

(d) unlawful entry of a structure, vehicle, or enclosure in which it is contemplated that the violation will be committed;

(e) possession of materials to be employed in the commission of the violation, which are specially designed for such unlawful use or which can serve no lawful purpose of the actor under the circumstances;

(f) possession, collection, or fabrication of materials to be employed in the commission of the violation, at or near the place contemplated for its commission, where such possession, collection, or fabrication serves no lawful purpose under the circumstances; or

(g) soliciting an innocent agent to engage in conduct constituting a violation.

(3) Liability for Attempt in Absence of Causation. Where an actor would be liable for a violation of the Code of Conduct but does not cause or is not causally accountable for the prohibited result under Code of Adjudication Section 110 (Causation Defined), he or she is liable for an attempt in violation of Code of Conduct Section 49 (Attempting Commission of a Crime).

(4) Complete and Voluntary Renunciation as a Defence to Attempt. An actor may not be held liable for attempting a crime, in violation of Code of Conduct Section 49 (Attempting Commission of a Crime), if the actor completely and voluntarily renounces the attempt before completion of the criminal conduct. An actor's renunciation is not 'complete and voluntary' if it is motivated in whole or in part by the actor's:

(a) decision to postpone the conduct until a more advantageous time,

(b) decision to transfer the criminal effort to another but similar objective or victim, or

(c) perception of circumstances that increase the probability of detection or apprehension.

*Section 112. Requirements for Violation of Code of Conduct Section 50
(Acting with Another Toward Commission of a Crime (Complicity, Conspiracy,
and Solicitation))*

(1) Unconvictable Perpetrator No Defence to Complicity. An actor may be held to have assisted in a violation, in violation of Code of Conduct Section 50 (Conspiracy), even if the person claimed to have committed the violation has not been prosecuted or convicted, has been convicted of a different violation or degree of violation, has an immunity to prosecution or conviction, or has been acquitted.

(2) Termination as a Defence to Complicity. An actor does not violate the prohibition against assisting a violation, contained in Code of Conduct Section 50 (Conspiracy) if the actor terminates his or her complicity prior to the completion of the criminal conduct, and:

    (a) wholly deprives his or her complicity of its effectiveness in assisting the criminal conduct,

    (b) gives timely warning to law enforcement authorities, or

    (c) otherwise makes proper effort to prevent the commission of the violation.

(3) Sufficiency of Unilateral Act for Conspiracy. An actor may be held to have agreed with another to commit a violation, in violation of Code of Conduct Section 50 (Conspiracy), even if the person with whom the actor agrees is not in reality agreeing to commission of the offence.

(4) Overt Act Requirement for Conspiracy. An actor does not violate the prohibition against agreeing with another to commit a violation, contained in Code of Conduct Section 5 (Conspiracy), unless one of them performs an overt act in pursuance of the conspiracy. This requirement does not apply if the object of the conspiracy has a base grade in Section 304 (Base Grade) of a first or second degree felony.

(5) Complete and Voluntary Renunciation as a Defence to Conspiracy and Solicitation. An actor may not be liable for agreeing with or soliciting another to commit a violation, in violation of Code of Conduct Section 50 (Conspiracy and Solicitation), if the actor prevents the crime under circumstances manifesting a complete and voluntary renunciation of his or her criminal purpose. A 'complete and voluntary' renunciation has the meaning given in Section 111(4) (Requirements for Violation of Code of Conduct Section 49 (Attempting Commission of a Crime)).

*Section 113. Requirements for Violation of Code of Conduct Section 51
(Creating a Prohibited Risk)*

An actor violates Code of Conduct Section 51 (Creating a Prohibited Risk) if, given the nature, degree, and circumstances of the risk, its creation is a gross deviation from the standard of conduct of a law-abiding person.

Section 114. Consent Defence

An actor does not violate the Code of Conduct if the victim consents and such consent:

    (1) negates an element of the violation, or

    (2) precludes occurrence of the harm sought to be prevented by the Code of Conduct provision defining the violation.

PART II. LIABILITY ASSESSMENT

ARTICLE 20. MINIMUM REQUIREMENTS FOR LIABILITY

Section 200. Minimum Culpability Required

(1) An actor's violation of the Code of Conduct is not criminal unless the actor is at least reckless as to each element of the violation as described in the Code of Conduct, except that negligence is the minimum culpability required:

(a) for a violation of the prohibition against causing the death of another person under Code of Conduct Section 3 (Injury to a Person); and

(b) as to the age of the victim for a violation of Code of Conduct Section 14(b) or (c) (Criminal Sexual Contact).

(2) In addition to the culpability requirements of subsection (1), to be liable for a violation of:

(a) Code of Conduct Section 49 (Attempting Commission of a Crime), the actor must have the purpose to engage in the conduct that would constitute the violation; and

(b) Code of Conduct Section 50 (Acting with Another Toward Commission of a Crime (Complicity, Conspiracy, and Solicitation)), the actor must have the purpose to facilitate the conduct constituting the violation.

(3) Definitions. 'Purposely', 'recklessly', and 'negligently' are defined in Section 401 (Definitions).

Section 201. De Minimis Violation

An actor's violation of the Code of Conduct is not criminal if the actor's conduct is too trivial to warrant the condemnation of a criminal conviction.

ARTICLE 21. DOCTRINES OF IMPUTATION

Section 210. Divergence Between Result Intended or Risked and Actual Result

When causing a result is an element of an offence, and the actual result differs from the result intended or risked by the actor, the required culpability as to causing the result is established if the difference is only that:

(1) a different person or property is injured, or

(2) the injury intended or risked would have been more serious than the actual injury.

Section 211. Inculpatory Mistake

Where an actor's ignorance or mistake negates the minimum culpability required by Section 200 (Minimum Culpability Required), the actor nonetheless is liable for the offence if he or she would be liable for a different offence had the situation been as he or she supposed.

Section 212. Accountability for Conduct of Another

(1) Legal Accountability. An actor is legally accountable for the conduct of another constituting an offence if, acting with the minimum culpability required for liability by Section 200 (Minimum Culpability Required):

(a) he or she causes an innocent or irresponsible person to engage in the conduct; or

(b) with knowledge that the other person is engaging in, or will engage in, the conduct constituting the offence, he or she:

    (i) aids, advises, or encourages the person,

    (ii) solicits the other person to engage in the conduct, or

    (iii) has a legal duty to prevent the conduct and fails to make a reasonable effort to do so.

(2) Exceptions to Accountability for Conduct of Another. An actor is not accountable for another's conduct under Subsection (1) if his or her conduct is inevitably incident to the commission of the violation, as a victim or otherwise, and is not prohibited by the Code of Conduct.

Section 213. Voluntary Intoxication

(1) Where an actor does not have the minimum culpability required for liability by Section 200 (Minimum Culpability Required) because the actor was voluntarily intoxicated, such lack of culpability is immaterial if he or she is unaware of a risk of which he or she would have been aware if sober.

(2) Definitions. For the purposes of this Section and Section 222 (Disability Excuse: Involuntary Intoxication):

(a) 'intoxication' means a disturbance of mental or physical capacities resulting from the introduction of substances into the body;

(b) 'voluntarily intoxicated' means the actor's intoxication was self-induced and not pathological;

(c) 'self-induced intoxication' means intoxication caused by substances, the tendency of which to cause intoxication the actor knows or reasonably ought to know, that the actor knowingly introduces into his or her body, unless he or she introduces them pursuant to medical advice; and

(d) 'pathological intoxication' means intoxication, grossly excessive in degree given the amount of the intoxicant, to which the actor does not know, and cannot reasonably be expected to know, he or she is susceptible.

ARTICLE 22. EXCUSES

Section 220. Disability Excuse: Involuntary Conduct

(1) An actor's violation of the Code of Conduct is excused if the actor's conduct constituting the violation is involuntary.

(2) 'Involuntary Conduct' Defined. For the purposes of this Section, conduct is 'involuntary' if it is:

(a) not the product of the effort or determination of the actor, or

(b) a reflex or convulsion.

(3) Habitual Conduct Not Necessarily Involuntary. The fact that conduct is habitual does not in itself make the conduct involuntary.

Section 221. Disability Excuse: Insanity

(1) An actor's violation of the Code of Conduct is excused if, at the time of the conduct constituting the violation, the actor:

(a) has a mental disease or defect, and
(b) by reason of such mental disease or defect, lacks substantial capacity to:

    (i) appreciate the criminality or wrongfulness of his or her conduct, or
    (ii) conform his or her conduct to the requirements of law.

(2) 'Mental Disease or Defect' Defined. For the purposes of this Section and Section 235 (Incompetency), 'mental disease or defect' is a physiologically confirmable abnormality of the mind, but does not include an abnormality manifested only by repeated criminal or otherwise anti-social conduct.

Section 222. *Disability Excuse: Involuntary Intoxication*
(1) An actor's violation of the Code of Conduct is excused if, at the time of the conduct constituting the violation, the actor:

(a) is involuntarily intoxicated, and
(b) by reason of such involuntary intoxication, lacks substantial capacity to:

    (i) appreciate the criminality or wrongfulness of his or her conduct, or
    (ii) conform his or her conduct to the requirements of law.

(2) 'Involuntary Intoxication' and 'Self-Induced Intoxication' Defined. 'Involuntary intoxication' means the actor's intoxication was not self-induced. 'Self-induced intoxication' is defined in Section 213(2)(c) (Voluntary Intoxication).

Section 223. *Disability Excuse: Immaturity*
(1) An actor's violation of the Code of Conduct is excused if, at the time of the conduct constituting the violation, the actor:

(a) is immature, and
(b) by reason of such immaturity, lacks substantial capacity to appreciate the criminality or wrongfulness of his or her conduct.

(2) 'Immaturity' Defined. For the purposes of this Section, 'immaturity' means a level of maturity typical of an individual less than sixteen years of age.
(3) Presumed Excuse for Actors Under Eleven. An actor of eleven years of age or less at the time of the conduct constituting the violation is presumed to satisfy the requirements of Subsection (1).
(4) Presumed Immaturity of Actors Under Sixteen. An actor more than eleven years of age but less than sixteen years of age at the time of the conduct constituting the violation is presumed to be immature as required by Subsection (1)(a).

Section 224. *Disability Excuse: Duress*
An actor's violation of the Code of Conduct is excused if, at the time of the conduct constituting the violation, the actor:

(1) was coerced to engage in the conduct by the use or threatened use of unlawful force against his or her person or the person of another, and
(2) a person of reasonable firmness in the actor's situation could not reasonably have been expected to have resisted such coercion.

Section 225. Disability Excuse: Impaired Consciousness

(1) An actor's violation of the Code of Conduct is excused if, at the time of the conduct constituting the violation, the actor:

(a) is in a state of impaired consciousness, and
(b) by reason of such impaired consciousness, lacks substantial capacity to:

(i) appreciate the criminality or wrongfulness of his or her conduct, or
(ii) conform his or her conduct to the requirements of law.

(2) 'State of Impaired Consciousness' Defined. For the purposes of Subsection (1)(a), a 'state of impaired consciousness' means a disturbance of consciousness resulting from a physiologically confirmable state or condition not specifically recognised or rejected as a basis for exculpation under any other Section in this Article.

(3) Presumed Impaired Consciousness. An actor who is unconscious, asleep, or under hypnosis is presumed to be in a state of impaired consciousness as required by Subsection (1)(a).

Section 226. Mistake Excuse: Mistake of Law

An actor's violation of the Code of Conduct is excused if, at the time of the conduct constituting the violation, the actor reasonably believes that the conduct does not constitute a violation because the actor:

(1) reasonably relies upon an official statement of law contained in a statute, judgment, or an administrative order or grant of permission, subsequently determined to be invalid or erroneous, or
(2) the actor diligently pursues all means available to ascertain the meaning and application of the Code of Conduct provision to his or her potential conduct and in good faith concludes that his or her conduct would not be a violation, in circumstances in which a reasonable person would also so conclude.
(3) 'Reasonable Belief' Defined. For the purposes of this Section, a 'reasonable belief' is a non-negligent belief. 'Negligently' is defined in Section 401(4) (Definitions).

Section 227. Mistake Excuse: Mistake as to Justification

(1) An actor's violation of the Code of Conduct is excused if, at the time of the conduct constituting the violation, the actor reasonably believes that the conduct constituting the violation is justified under Part IV of the Code of Conduct.

(2) 'Reasonable Belief' Defined. 'Reasonable belief' is defined in Section 226(3) (Mistake Excuse: Mistake of Law).

Section 228. Rebuttable Presumptions

The presumptions afforded an actor in Section 223(3) and (4) (Disability Excuse: Immaturity) and Section 225(3) (Disability Excuse: Impaired Consciousness) may be rebutted by the prosecution by proof by a preponderance of the evidence that the actor is mature or not in a state of impaired consciousness, respectively.

ARTICLE 23. NONEXCULPATORY DEFENCES

Section 230. Timing of Assertion of Nonexculpatory Defence

Any defence contained in this Article must be raised by the defendant before trial. A failure to assert such a nonexculpatory defence before trial shall be deemed a waiver of that defence, but shall not preclude the defendant from raising any other appropriate defence.

Section 231. Waiver of Nonexculpatory Defence

Where an actor would otherwise satisfy the requirements of a nonexculpatory defence in this Article, the actor may elect to waive the nonexculpatory defence in order to allow the trier of fact to reach a verdict other than 'Not Punishable' as provided in Section 413 (Verdict Form: Not Punishable).

Section 232. Diplomatic Immunity

An actor may not be prosecuted for a violation of the Code of Conduct if he or she has been granted immunity from prosecution pursuant to the procedures of the Diplomatic Relations Act of 1978.

Section 233. Prosecution Barred by Former Prosecution

(1) An actor may not be prosecuted for a violation of the Code of Conduct if:

(a) he or she was previously prosecuted for a violation of the same provision of the Code of Conduct;

(b) the present violation is based on the same facts; and

(c) the previous prosecution:

    (i) resulted in a conviction,

    (ii) resulted in an acquittal,

    (iii) was terminated after jeopardy attached, or

    (iv) was terminated by a final order or judgment for the defendant, if the order or judgment necessarily required a determination inconsistent with a factual or legal proposition required for conviction of the violation.

(2) Attachment of Jeopardy. The point in time at which 'jeopardy attached', as referred to in subsection (1)(c)(iii), is defined by the applicable Rules of Criminal Procedure.

Section 234. Governmental Immunity

An actor may not be tried for a violation of the Code of Conduct if he or she has judicial, legislative, or executive immunity from liability for such violation.

Section 235. Incompetency

(1) An actor may not be tried for a violation of the Code of Conduct if, as a result of a mental disease or defect, the actor lacks the capacity necessary to:

(a) understand the nature of the proceedings against him or her, or

(b) adequately assist counsel in the preparation of a defence.

(2) 'Mental Disease or Defect' Defined. 'Mental disease or defect' is defined in Section 221(2) (Disability Excuse: Insanity).

Section 236. *Period of Limitation for Commencement of Prosecution*

(1) An actor may not be tried for a violation of the Code of Conduct if:

(a) the violation is a misdemeanor or a petty misdemeanor and the court determines that the conduct constituting the violation occurred more than three years prior to the date of commencement of the prosecution, or

(b) the violation is a felony and the court determines that the conduct occurred more than seven years prior to the date of commencement of the prosecution, unless the conduct constitutes a violation of Code of Conduct Section 3 (Injury to a Person) that results in the death of another person.

(2) Commencement of Prosecution. For the purposes of this Section, 'commencement of the prosecution' can be achieved by any of the following:

(a) return of an indictment,

(b) filing of an information, or

(c) issuance of a warrant or other process, provided that such warrant or process is executed without unreasonable delay.

Section 237. *Entrapment*

An actor may not be punished for a violation of the Code of Conduct if:

(1) the conduct constituting the violation is induced by a law enforcement officer,

(2) the actor was not predisposed to commit the violation, and

(3) the officer's conduct created a substantial risk that a reasonable person not predisposed to commit the violation would have been induced to do so.

Article 24. Causing the Conditions of One's Own Defence

Section 240. *Causing the Conditions of One's Own Justification or Excuse Defence*

(1) When an actor causes the conditions that give rise to a justification under Part IV of the Code of Conduct or to an excuse under Article 22 of the Code of Adjudication, the actor gains the benefit of the defence despite his or her conduct in causing the defence conditions, but

(2) the actor may be held liable for the violation of the Code of Conduct based upon his or her conduct in causing the defence conditions if, at the time of causing those conditions, the actor has the culpability as to bringing about the violation that is required by Section 200 (Minimum Culpability Required).

(3) As provided by Section 310 (Adjustment for Greater Culpability), the grade of liability for causing the defence conditions under Subsection (2) increases if the actor was knowing or purposeful as to causing the violation.

(4) Defence to Liability for Causing the Conditions of One's Own Defence. An actor may have a justification or excuse defence to liability under Subsection (2) for his or her conduct in causing the defence conditions.

Section 241. Causing the Conditions of One's Own Nonexculpatory Defence

When an actor establishes a nonexculpatory defence under Article 23 and the actor caused the conditions of that defence, such defence is not available to the actor. This Section is not intended to supersede any international treaties.

PART III. GRADING

ARTICLE 30. BASE GRADE OF OFFENCE

Section 300. Grade of Offence

The grade of an actor's offence shall be the base grade provided in Section 304 (Base Grade), as adjusted by the provisions of Article 31.

Section 301. Grade Levels

This Code recognises:

(1) Eight grades of felonies:

First degree felony	F1 (most serious offence)
Second degree felony	F2
Third degree felony	F3
Fourth degree felony	F4
Fifth degree felony	F5
Sixth degree felony	F6
Seventh degree felony	F7
Eighth degree felony	F8

(2) Five grades of misdemeanors:

First degree misdemeanor	M1
Second degree misdemeanor	M2
Third degree misdemeanor	M3
Fourth degree misdemeanor	M4
Fifth degree misdemeanor	M5

(3) One grade of petty misdemeanor:

Petty misdemeanor	PM (least serious offence)

Section 302. Grade of Offence When Divergence Between Result Intended or Risked and Actual Result

Where an actor satisfies the requirements of Section 210 (Divergence Between Result Intended or Risked and Actual Result) and the grade of the offence for the result intended or risked by the actor's conduct is lower than the grade of the offence actually committed, the grade of the actor's offence is the grade of the offence for the result intended or risked.

Section 303. Grade of Offence If Inculpatory Mistake

Where an actor satisfies the requirements of Section 211 (Inculpatory Mistake) and the grade of the offence under his or her mistaken belief is lower than the grade of the offence actually committed, the grade of the actor's offence is the grade of the offence under his or her mistaken belief.

Section 304. Base Grade

An offence has the base grade indicated below. Unless otherwise provided, the grade given assumes a reckless violation.

Code of Conduct section violated:	Additional grading categories:	Base grade
3. Injury to a Person	(a) Death	F3
	(b) Death (negligently)	F4
	(c) Serious or permanent bodily injury	F5
	(d) Bodily injury	M1
6. Assisting Another's Suicide	Neither (a) nor (b)	F3
	(a) Terminal illness (but assistance not voluntarily requested)	F5
	(b) Assistance voluntarily requested (but no terminal illness)	F5
7. Criminal Harassment		M3
8. Violation of Privacy		M4
9. Criminal Threat of Committing a Crime	(a) Threatens a felony	F6
	(b) Threatens a misdemeanor	M2
10. Criminal Threat of Exposure		M2
11. Criminal Threat of Official Action		M2
12. Criminal Restraint		F5
13. Welfare of Child		M1
14. Criminal Sexual Contact	(a) Sexual intercourse with a person under eleven years of age	F3
	(b) Sexual contact with a person under eleven years of age	F5
	(c) Sexual intercourse without consent	F4
	(d) Sexual contact without consent	M1
	(e) Sexual intercourse with a person under sixteen years of age if the actor is four or more years older than the victim	F7
	(f) Sexual contact with a person under sixteen years of age if the actor is four or more years older than the victim	M2
	(g) Sexual intercourse with a person in the actor's custodial or mental health care	F7

Code of Conduct section violated:	Additional grading categories:	Base grade
	(h) Sexual contact with a person in the actor's custodial or mental health care	M2
17. Indecent Exposure		M4
19. Abortion		F6
20. Bigamy		M5
21. Interference with Custody		M2
22. Duty to Provide Support		M4
23. Incest		F7
24. Damage to or Theft of Property	(a) Value of property damaged or stolen exceeds $100,000	F3
	(b) Value of property greater than $10,000 and less than or equal to $100,000	F6
	(c) Value of property greater than $1,000 and less than or equal to $10,000	F8
	(d) Value of property greater than $500 and less than or equal to $1,000	M3
	(e) Value of property greater than $100 and less than or equal to $500	M5
	(f) Value of property less than or equal to $100	PM
25. Criminal Trespass	(a) Dwelling or occupied structure	M1
	(b) Land	PM
26. Duty to Prevent Catastrophe		M3
27. Failure to Return Lost or Mistakenly Delivered Property		M5
28. Forgery, Bad Checks, and Fraudulent Practices		M2
29. Destruction or Damage of Certain Objects	(a) Irreparable damage, destruction, or defacement	M4
	(b) Other	M5

Code of Conduct section violated:	Additional grading categories:		Base grade
30. Disorderly Conduct			PM
31. Indecent Behavior			PM
32. Creating a Public Alarm or Panic			M3
33. Obstructing a Public Passage			PM
34. Prostitution			M4
36. Obscenity			M4
37. Criminal Possession	(a) Weapon		M4
	(b) Controlled substance		M2
	(c) Drug paraphernalia		—*
	(d) Stolen property	Base grade of offence according to scale used in Section 24 (Damage to or Theft of Property)	M5
38. Cruelty to Animals			M4
39. Abuse of Corpse			M4
40. Obstruction of Law			M3
41. Avoiding Lawful Detention			M3
42. Failure to Appear			M5
43. Abuse of Non-Public Information by Public Official			M2
44. Providing False Information	(a) If under oath		F8
	(b) If not under oath		M1
45. Bribery and Criminal Compensation			F6
46. Governmental Oppression			F8
47. Tampering with Records			M3

* The Table follows the Model Penal Code's lead in not taking a position on the precise substances that are to be controlled or on the appropriate grading for various drug-related crimes.

Code of Conduct section violated:	Additional grading categories:	Base grade
48. Impersonating a Public Official		M4
49. Attempting Commission of a Crime	Two grades less than the grade for the completed offence	
50. Acting with Another Toward Commission of a Crime (Complicity, Conspiracy, and Solicitation)	Grade adjusted as provided in Section 311 (Extent of Participation in Assisting an Offence by Another)	
51. Creating a Prohibited Risk	One grade less than the grade for the offence if the harm risked had resulted	

ARTICLE 31. ADJUSTMENTS TO BASE GRADE

Section 310. Adjustment for Greater Culpability

(1) The grade of an offence increases:

(a) two grades if the actor is purposeful as to the core elements, or
(b) one grade if the actor is knowing as to the core elements.

(2) Definitions. For the purposes of this Section:

(a) The 'core elements' are those facts that establish the violation in the Code of Conduct and its grade in Section 304 (Base Grade).
(b) Purposely', 'knowingly', 'recklessly', and 'negligently' are defined in Section 401 (Definitions).

SECTION 311. ADJUSTMENT ACCORDING TO EXTENT OF PARTICIPATION IN ASSISTING AN OFFENCE BY ANOTHER

Where the actor assists another to commit an offence, in violation of Code of Conduct Section 50 (Acting with Another Toward Commission of a Crime (Complicity)), the grade of the actor's offence:

(1) increases two grades if the actor is an organizer,
(2) increases one grade if the actor is a manager,
(3) is unaffected if the actor is a participant,
(4) decreases one grade if the actor is a supporter.
(5) Definitions. For the purposes of this Section:

(a) The actor is an 'organizer' if he or she directed, supervised, or managed one or more persons who satisfy manager criteria;
(b) The actor is a 'manager' if he or she shared management responsibilities on an equal basis with one or more actors in any one of the following:

      (i)   the selection of the criminal objective,

     (ii)   the identification of resources necessary to achieve the criminal objective, or

    (iii)   the planning, financing, or scheduling of the activities necessary to achieve the criminal objective;

  (c) The actor is a 'participant' if he or she was involved in any way in the design or implementation of the conduct constituting the offence; and

  (d) The actor is a 'supporter' if he or she was a minor participant in a criminal scheme and was to be compensated by a fixed amount rather than a percentage of the profits of the criminal objective.

Section 312. Adjustment for Ineffective Renunciation of Attempt, Conspiracy, or Solicitation

(1) The grade of the actor's offence decreases one grade if the actor completely and voluntarily renounces his or her attempt, conspiracy, or solicitation but is unable to prevent commission of the offence.

(2) 'Complete and Voluntary' Defined. A 'complete and voluntary' renunciation has the meaning given in Section 111(4) (Requirements for Violation of Code of Conduct Section 49).

Section 313. Adjustment for Partial Disability

The grade of the actor's offence decreases one grade if, at the time of the conduct constituting the offence, the actor suffers a substantial impairment of cognitive or control dysfunction, as defined in a provision in Article 22, but to a degree insufficient to merit a complete excuse.

Section 314. Adjustment for Selection of Victim

(1) The grade of the actor's offence increases one grade if the actor selects the victim of the offence because the victim is:

  (a) younger than sixteen years of age;

  (b) older than sixty-five years of age;

  (c) suffering from a physical or mental disability; or

  (d) of a particular race, religion, ancestry, gender, sexual orientation, or national origin, and by choosing the victim the actor hopes to intimidate or humiliate the other members of the group of which the victim is a member.

(2) The grade increase provided by this Section does not apply if the characteristic defined in Subsection (1) is an element of the violation.

PART IV. GENERAL PROVISIONS

ARTICLE 40. MISCELLANEOUS

Section 400. Principles of Construction

(1) Each term in the Code of Conduct and the Code of Adjudication shall be interpreted according to a definition provided for the term or, if none is provided, shall be given its common and plain meaning.

(2) Any remaining ambiguities shall be resolved to best further the Code's goal of imposing liability according to the degree of an actor's blameworthiness, including the degree of the actor's culpability and the extent of any harm that results from the actor's conduct.

Section 401. Definitions

For the purposes of this Code of Adjudication:

(1) A person acts 'purposely' with respect to an element of a violation when:

(a) if the element involves the nature of his or her conduct or a result thereof, it is his or her conscious object to engage in conduct of that nature or to cause such a result, and

(b) if the element involves the attendant circumstances of the conduct, he or she is aware of the existence of such circumstances or he or she believes or hopes that they exist.

(2) A person acts 'knowingly' with respect to an element of a violation when:

(a) if the element involves the nature of his or her conduct or the attendant circumstances, he or she is aware that his or her conduct is of that nature or that such circumstances exist, and

(b) if the element involves a result of his or her conduct, he or she is aware that it is practically certain that his or her conduct will cause such a result.

(3) A person acts 'recklessly' with respect to an element of a violation when he or she consciously disregards a risk that the element exists or will result from his or her conduct. The risk must be of such a nature and degree that, considering the purpose of the actor's conduct and the circumstances known to him or her, the actor's failure to perceive it involves a gross deviation from the standard of conduct that a law-abiding person would observe in the actor's situation.

(4) A person acts 'negligently' with respect to an element of a violation when he or she should be aware of a risk that the element exists or will result from his or her conduct. The risk must be of such a nature and degree that, considering the purpose of the actor's conduct and the circumstances known to him or her, the actor's failure to perceive it involves a gross deviation from the standard of conduct that a law-abiding person would observe in the actor's situation.

(5) 'Element of an Offence' Defined. An 'element of an offence' means such:

(a) conduct,

(b) attendant circumstances, or

(c) a result of conduct,

as is contained in the definition of a violation.

(6) 'Conduct' Defined. 'Conduct' means a physical act or omission.

(7) 'Circumstance' Defined. 'Circumstance' means a characteristic of the conduct or a condition or environment under which the conduct occurs.

(8) 'Result' Defined. 'Result' means a circumstance changed by the conduct of the actor.

(9) Other Definitions. The following terms are defined in the following sections:

(a) In the Code of Conduct:

'Consent' in Section 5,

'Deadly force' in Section 53,

'Family member' in Section 23,
'Intimate parts' in Section 16,
'Property' in Section 24,
'Public place' in Section 18,
'Sexual act' in Section 35,
'Sexual contact' in Section 15, and
'Unlawful force' in Section 54.

(b) In this Code of Adjudication:
'Causation' in Section 110,
'Complete and voluntary' renunciation in Section 111(4),
'Immaturity' in Section 223(2),
'Included offence' in Section 402(2),
'Intoxication' in Section 213(2)(a),
'Involuntary conduct' in Section 220(2),
'Involuntary intoxication' in Section 222(2),
'Manager' in Section 311(5)(b),
'Mental disease or defect' in Section 221(2),
'Organizer' in Section 311(5)(a),
'Participant' in Section 311(5)(c),
'Pathological intoxication' in Section 213(2)(d),
'Reasonable belief' in Section226(3),
'Self-induced intoxication' in Section 213(2)(c),
'State of impaired consciousness' in Section 225(2),
'Substantial step' in Section 111(2),
'Supporter' in Section 311(5)(d), and
'Voluntarily intoxicated' in Section 213(2)(b).

Section 402. Limitations on Convictions for Multiple Offences

(1) When the same conduct of an actor satisfies the elements of more than one offence, the actor may be held liable for each offence, unless:

(a) one offence is included in another as defined in Subsection (2) of this Section, or

(b) inconsistent findings of fact are required to satisfy the elements of the offences.

(2) 'Included Offence' Defined. For the purposes of this Section, an offence is 'included' in another if it consists of attempting, conspiring, or soliciting the other.

ARTICLE 41. VERDICT FORMS

Section 410. Verdict Form: No Violation of Prohibitions or Duties

If the trier of fact finds no violation of the prohibitions or duties described in Parts II and III of the Code of Conduct, then the verdict shall be 'No Violation'.

Section 411. Verdict Form: Justified Violation of Prohibition or Duty

If the trier of fact finds that the actor's conduct constitutes a violation of a prohibition or duty under Parts II or III of the Code of Conduct, but finds that the violation is justified under Part IV of the Code of Conduct, then the verdict shall be 'Justified Violation'.

Section 412. Verdict Form: Blameless Violation

If the trier of fact finds that the actor's conduct constitutes an unjustified violation of the Code of Conduct, but:

(1) the minimum requirements for liability contained in Code of Adjudication Article 20 have not been satisfied, or
(2) the actor's conduct is excused under Code of Adjudication Article 22, then the verdict shall be 'Not Guilty by Reason of Blameless Violation'.

Section 413. Verdict Form: Not Punishable

If the trier of fact finds that the actor is not subject to prosecution, triable, or punishable because of a provision in Code of Adjudication Article 23, then the verdict shall be 'Not Punishable'.

Section 414. Verdict Form: Guilty

If the trier of fact finds that the actor violated the Code of Conduct without justification, satisfies the minimum requirements of liability under Code of Adjudication Article 20, and has no defence under Code of Adjudication Articles 22 or 23, then the verdict shall be 'Guilty'. The verdict shall indicate the grade of the offence as provided by Part III of the Code of Adjudication.

Index